Bailey Isla

Memories, Pictures & Lore

Nancy Jensen

Nancy Orr Johnson Jensen

Mayhaven Publishing
P O Box 557
Mahomet, IL 61853 USA

Original Cover Art by Brad McFadden, Orr's Island, Maine 2002

Second Printing 2003
ISBN 1-878044-96-6
Library of Congress Number: 2003102326
Printed in Canada

We thank the following and those listed in the Sources, for the use of material reprinted in this book.

"Ragged Island" by Edna St. Vincent Millay. From *COLLECTED POEMS*, Harper Collins. Copyright © 1954, 1982 by Norma Millay Ellis. All rights reserved. Reprinted by permission of Elizabeth Barnett, literary executor.

The Times Record (Brunswick, Maine) for their permission to use various items from their newspaper.

Charlie York: Maine Coast Fisherman by Harold B. Clifford. International Maine Publishing Co. 1974. Camden, ME. Reprinted by permission of the McGraw-Hill Companies.

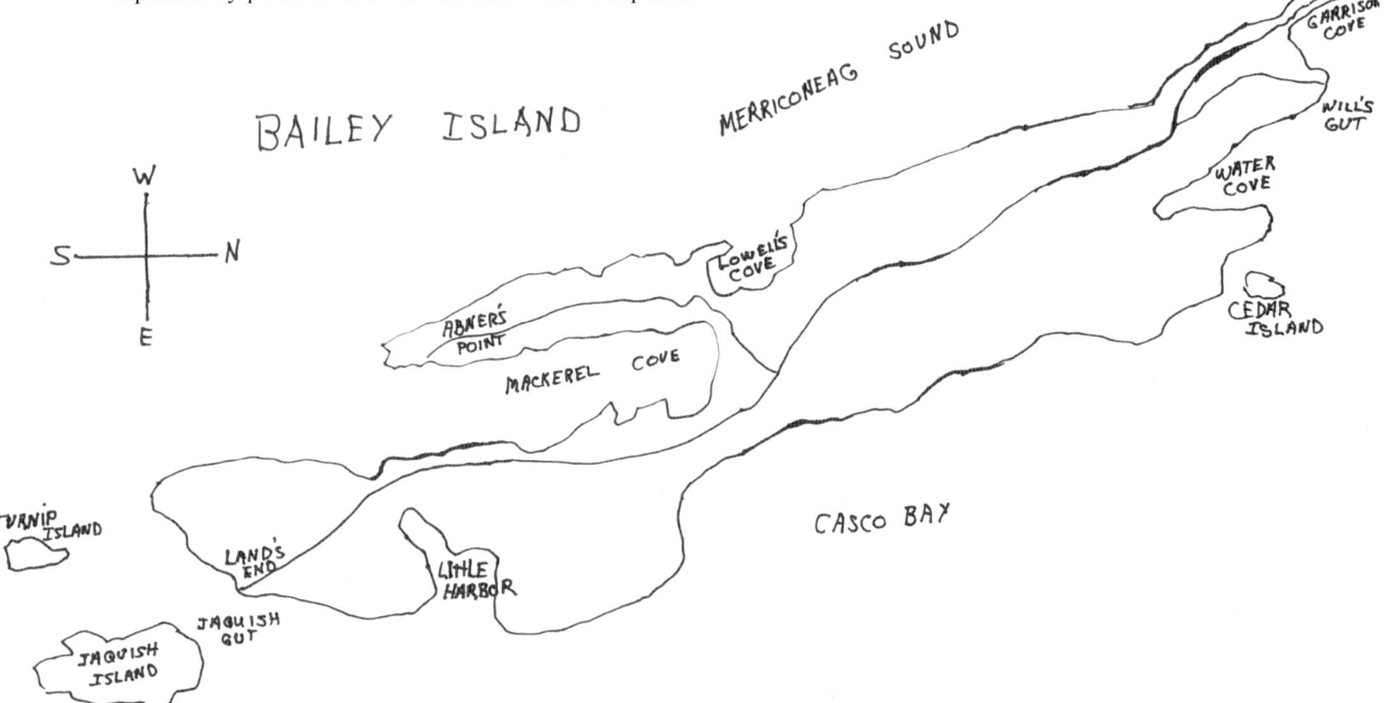

I dedicate this book to my father, Linwood Johnson, whose heritage is Harpswell of which Bailey Island is a part. I have great respect for the knowledge he had of the entire Harpswell area. I am grateful for the information he gathered and saved, and appreciate the love he had for the people he knew and worked for.

Jim Herrick, one of Bailey's elder residents said of my father, "Linwood was an island character, as much a part of the island as the solid cliffs that face the sea, unshakable as the upended rocks—a backbone of the island."

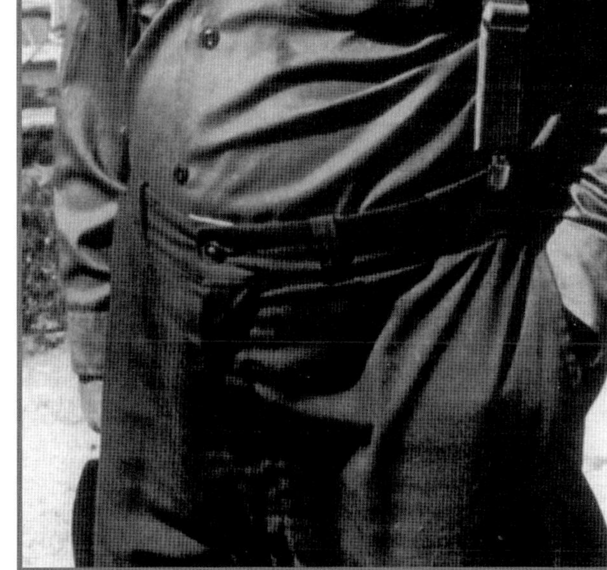

Photo by Don Hinckley

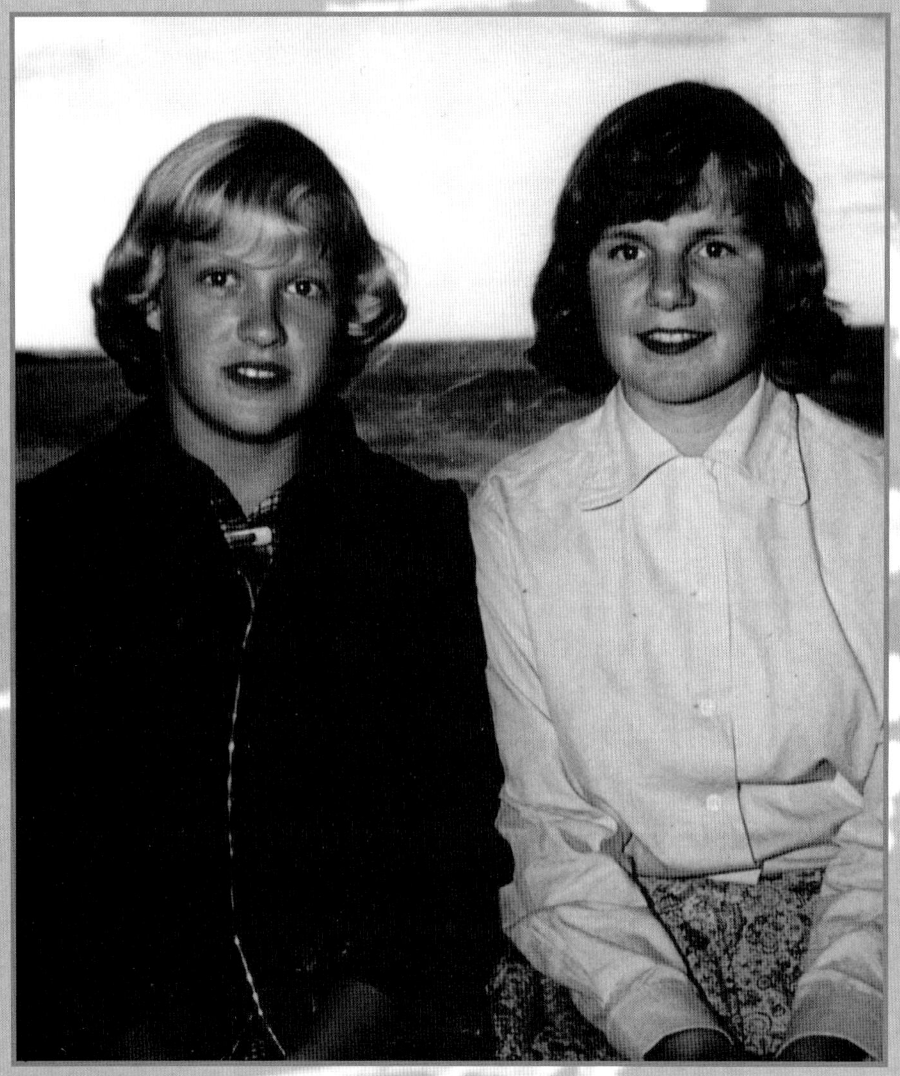

Left to Right: Janet Freeman and me, Nancy Orr Johnson, Lowell's Cove, Bailey Island, Maine, 1952.

Photo by Royal Root

Acknowledgements

In preparing for the writing of this book, I spent many hours with my best friend, Janet Freeman Baribeau, who now lives in Brunswick, Maine. As children we were always together. I often spent the night at her house and ate many a meal there. After high school we went our separate ways and did not get together until just a few years ago when we took a writing class together. Not much has changed. We still share the same stories and laugh 'til we cry.

Soon after we renewed our friendship, we toured around Maine, gathering information from such places as the Maine Folklife Center at the University of Maine in Orono, The Cumberland County Registry of Deeds in Portland, the Bowdoin College Library, the Curtis Memorial Library and the Pejepscot Historical Society, all in Brunswick. We also enjoyed visits with some very dear island folks who offered much information: Clayt Johnson, Grace Leeman, Harriet Huff, Jean Doughty, Mrs. Jesse Johnson, Jim Herrick and many others. For these wonderful experiences, I thank Janet.

I'm especially thankful to Barbara Munsey for taking the time to talk to me about people and events on Bailey Island. I also appreciate the use of her school pictures.

Special thanks goes to my husband, Hal, whose patience is incredible. He often dropped whatever he was doing to listen to a new thought or idea that I had for this writing. He'd then take the time to go over it with me, time and again.

I am grateful to all of those who gave me information and corrected me on some details, especially my family. My brother Ralph, a Bailey Island lobsterman, is one of the finest storytellers around. Many of his best stories he told while standing by his truck in the front dooryard at Lowell's Cove. My other brother, Steve, also a fisherman, has colorful knowledge of island history. He helped identify people and places in the old photos. My sisters, Ruth and Karen, reviewed the manuscript for detail and made helpful suggestions. I really appreciate their efforts.

On one occasion my niece, Ginny Leeman, went with me to visit Jesse Johnson. It was in 2001, a year before Jesse's death. I also spent a few afternoons with my sister-in-law, Shari Johnson, at a number of local cemeteries locating ancestors.

I am especially grateful to David Hackett, III and Gerry York of the Harpswell Historical Society for sharing their knowledge of the town history.

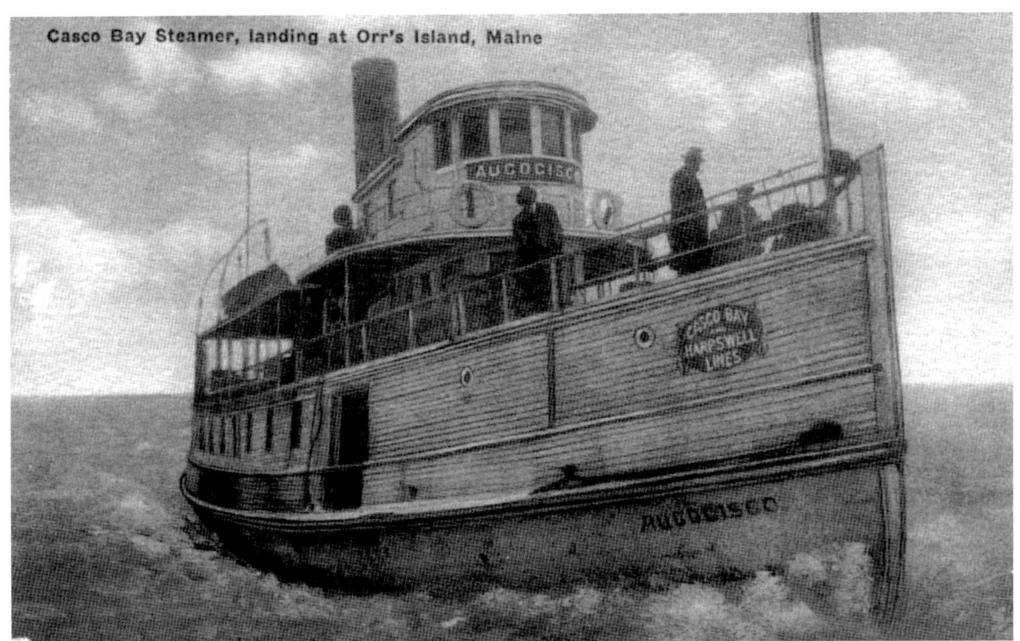
Casco Bay Steamer, landing at Orr's Island, Maine
AUCOCISCO
CASCO BAY
HARPSWELL
LINES

Introduction

As I reflect on my past and growing up, I'm proud of my heritage and feel fortunate to have been raised on Bailey Island. To learn of the outside world through visitors to our island provided a unique experience. Perhaps those visitors influenced me most and contributed to my need to explore the world beyond Bailey Island.

After I attended Gorham State Teachers College—now University of Southern Maine—I got my first teaching job in Brunswick. Although I loved the area, I had to move on. So, off to Washington, D.C. I went and visited Margaret Chase Smith, then a U.S. Senator. I told her of my desire to travel and teach outside of Maine. She recommended that I apply to teach overseas with the Department of Defense.

I landed a job in Berlin, Germany one year after the infamous wall went up. Five years later I returned to the states with a husband, Hal Jensen, also a teacher in Berlin. We settled in Illinois, 25 miles west of Chicago and raised our family there.

Since then my husband and I have traveled extensively, visiting numerous cultures of the world. Still I return to Bailey Island several times a year. When in Illinois there's hardly a day goes by that I don't think about Bailey Island: the beauty, the memories, the people.

My children have always enjoyed listening to me tell experiences of my childhood: my activities with my friends, my freedoms on the island and my family's day-to-day life back then. You might say that my children are actually responsible for encouraging me to write down some of these memories, which I now present to you along with some wonderful tales of island history. In addition, I've included many pictures from my father's collection. Others are my own photos.

Since my parents have recently passed away my siblings and I have gone through the many volumes of documents and pictures. It is a most valuable collection of historical information and will be given to the Harpswell Historical Society.

It has been difficult and confusing putting this together in one volume because it covers a timespan of over 150 years. The book includes pictures from the late 1800's to recent photos. The shifting of time from page to page may seem confusing. On one page you might see a picture of my eighth grade graduating class in 1952 and the next page you'll see an 1887 photo of the main road on Bailey Island. Intermingled are stories of Bailey Island as it is being developed and memories of my own experiences. The order of the work basically follows a pattern of north to south on the island. No attempt has been made to place events and occurrences on a time line.

Efforts to include all appropriate information without making errors was a difficult task, especially when names and dates are not recorded the same on all accounts. I apologize for any deletions, omissions or errors.

The Island Landscape

"Westward of this river is the Countrie of Aucocisco in the Bottome of a large, deep Bay, full of many great Isles, which divide it into many good Harbours."

Unknown Author

It has been said that there are more islands in Casco Bay than in any other body of water in the U.S. An early English report referred to the islands of Casco Bay as the Calendar Isles, meaning there were as many islands in the bay as there are days in the year. Some of these may be merely ledges with very little vegetation. The state of Maine counts 222 islands "big enough for a man to get out and stand on."

Some of these islands are named for the animal kingdom: Cow, Ram, Horse, White Bull, Little Bull, Brown Cow, Horse No. 2, and Bear. Others are named for birds: Crow, Goose, Goslin and Eagle; things from the sea: Crab, Whaleboat and Haddock Ledge; and from the farm: House, Pumpkin, Turnip and Gooseberry.

One of these islands in Casco Bay is Bailey Island. Bailey Island lies 15 miles south of Brunswick, Maine. It is part of the Town of Harpswell which consists of the Harpswell peninsula, three major islands, (Bailey Island, Orr's Island and Great Island), and many smaller islands.

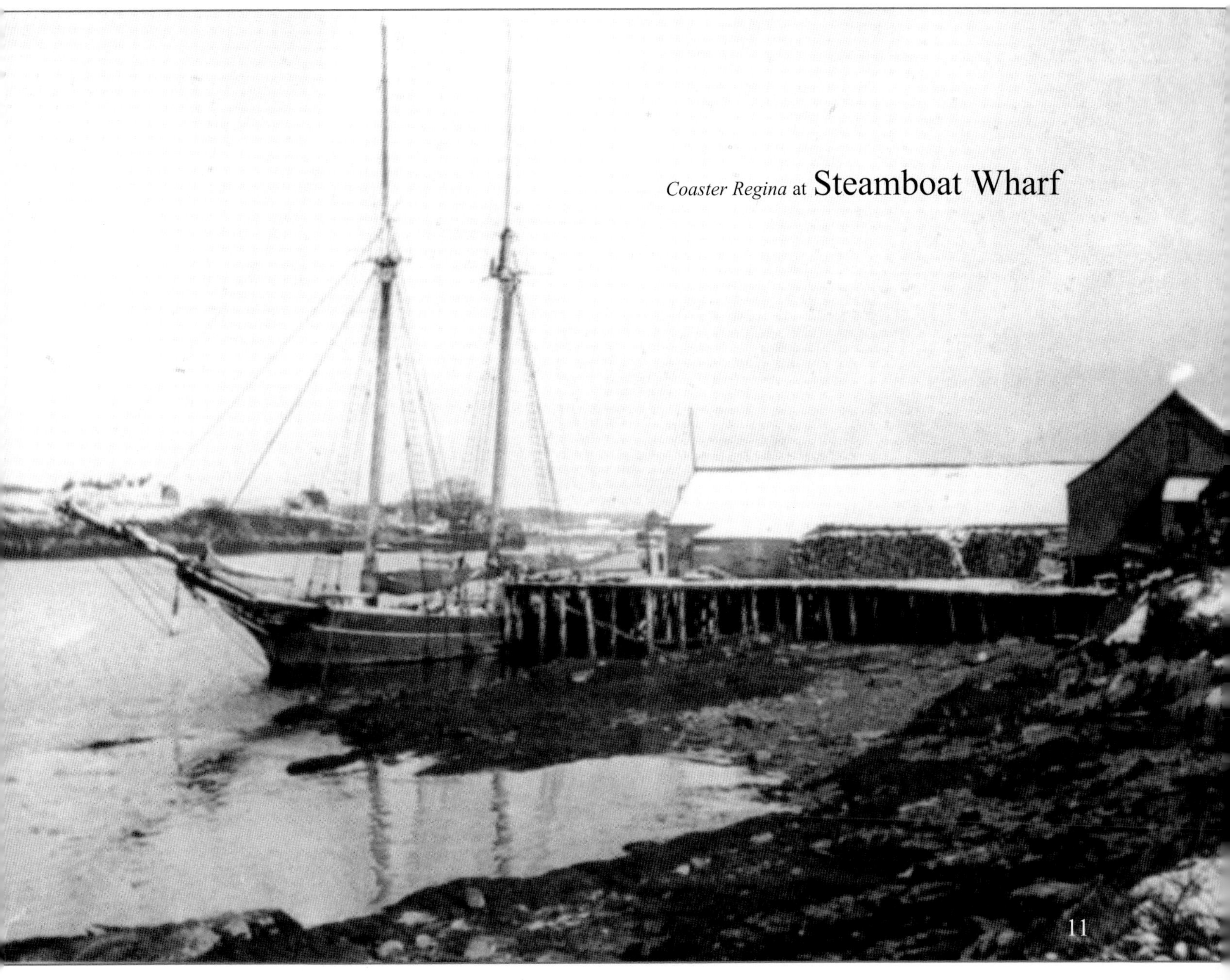

Coaster Regina at Steamboat Wharf

Bailey Island is about two and a half miles long and merely a half mile at its widest. There are many bays, coves and tidal inlets around the island. The mean range of tide is 8.0 feet but tides of 11 feet are not uncommon.

Here and there small stands of spruce, fir and pine cover what is mostly ledge beneath. Bayberry bushes and pine juniper are commonly found in exposed areas. Sea Lavender and Wild Sweet Peas grow around the upper beaches where the ledge meets the sand. In the summer wild blueberries, strawberries, choke cherries, blackberries and gooseberries can be found. Wild roses bloom throughout the summer along the roadways and in the pastures. Indian Pipes, Devil's Paintbrush, Touch-Me-Nots, Buttercups, Daisy Fleebane, Field Pussytoes, Ox-eye Daisies and Columbine grow in the fields.

On a clear day, looking west from a high spot on Bailey Island, one can see Mt. Washington, the highest point in New England, about seventy-five miles away. Looking to the east is Pond Island, Ram Island and Ragged Island. At the south end of Bailey Island, Jaquish Island, Mark Island, Turnip Island and Halfway Rock can be viewed.

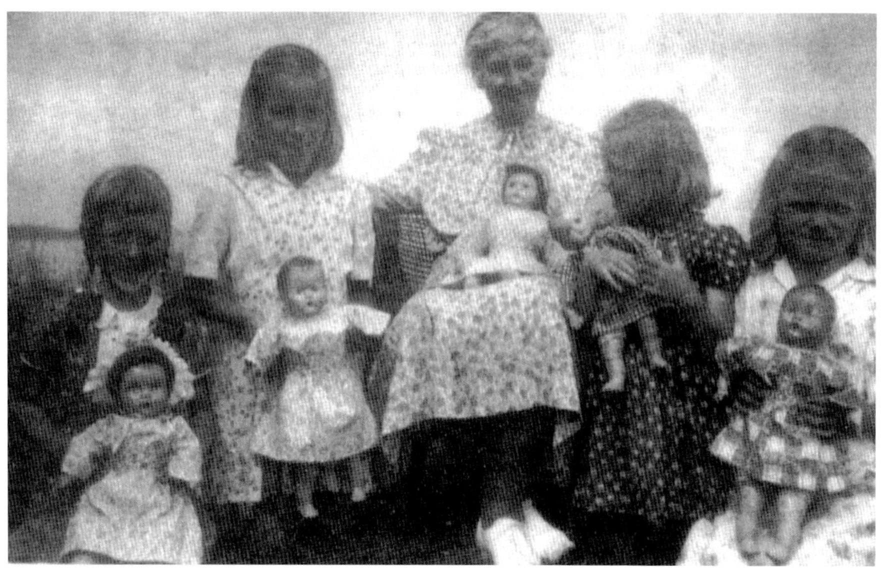

Mrs. Proal's summer sewing class with their dolls. 1944. Left to Right: Donna Leeman, Ruth Johnson, Mrs. Proal, Sandra Stevens and me.

I grew up on Bailey Island in the 1940's and 50's. During the post-war era money was scarce and times were hard. My home was simple with no indoor plumbing or running water. There was not much money for food, so my folks relied on the generosity of others on the island. Islanders always looked out for one another. My memories reflect the small world I lived in, the fun I had and the influences from outsiders.

Grade school, Sunday School, Summer Bible School, the Methodist Youth Fellowship and the Merriconeag Grange were very important in those early years.

Summer was the best time of the year, for then the summer folks from away would come to their cottages, many of them with children my age. This provided a window to the outside world, a world I only imagined. This was also a more prosperous time for my family and other islanders who worked for these people sewing, cleaning houses, cooking, doing laundry, painting houses and doing carpentry.

I suffered many childhood diseases such as chicken pox, whooping cough, old-fashioned measles, German measles and mumps. Dr. Webb from Brunswick and Miss Higgins, the town nurse, held a clinic each year at the Bailey Island school in late summer to give island children pre-school immunizations. This was the only doctor or nurse most of us ever knew. Dr. Pete Smith, who had a summer place on the island, gave free dental checkups to the island children. He cleaned our teeth and if there were any cavities he took care of them.

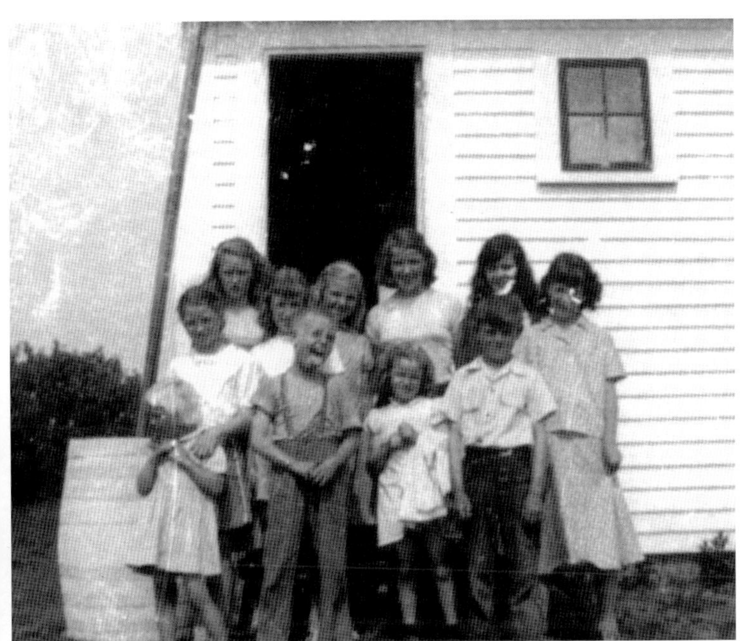

Back row, left to right: Patricia Shea, Donna Leeman, me, Alice Herrick, Denise Beaulieu and ?. Front row, left to right: Karen Johnson, Sandra Stevens, Steve Johnson, Joyce Murray and Jeff Johnson.

Ancestors

"It is wise for us to recur to the history of our ancestors. Those who do not look upon themselves as a link connecting the past with the future do not perform their duty to the world."

Daniel Webster

When I researched the ancestry on my father's side the names Johnson, Orr, Stover, Sinnett and Merriman came up repeatedly. Rev. Charles N. Sinnett wrote their family genealogies in the early 1900's. He was a relative of mine and a native of Bailey Island who moved away in his adult years. He wrote more than 125 family histories and genealogies, many of them of Harpswell clans.

It was no easy task to follow all these names. Variations of Sinnett were Sinnet, Sinnott, Sennett, Synnott and Synott. Variations of Merriman were Merryman and Meryman. In addition, in the early years along the coast of Maine many men were seafaring souls and therefore had the title of Captain, which only added to the confusion. I uncovered the following names: Captain James Sinnett, Captain Johnson Stover, James Stover, Captain David Sinnett, Captain David Johnson, Captain Sinnett Orr, Michael Sinnett, William Orr Sinnett and Joseph Orr. One of my great-grandfathers was Sinnett Orr Johnson and another was Captain James Lewis Orr. My great-great-grandfather, Captain Lemuel Hinckley Stover, married Jane Johnson Sinnett. Perhaps you can now appreciate the confusion!

Jacob Johnson, born in 1715, came from England to settle in Harpswell around the year 1735. He is buried at the Bailey Island Cemetery, his tombstone the oldest in the cemetery.

Several stories surrounded my ancestor Jacob Johnson. One story claimed that he was English and his real name was Hatheway, taking the Johnson name to remain undiscovered when he escaped from an English man-of-war. Rev. Charles Sinnett liked the philosophy: "Hatheways we may be—but the Johnson name is one that we love."

My ancestor Michael Sinnett was born around 1730 in the County of Wexford, Ireland. When he was a young boy he went with a few friends to Dublin. They went down to the docks where ships were tied up. They were invited aboard, shown around, fed and treated well but when it was time to leave, they were told to stay on the ship. They were bound, kidnapped and taken to America to help in the colonies. Joseph Orr of Orr's Island was in Boston soon after the ship came in and paid the passage money for Michael Sinnett to go to America. Michael died in 1800 at Orr's Island.

Another of my ancestors, Sylvester Stover, probably came to York, Maine from Devonshire, England, around 1653.

My ancestor Orr may have come from a Scottish clan named McClaine living in the Highlands of Scotland about the year 1500. For some reason, religious or political, his clan had to leave Scotland. As they traveled south in Scotland, they came to the River Awe in Argyle County. When they had crossed, the head of the clan called the crowd around him and said, "We have now crossed the River Awe, we will shake the Scotch dust from our feet and will also change our name and call it Awe." Many years later it was changed to Orr. They traveled south, very likely to some place near the Mull of Cantyre and there crossed over to the North of Ireland, settling at Coleraine.

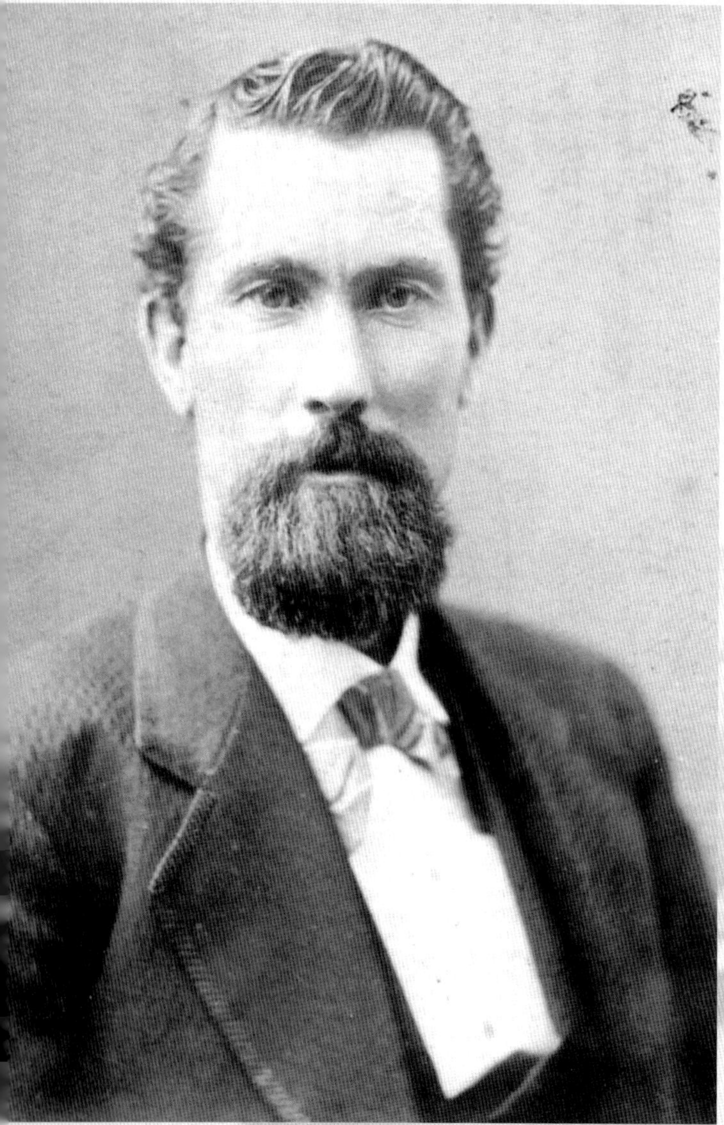

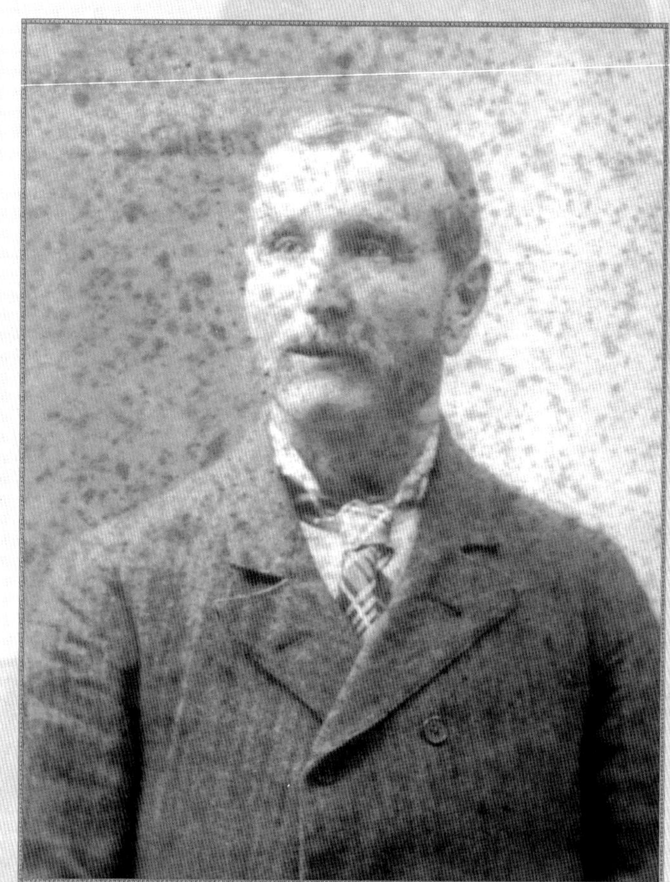

Great-grandfather Captain James Lewis Orr.
1846-1900

At left: Great-grandfather Sinnett Orr Johnson.
1836-1877

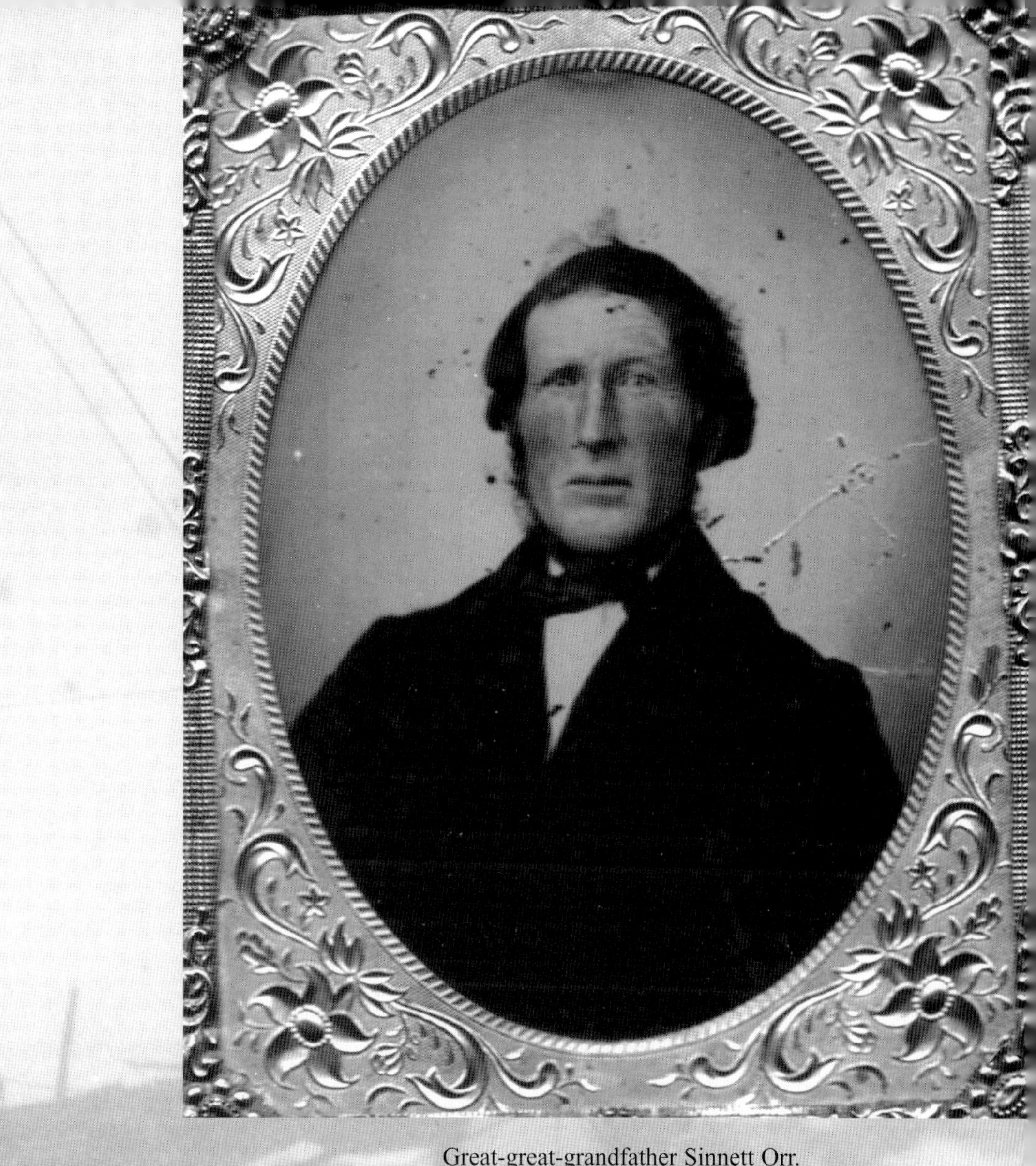

Great-great-grandfather Sinnett Orr.
1817-1897

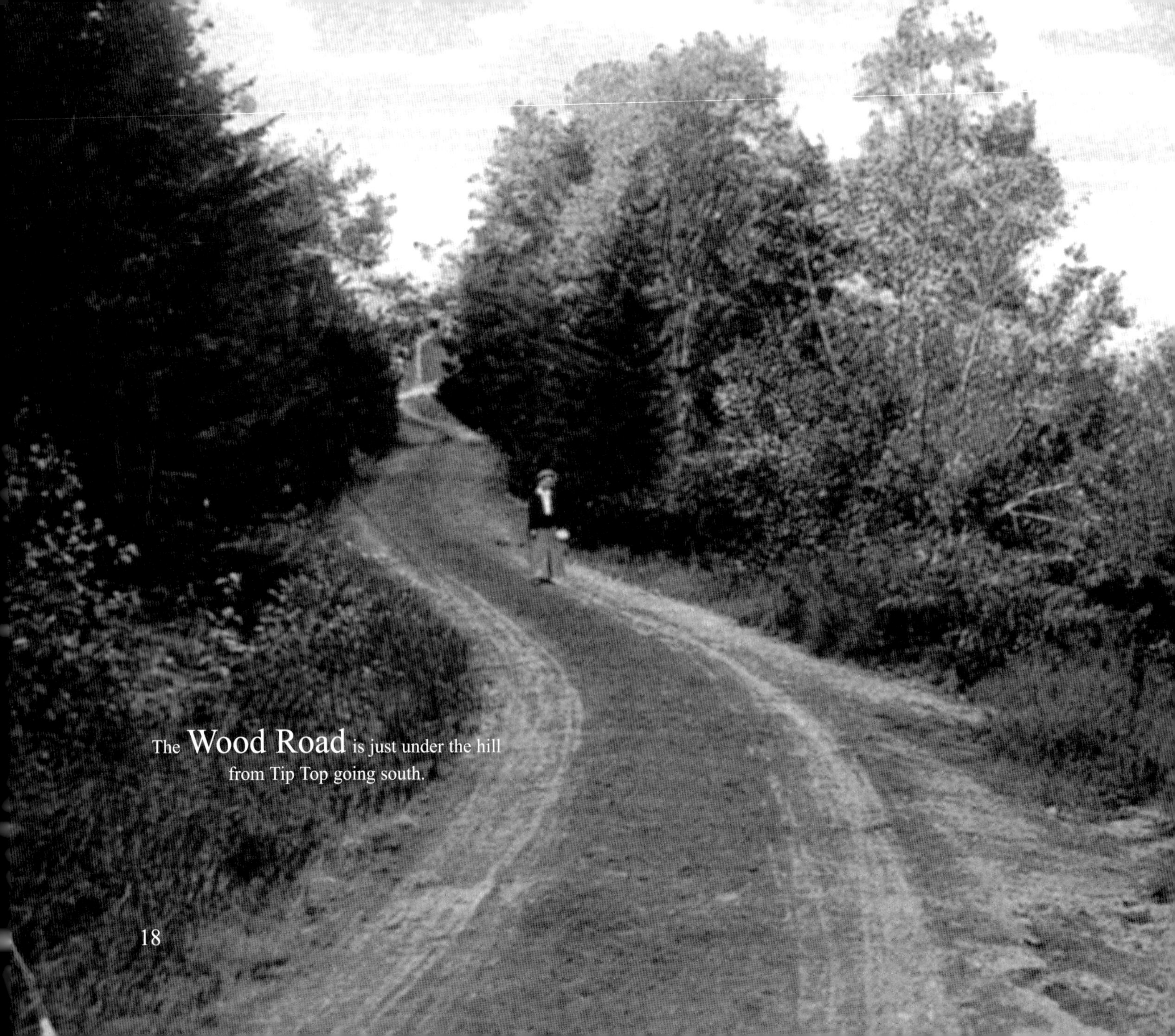

The Wood Road is just under the hill from Tip Top going south.

Newwaggin Becomes Bailey Island

Bailey Island was originally called "Newwaggin," a name given by the Abenaki Indians who came to Casco Bay each spring from their inland winter encampments. Here they would work, gather food and reunite with other Abenaki tribes. The islands were rich with shellfish, cod, mackerel, halibut, lobsters and crabs. The name "Casco," derived from an Indian word, "Aucocisco," means "a resting place."

The first settler, Will Black, after "fulfilling 20 years of quiet possession" under the ancient law of "squatter's rights," legally took possession and received title to the whole island. He registered the transaction in the Act of Incorporation of Harpswell at Harpswell Court. It then became known as Will's Island.

In 1742 Hannah Curtis married Timothy Bailey and with her influence had her new husband appointed deacon of the North Yarmouth parish. Hannah wanted Will's Island for her new home. Will Black's legal title to the island was conveniently discredited and for one pound of tobacco and a gallon of rum, Timothy Bailey bought the island from the North Yarmouth Proprietors; hence, Bailey's Island. Will Black felt intimidated by the Baileys so he packed up and left for Orr's Island over the narrow strait connecting the two islands. The strait is still known as Will's Strait or Will's Gut.

Somewhere along the way—why the change took place is unknown—Bailey's Island became Bailey Island, as it is known today.

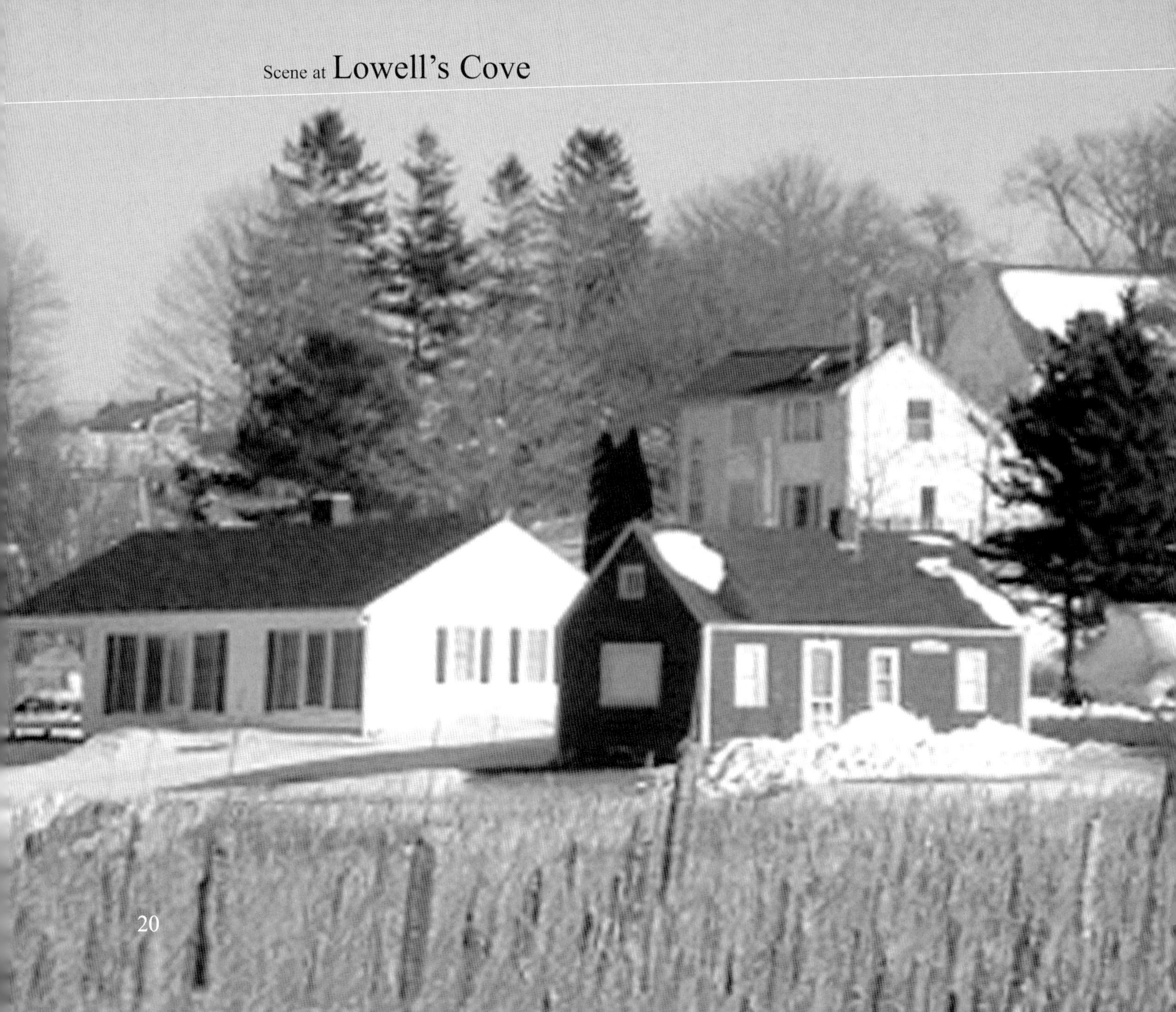
Scene at Lowell's Cove

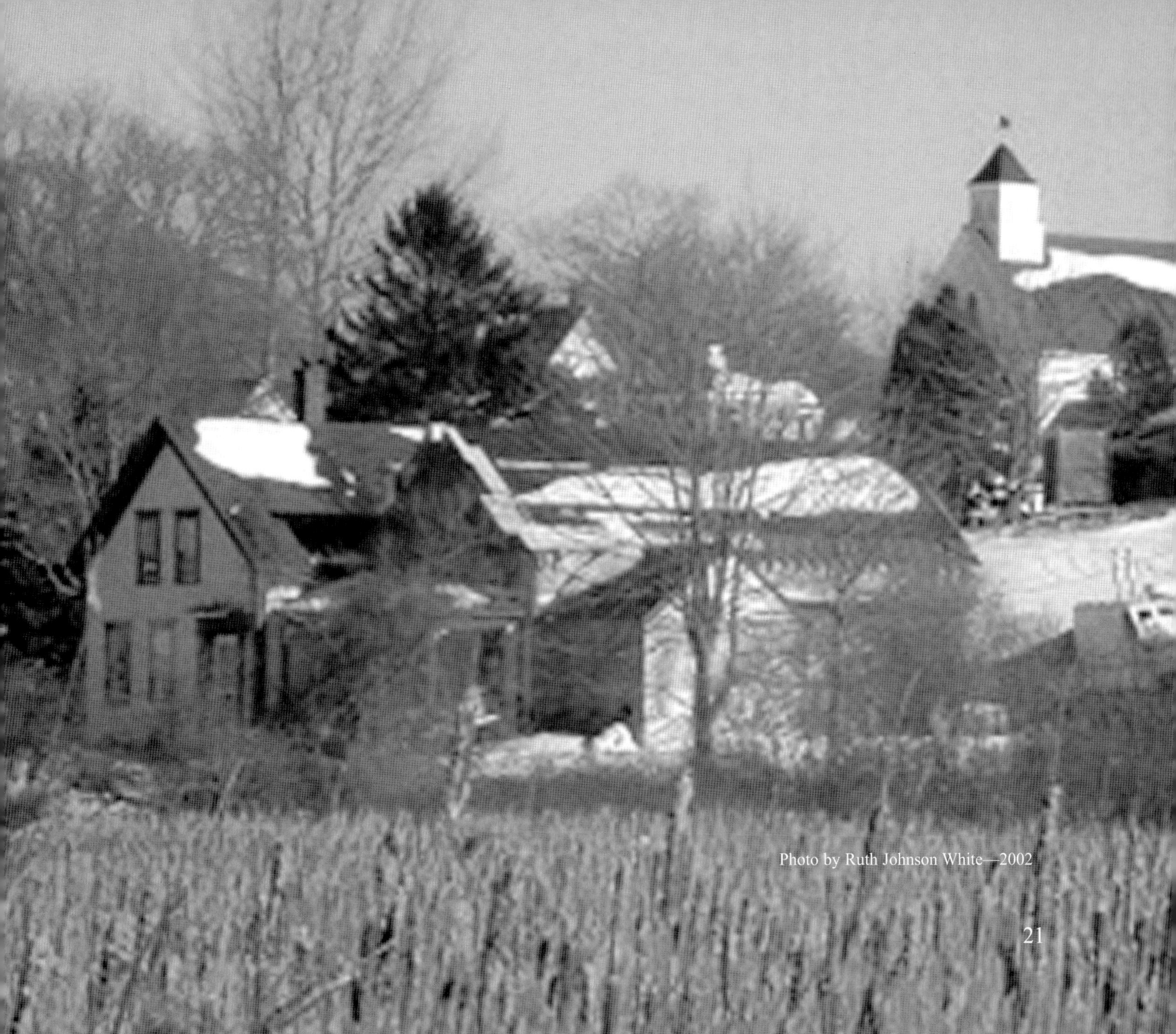

Photo by Ruth Johnson White—2002

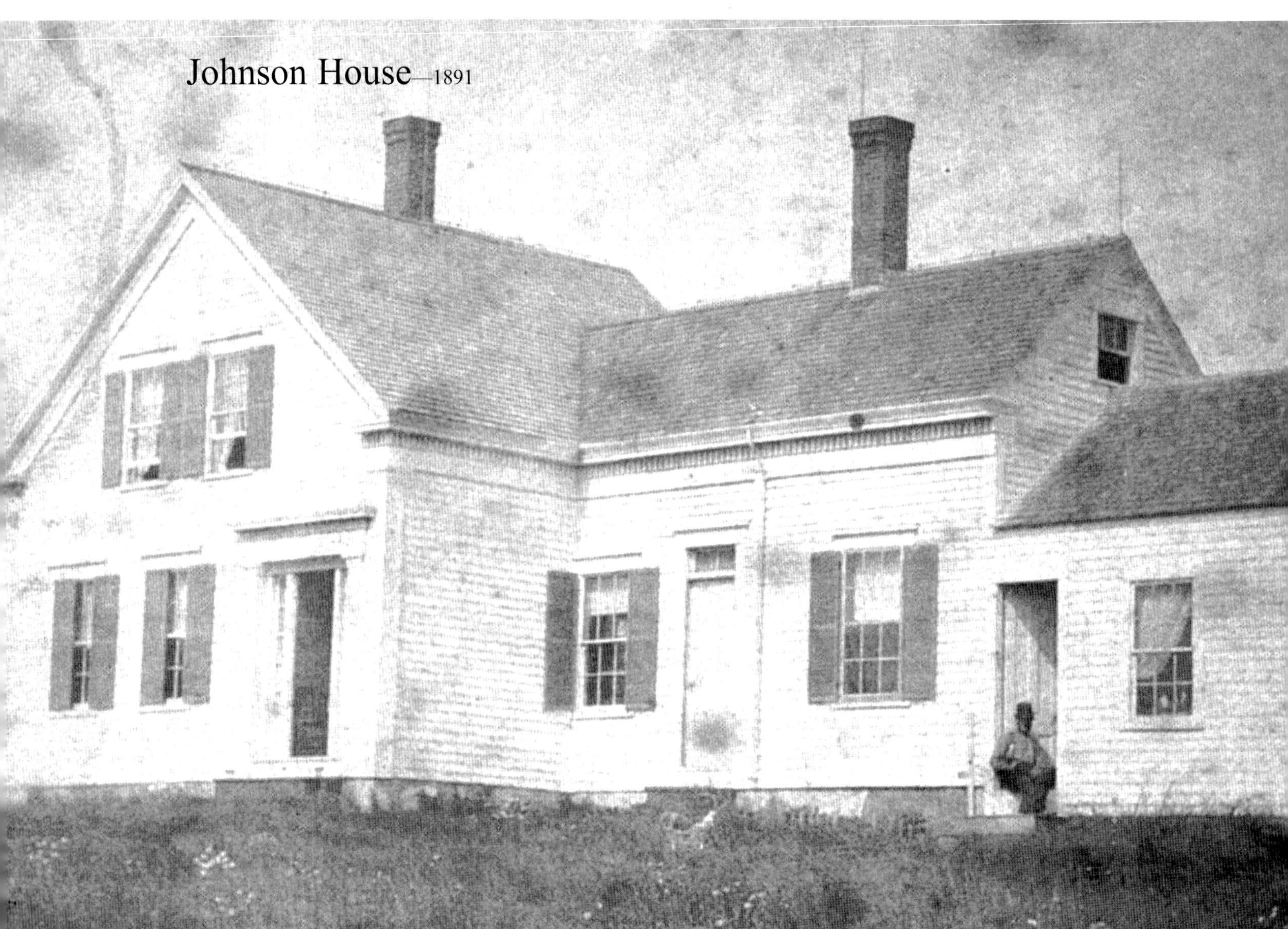

Johnson House—1891

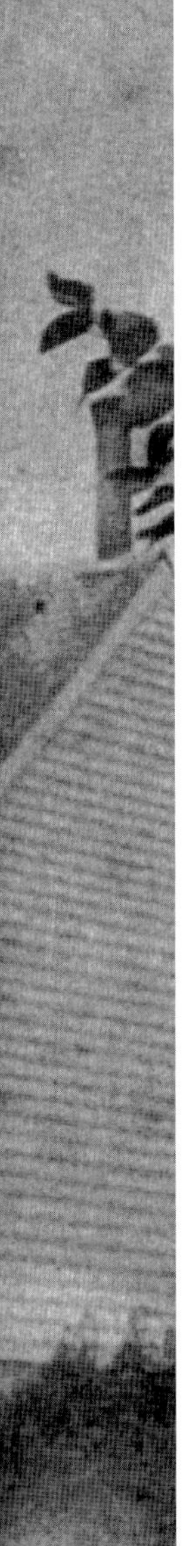

We lived in one of the oldest houses on the island. Built in 1852, it overlooks Lowell's Cove, facing west. Grandfather and Grandmother Johnson lived downstairs and we lived upstairs: seven of us in three rooms.

Before younger sister Karen was born, my sister Ruth and I slept in one of the two back bedrooms and brothers, Ralph and Steve, slept in the other one. In the winter we spent cold nights in bed with heavy coats spread over us and heated bricks at our feet. The frost on the windows was so thick we often carved a couple of pictures before we jumped into bed.

Mom and Dad slept in the front room facing the ocean. It was a multi-purpose room, a place to cook, eat, sleep, bathe, socialize, and do homework. That small room was furnished with a big Atlantic cook stove, a metal kitchen table and chairs, a table for two pails of water with a dipper for drinking, a wash basin, and a pull-out cot with a one-inch mattress for Mom and Dad to sleep on at night and the family to sit on during the day. We also had a big comfortable chair with wooden arms. There weren't any cupboards or closets so everything was stacked on the table or the stove. The wide-planked wooden floors were painted a dark brown.

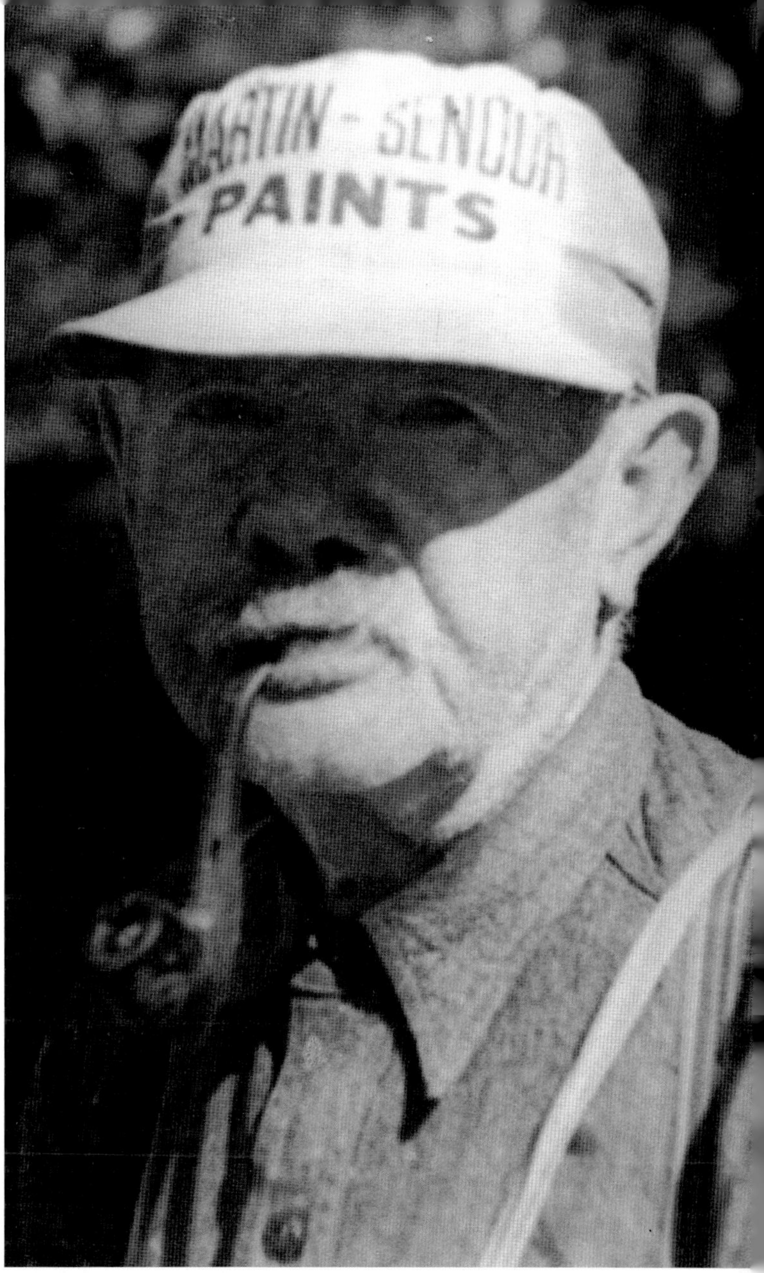

Right: Grandfather Orrin L. Johnson.

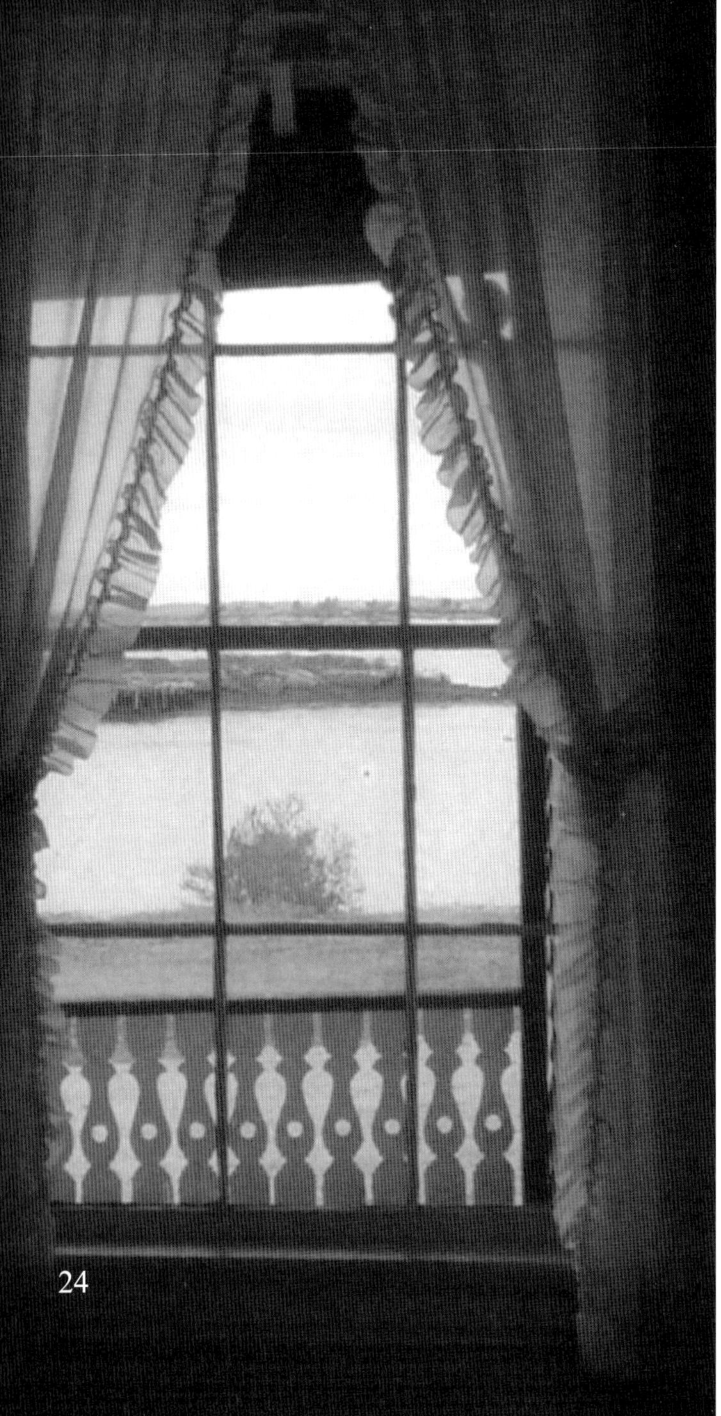

A view from the downstairs kitchen where Grandmother and Grandfather lived.

Those of us who were old enough and strong enough had to carry water from the outside well to our upstairs living quarters. Of course that meant carrying the water back out after using it.

Photo by Nancy Jensen

The best view of the bay was from this front room window of our upstairs living quarters.

In the winter there were storm windows on the two windows facing west. I can still hear them rattling and the wind howling when there was a strong Nor'easter.

Photo by Nancy Jensen

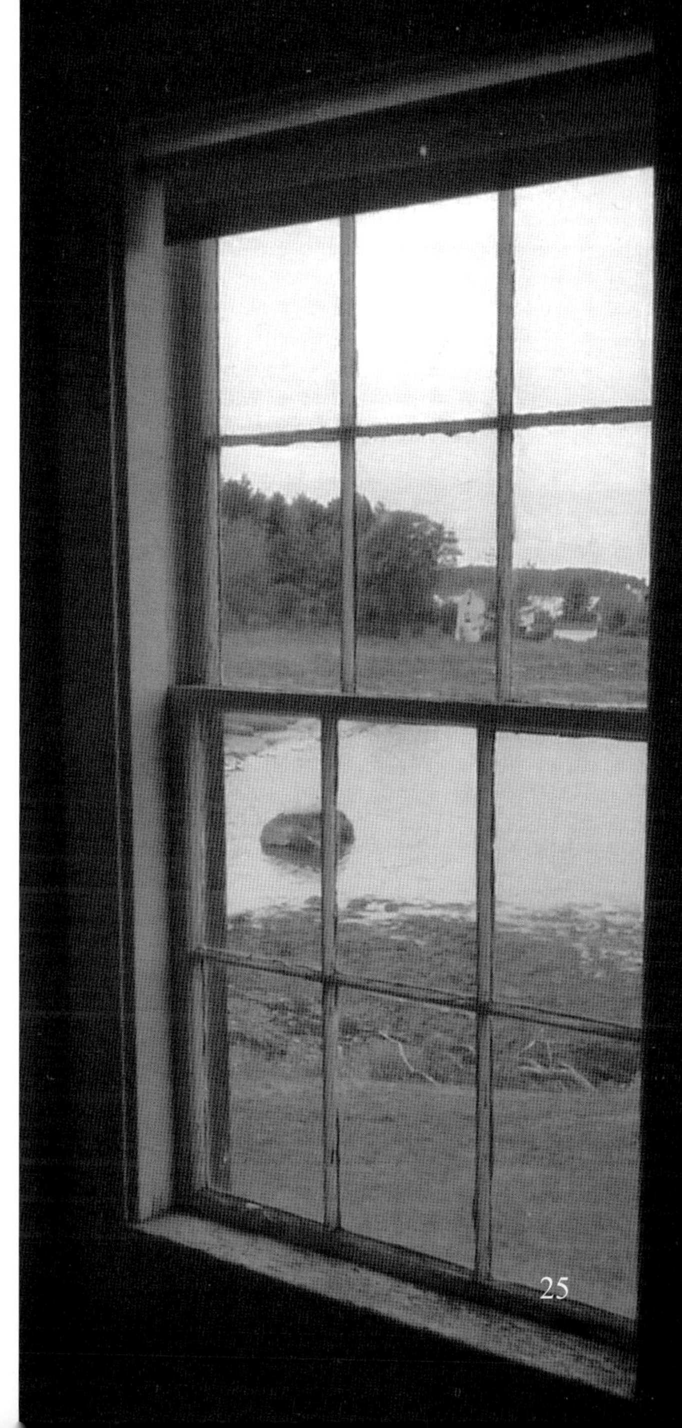

Next to our house was the Folsom House, built in 1797 (some records say 1812). During the years I lived on Bailey Island this building was used as a paint shed for my father. It was stacked with paint cans, containers of linseed oil, large metal pails and cardboard boxes of orange and white lead for coloring the paint. Grampy and Dad always mixed their own paint. Brother Ralph remembers going in there barefoot and making footprints on the floor.

Attached to the Folsom House was an outhouse. The only way to get there was to walk through the maze of paint stuff in the paint shed. The outhouse was lined with posters and pictures. Ralph remembers the ads for Portland Light Pipe Tobacco and RCA Victor with the beagle with his ear up to the horn. Yes, the Sears catalog was right there, too.

In an interview in 1980 with architectural historian James Schimmer published in the *Brunswick Times Record*, Dad said the Folsom House was first built to be used as a home. Then it was a grocery store. In the late 1870's it was Lewis Orr's fish house. It became a paint shop for Grampy Johnson in 1907 and remained so for him and my father until the early 1960's when a friend of our family returned to the island to retire and had it rebuilt as her home.

Photo of porch detail by Steve Black

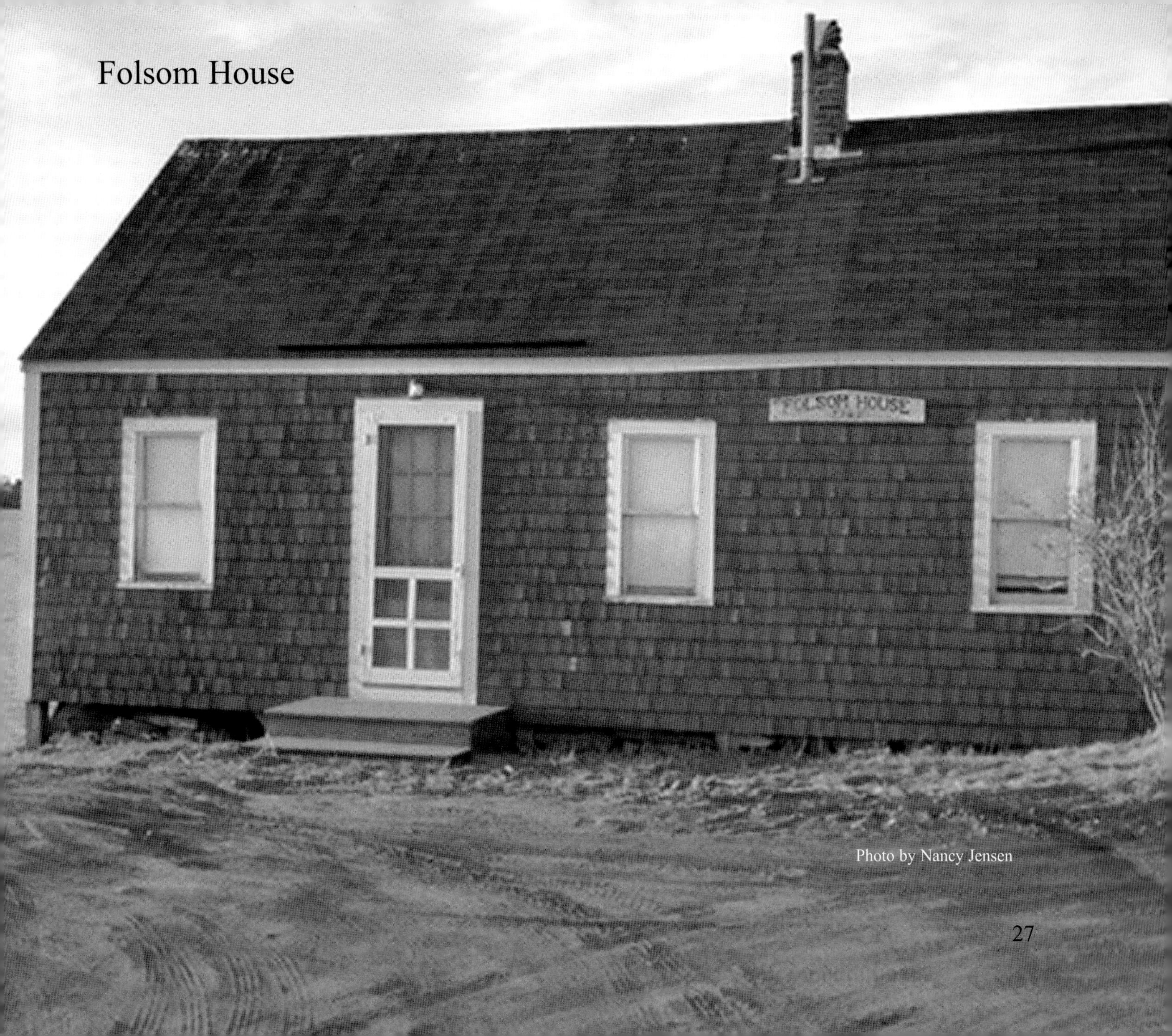

Folsom House

Photo by Nancy Jensen

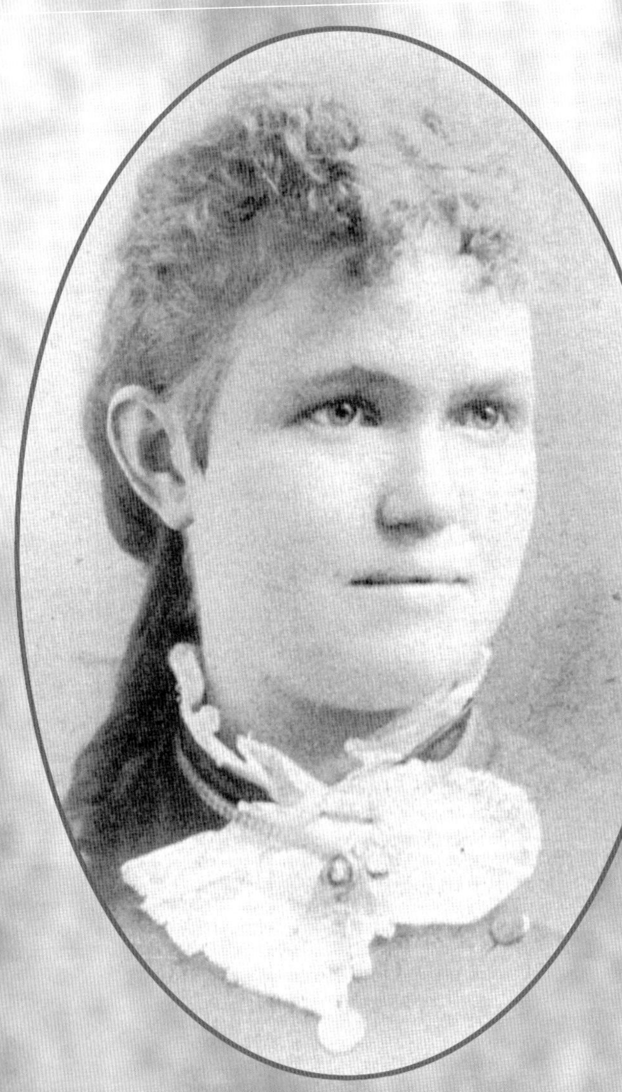

Great-grandmother, Mary Louise Orr, was a very talented and creative person. There was no television or radio in her day, so Mary Louise used her time to make quilts. She was also an artist, and with that talent she designed a Crazy Quilt that was shown at many island gatherings for years afterwards.

The quilt, which she completed in one year, was made of deep red velvet and silk. The squares featured padded flowers of velvet and silk. Mary painted animals of the island as well as portraits of ladies on velvet pieces. Amazingly, the paint has not cracked or deteriorated. On some squares were silk ribbons bearing the signatures of John Greenleaf Whittier, President Harrison's wife, and other notable people.

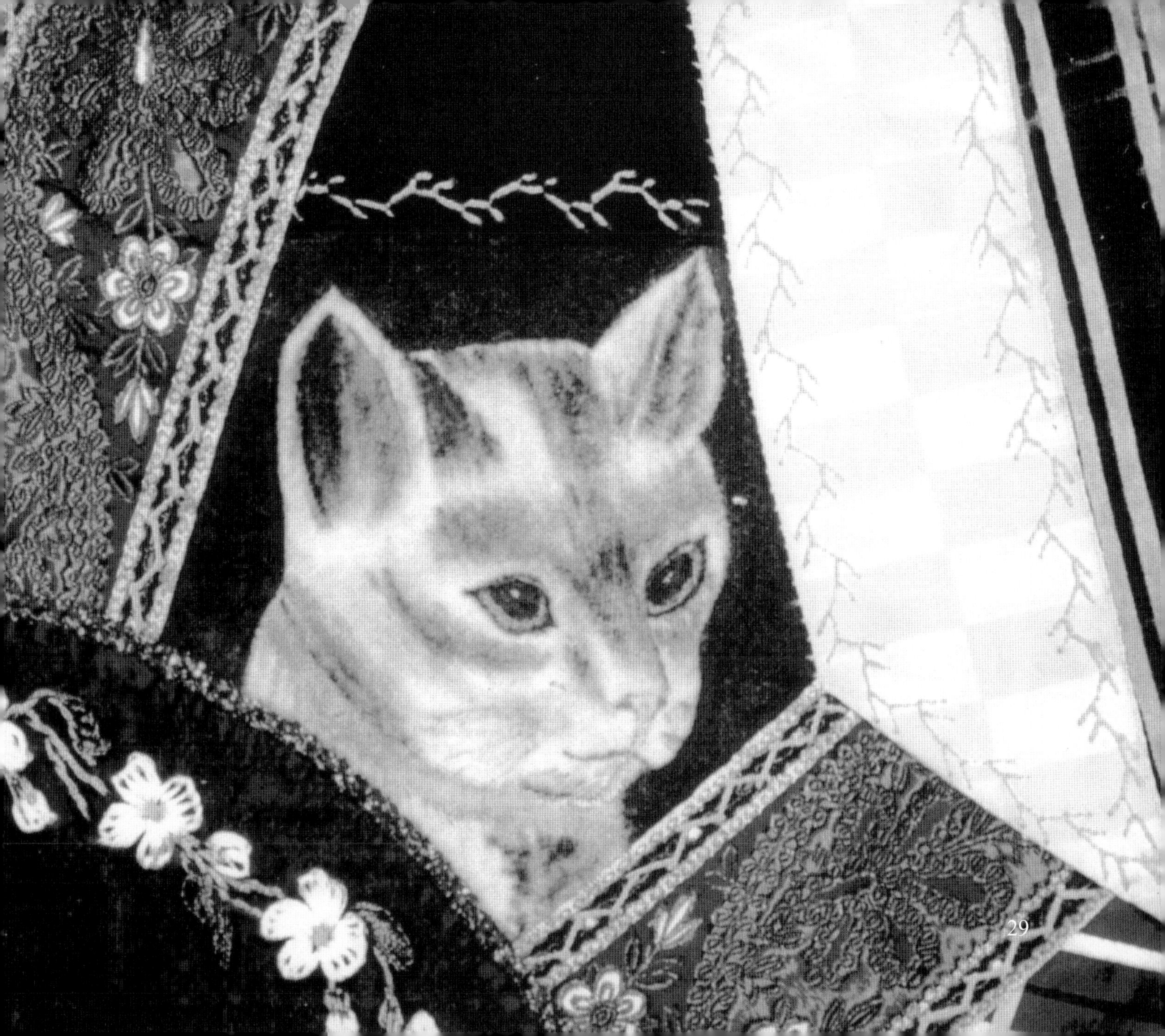

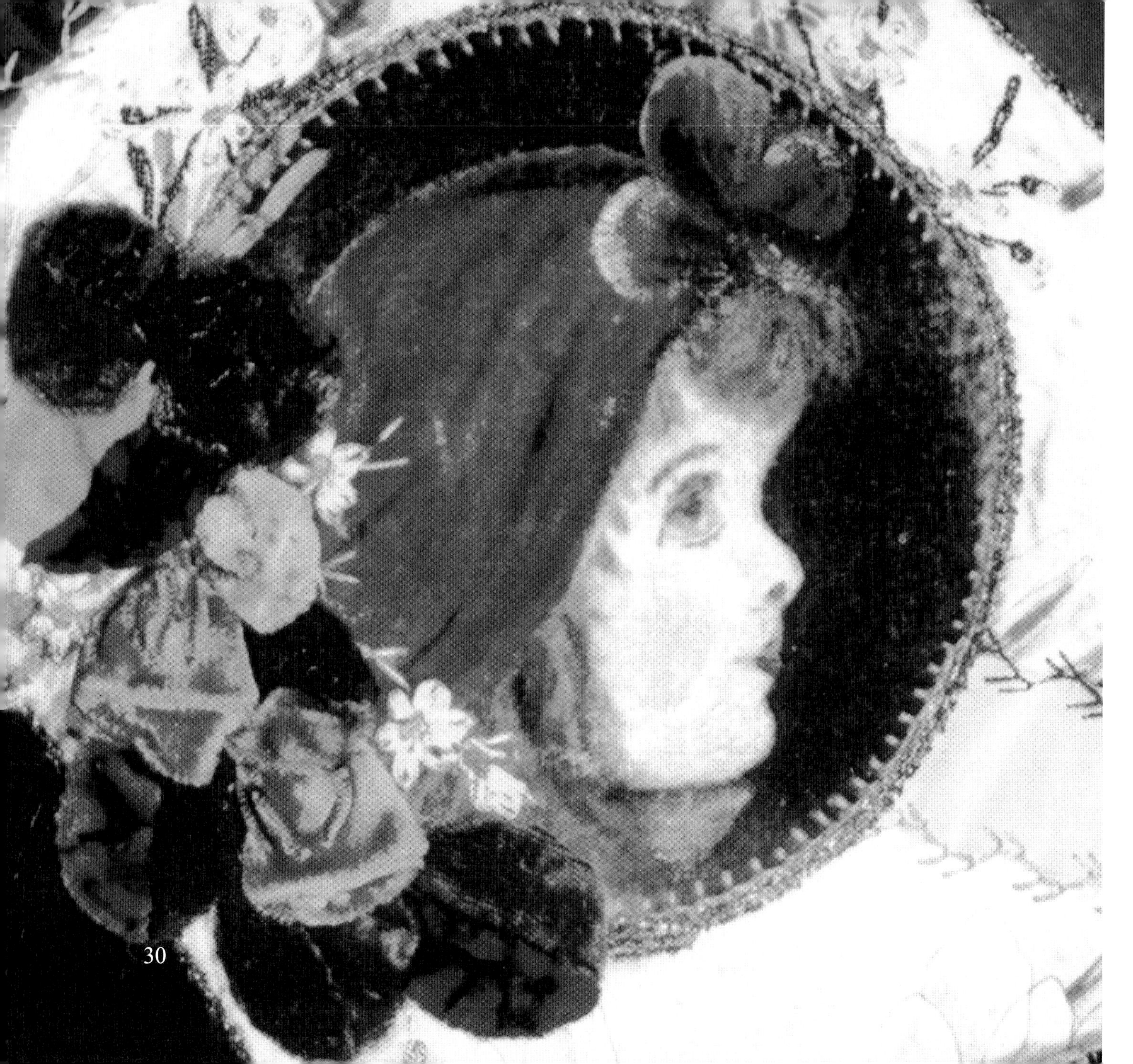

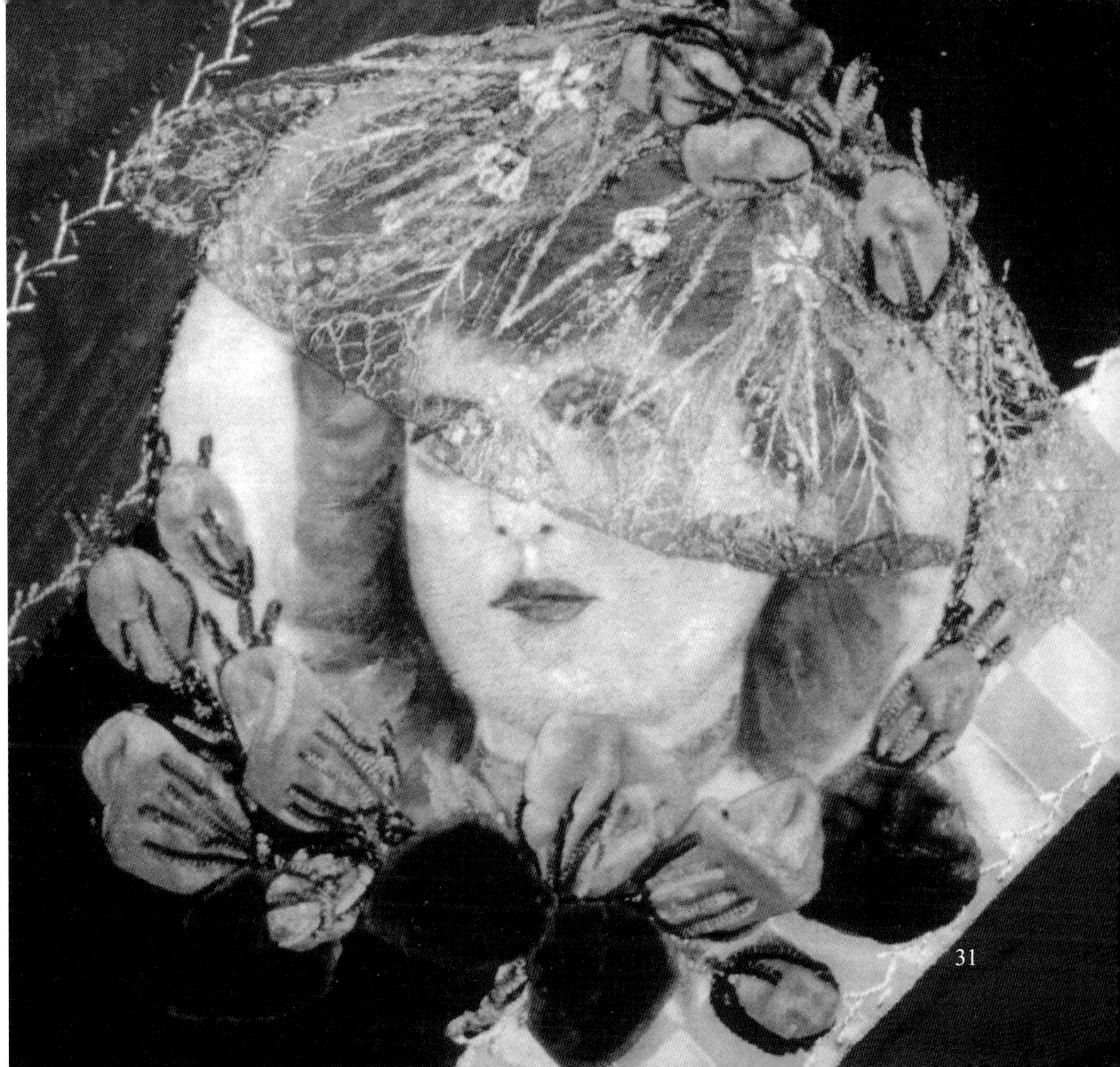

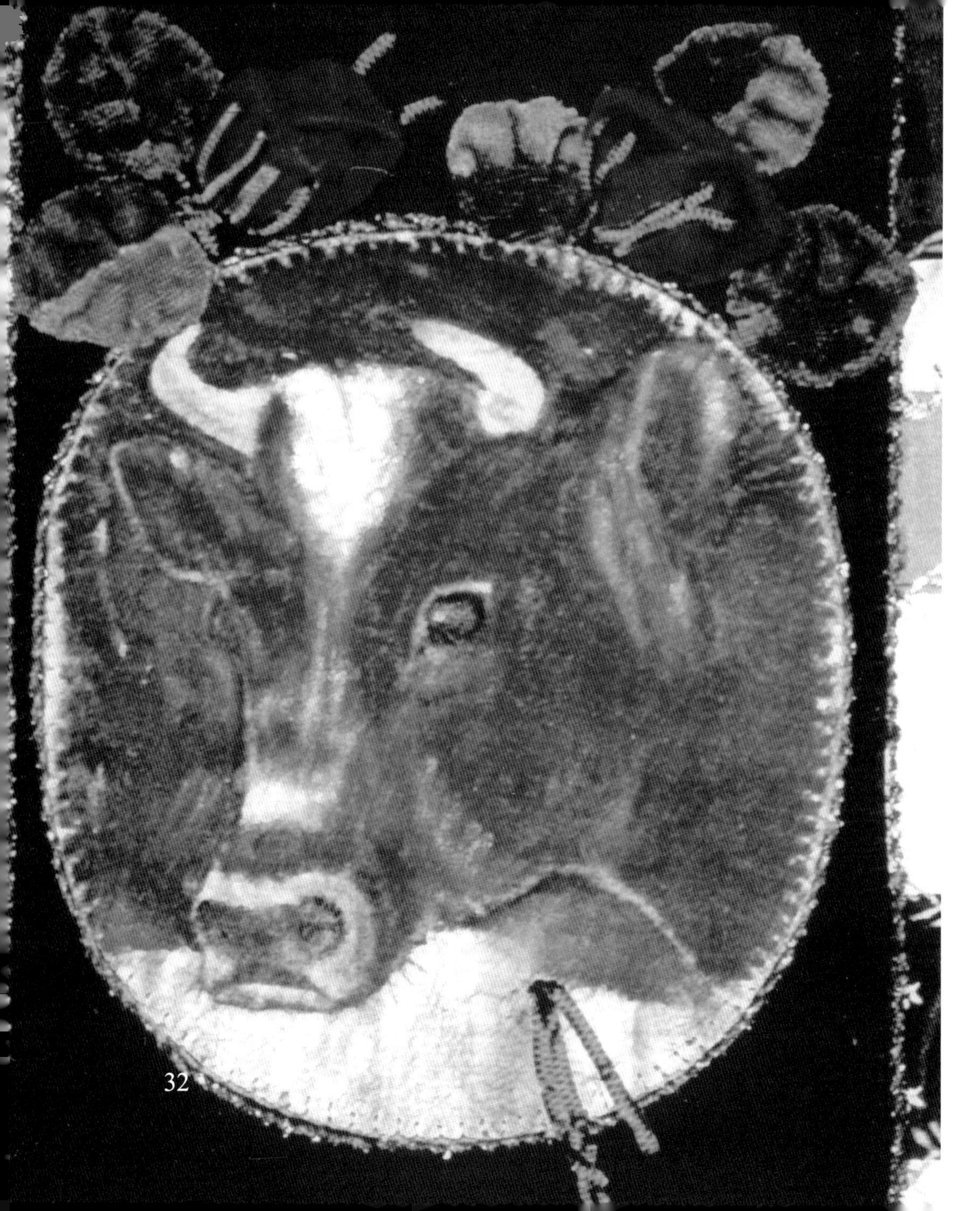

Grandmother Ethel was eight years old in 1890 and did not go to school because she was ill, perhaps from asthma which she suffered from for many years. She wrote to Helen Keller asking for her signature for her mother's quilt. Helen, ten years old, could only use pencil because of the style of writing she was learning, Square Handwriting, so she wouldn't write on the silk ribbon Grandmother had supplied for fear the pencil markings would rub out. However, Helen made a small glass-beaded basket for Grandmother. Helen and Ethel wrote back and forth for a short period of time. Grandmother's quilt is now in the Maine State Museum in Augusta, along with the letters from Helen Keller. One letter is reproduced on the following pages.

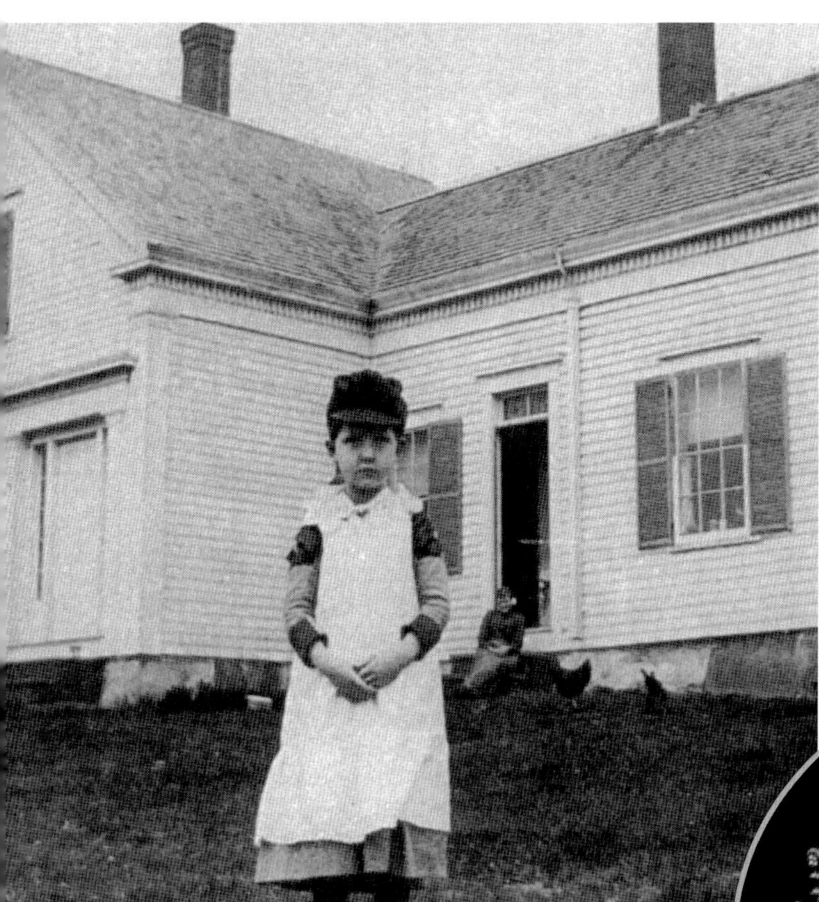

Above: Grandmother Ethel Johnson at about eight years when she corresponded with Helen Keller.
At right: basket beaded by Helen Keller for Grandmother Ethel in 1890. The basket remains in a private collection.

So. Boston, March 15, 1890.

My sweet Little Friend,

The box of pretty
things you sent me, and your dear
mother's letter have been received,
and I do not know how to tell you
how happy they made me. I love
dearly to see things that have come
from far away lands. Geography
is a beautiful study - you will enjoy it I am sure, when you are
well enough to go to school. A long
while ago when I was a small child
I did not know anything about
the beautiful world, and all the
strange and wonderful things
that I know about now. I was
not perfectly happy then. You
must ask your kind mamma to

tell me about Baileys Island when
she writes to me again. I hope Polly
has learned to say Helen by this
time. All of my friends were
greatly interested in my pretty
treasures. I am very glad that
my mother sent you a little bead
basket. Now I must tell my dear
little Ethel good-bye for I have
several letters to write before dinner.

With much love and a kiss,
From your little friend
Helen A. Keller.

Here, and on the previous page, is a copy of one of the letters written to Grandmother Ethel by the famous and admired Helen Keller.

Dad was a house painter. Most of his work was done in the summer, painting cottages on all three islands. He was also an amateur historian. His collection of documents and pictures, many used in this book, came down through the family. He always lived in the Johnson House on Lowell's Cove, as did his parents and grandparents before him.

Mom was a fine seamstress, sewing clothes and making furniture slipcovers for the summer folks. She also was a cook and worked at the local restaurants. It was a hard life for them, managing the household, caring for five children and working many hours a day.

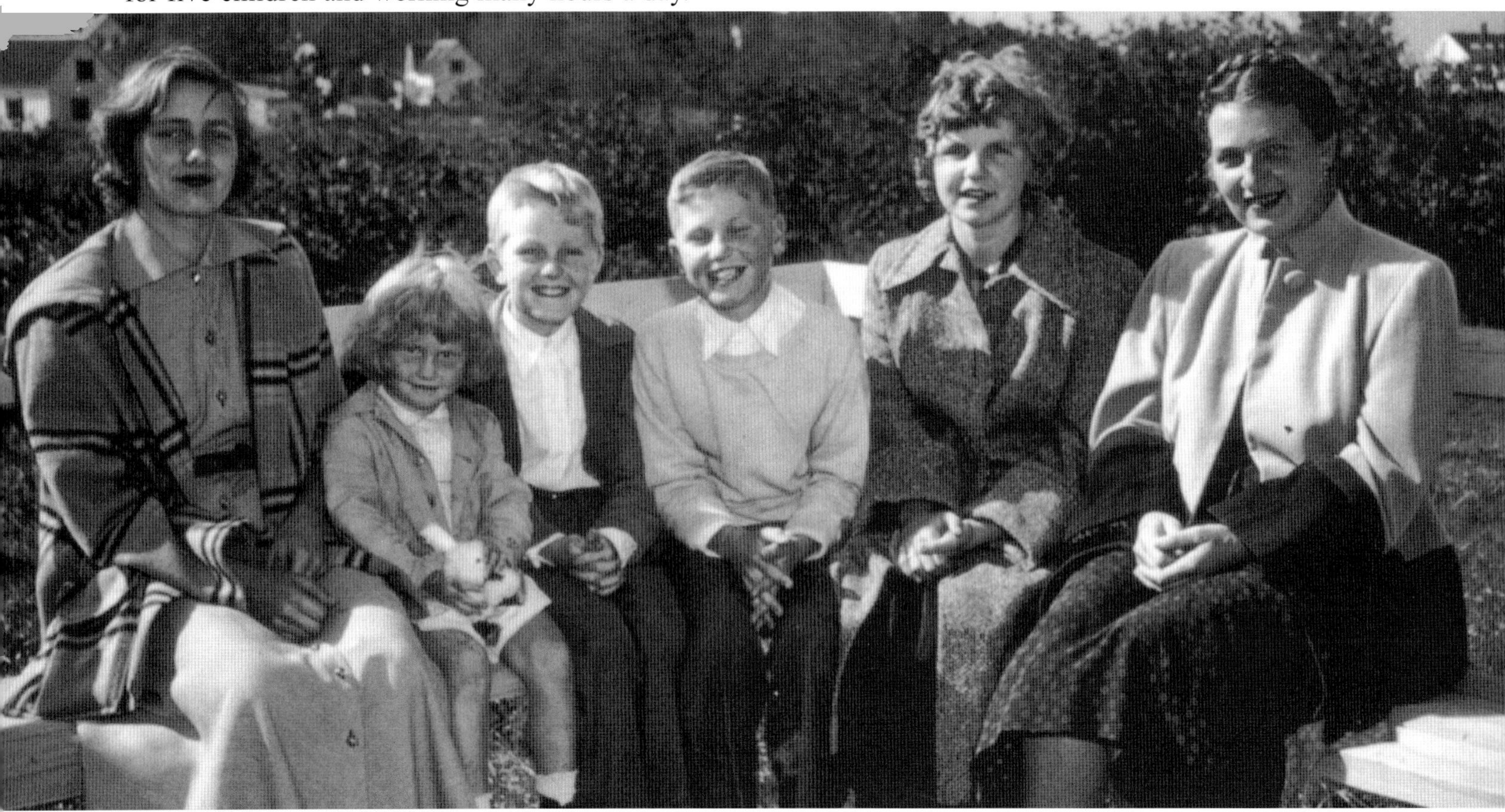

Ruth, Karen, Steve, Ralph, me and Mom, Virginia Johnson. Early 1950's. Photo by Royal Root

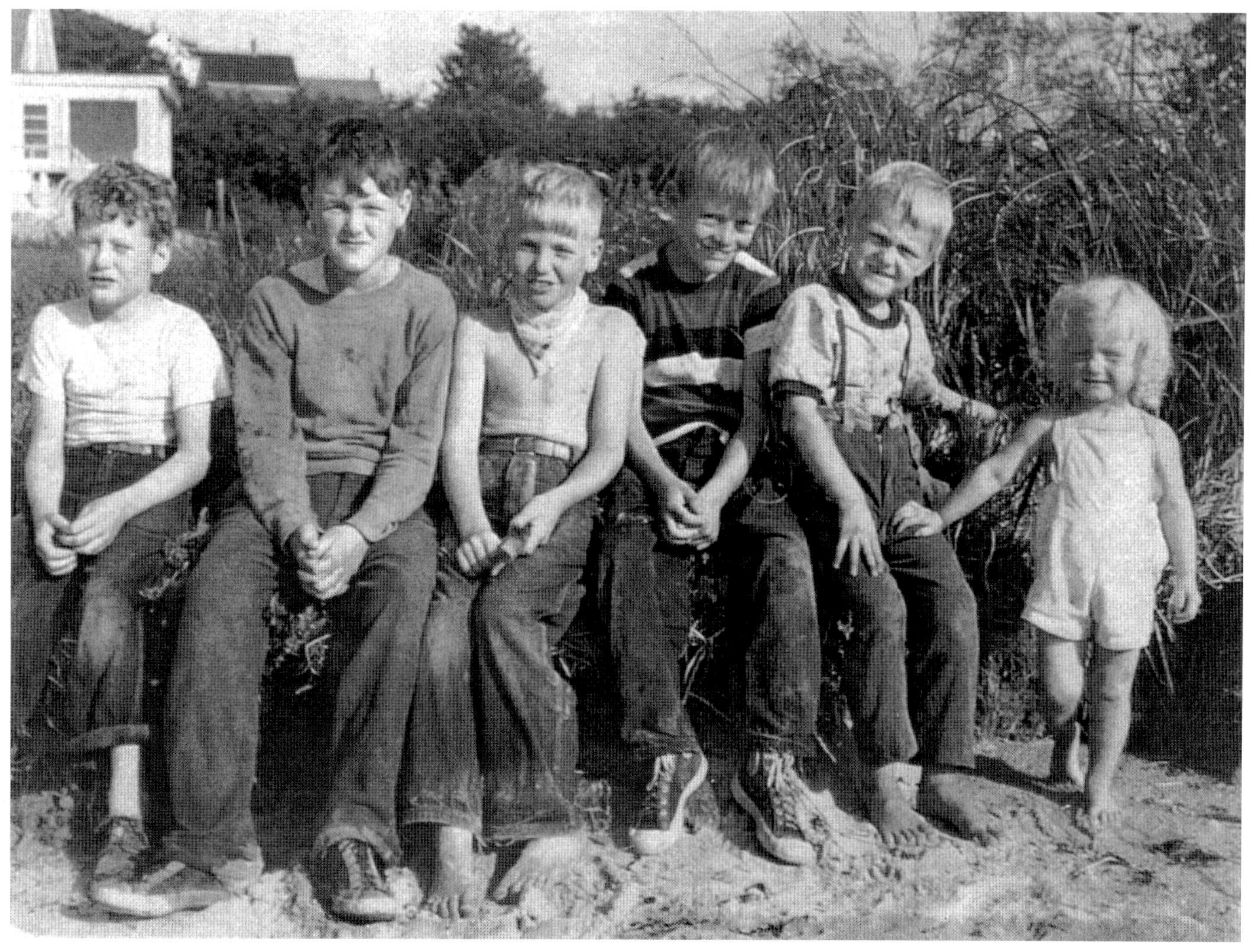

Three Johnson families are represented here. Left to right: Clifford and Arthur, Bunk and Ellen's sons. Jeff, son of Larry and Eileen is sitting between my brothers Ralph and Steve. Little sister Karen is by their side. Early 1950's.

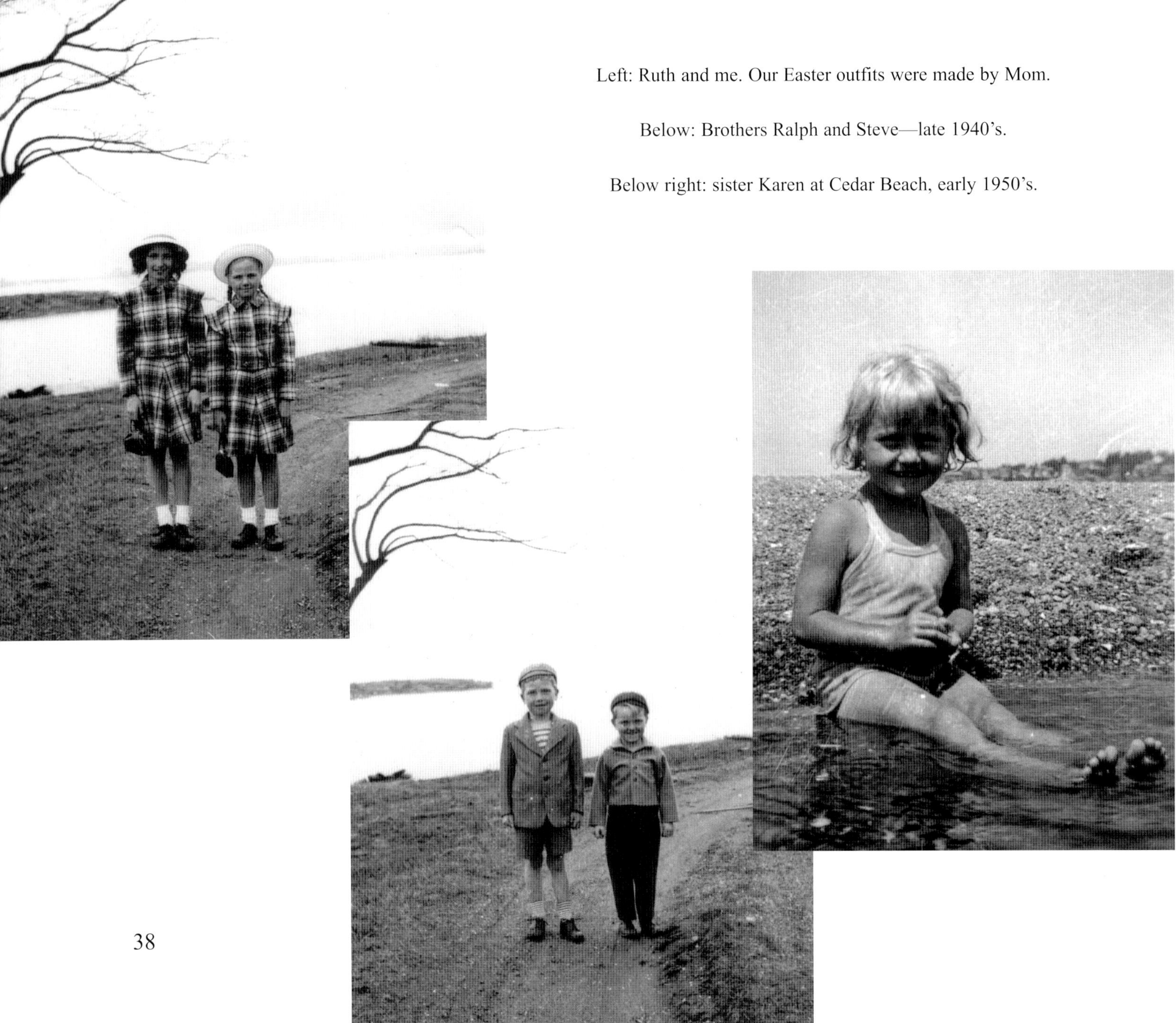

Left: Ruth and me. Our Easter outfits were made by Mom.

Below: Brothers Ralph and Steve—late 1940’s.

Below right: sister Karen at Cedar Beach, early 1950’s.

Johnson Family Tree—about 1950.

Foreground: Virginia, Karen and Linwood Johnson.
Above left to right: Sally Murray, and me, Ruth and Steve Johnson.
Brother Ralph was not present when this photo was taken.

Photo by Royal Root

Royal Root was a distinctive summer resident of Bailey Island, known for his photography and for tuning islander pianos. I remember him sitting at Grandmother's piano, eating his lunch—spoonfuls of peanut butter from a jar.

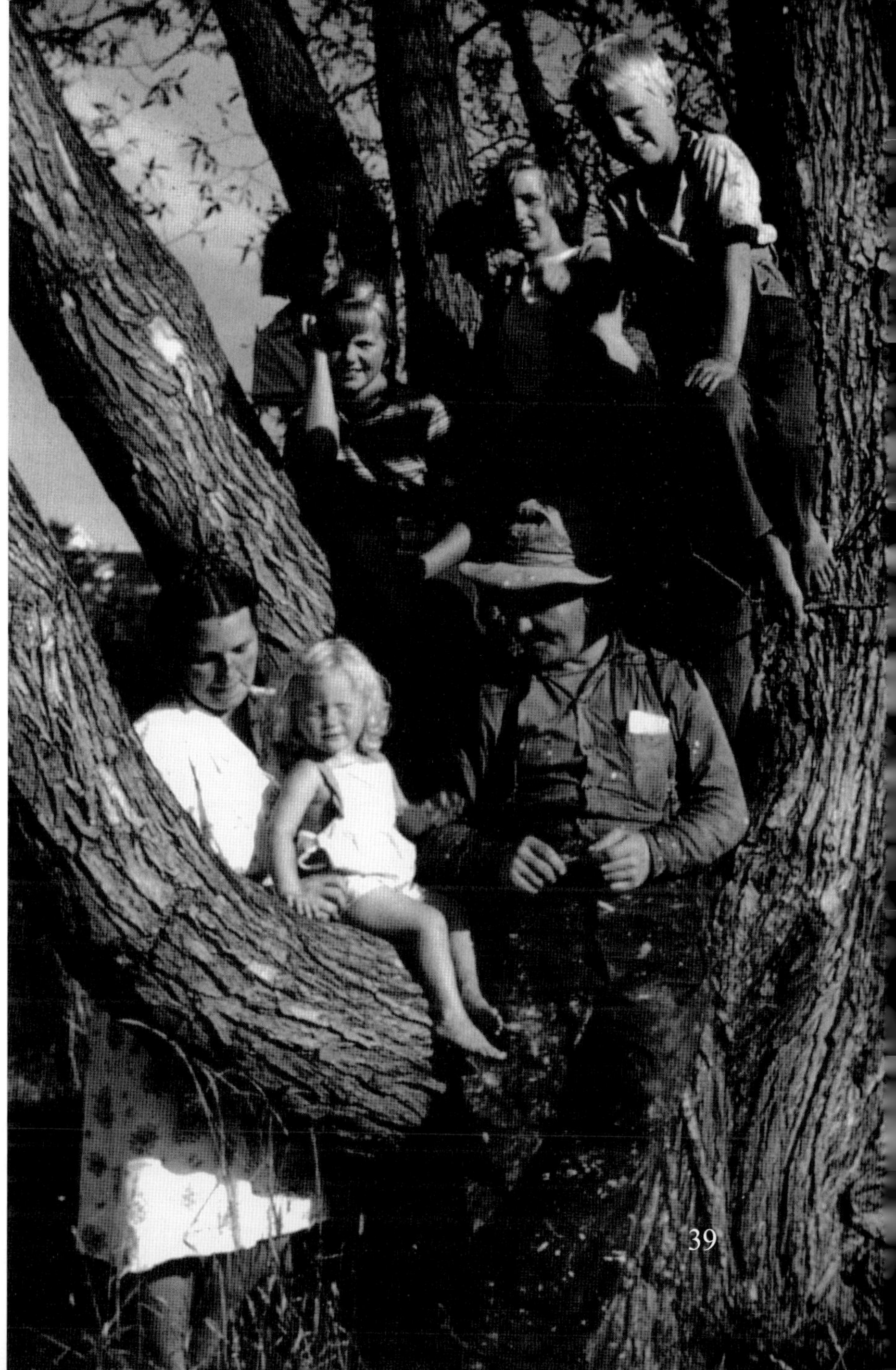

The Jot House

This sketch is from the *Johnson Genealogy* by Charles Sinnett, 1907.

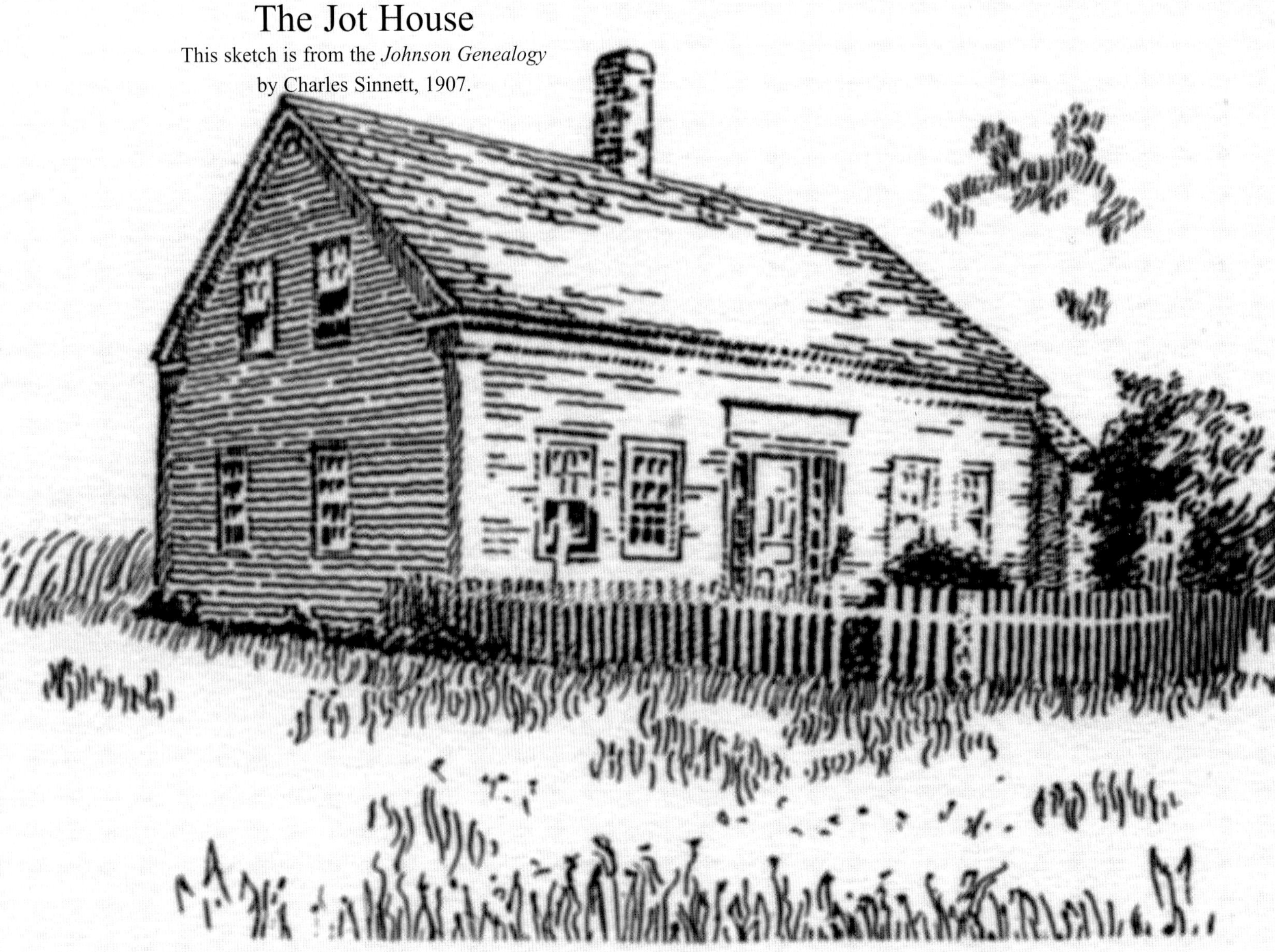

Home of David Johnson, Bailey Island, Me. Built in 1763.

The Ten Oldest Buildings on Bailey Island

The Jot House—1763 (Bob Leeman's house across the street and north of the cemetery)
Captain David Sinnett's House—1788 (Harvey Johnson's house on east side of road, going south)
Nubble—1790 Jacob Johnson (Under the hill from Tip Top on the right, going south)
Folsom House—1797 (Cape Cod-style house on Lowell's Cove)
George Washington Doughty House—1799 (On Ocean Side Road opposite fire station)
James Sinnett on Main Rd—1814 (Labrador Jim's house opposite Catholic Church)
Abner Johnson House—1822 (West side of Mackerel Cove by marina)
Jesse Johnson House—1839 (On top of hill in back of Union Church)
The Homestead—1842 (Last house on the right of Highway 24 at the south end)
Linwood Johnson House—1852 (Lowell's Cove, beside the Folsom House)

Of the ten oldest buildings on Bailey Island, nine are still standing as of this writing. The Jot House, built in 1763, is the oldest. It stands on the opposite side and just north of the cemetery on 24. The rooms are plastered with lime made from mussel shells brought ashore from Pond Island.

Will's Gut, Will's Cut or Will's Strait are names given for the narrow channel between Bailey and Orr's Island. Heavy currents are created as the tides flow in and out. The proposed cribstone bridge, approved by the Maine State Legislature in 1883, would connect the two islands.

In the days before the cribstone bridge, a Friendship dory was based on the north end of Bailey Island. The ferryman of the day would transport people back and forth across Will's Gut, or Will's Strait. If you were on Orr's Island and you wanted to go to Bailey Island you'd hoist a dingy old white flag to the top of a pole, which was mounted on the fish house there. When the ferryman saw the flag he would row across the gut to pick up the passengers. To go from Orr's to Bailey's cost fifteen cents. The return trip to Orr's cost twenty-five cents. Orr's Islanders were known to say, "After you've been on Bailey's for an hour, it's worth a quarter to get back!"

An unidentified child in a ferry between Bailey Island and Orr's Island—before 1925.

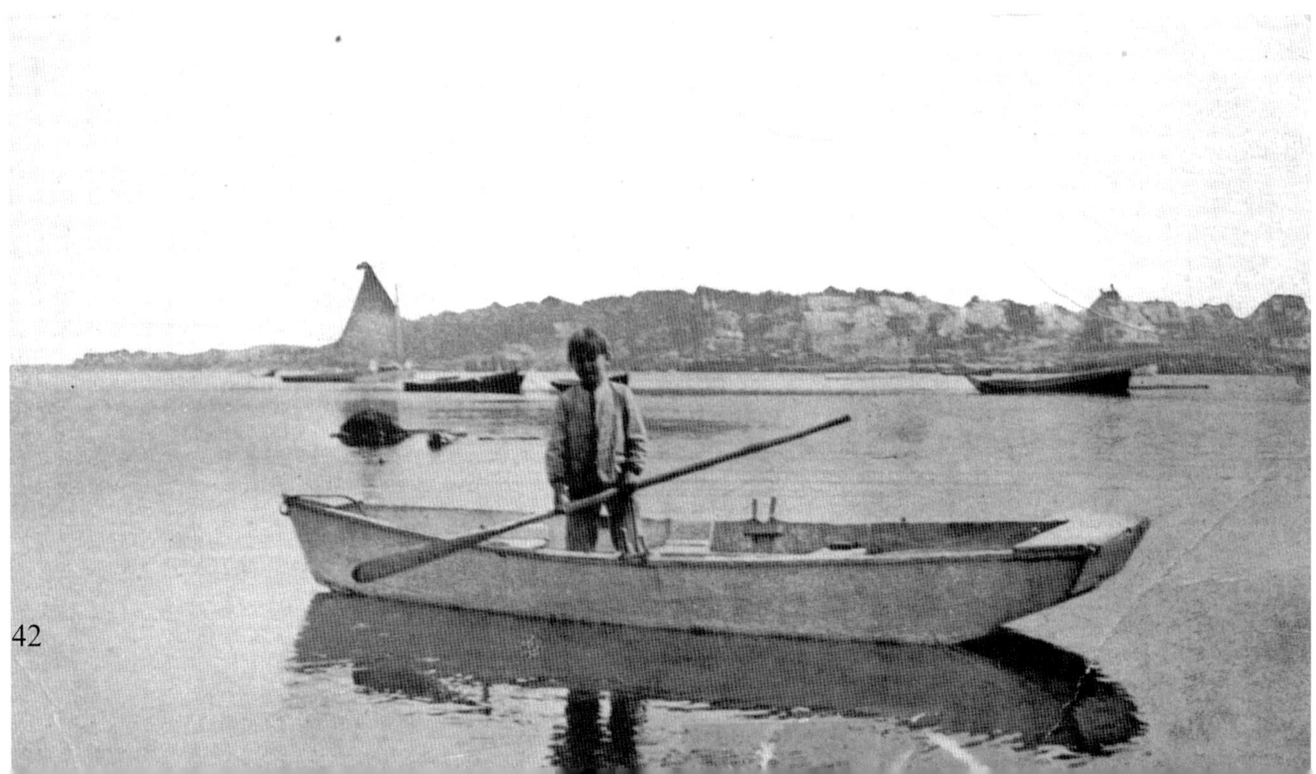

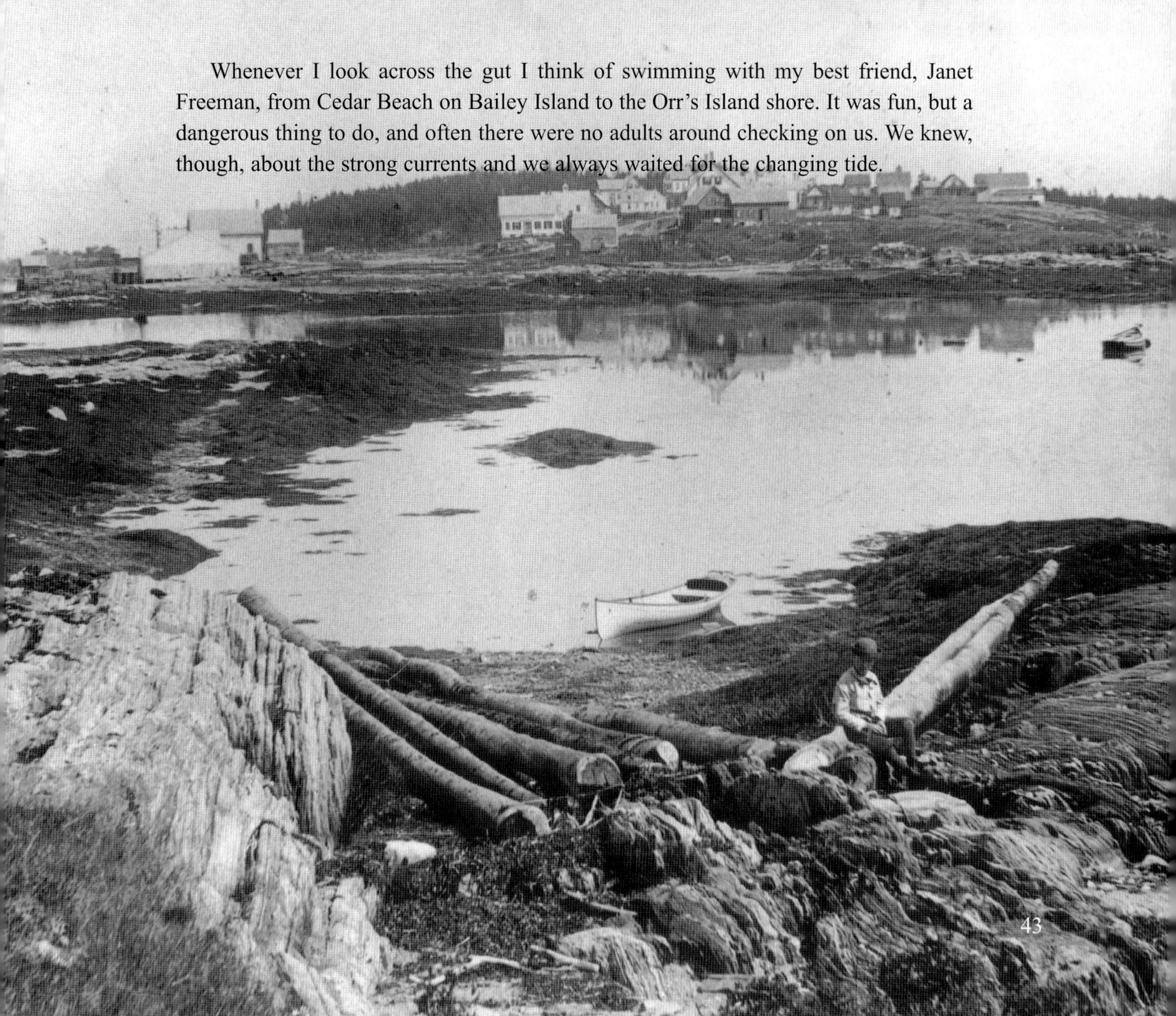

Whenever I look across the gut I think of swimming with my best friend, Janet Freeman, from Cedar Beach on Bailey Island to the Orr's Island shore. It was fun, but a dangerous thing to do, and often there were no adults around checking on us. We knew, though, about the strong currents and we always waited for the changing tide.

Today, crossing the Cribstone Bridge from Orr's Island to Bailey Island, one can see Cook's Lobster House on the point. Lobster boats are moored in Garrison Cove, named for a garrison house built there before 1756 by Deacon Bailey as protection against the Indians.

A fish house at the head of Garrison Cove at the turn of the century.

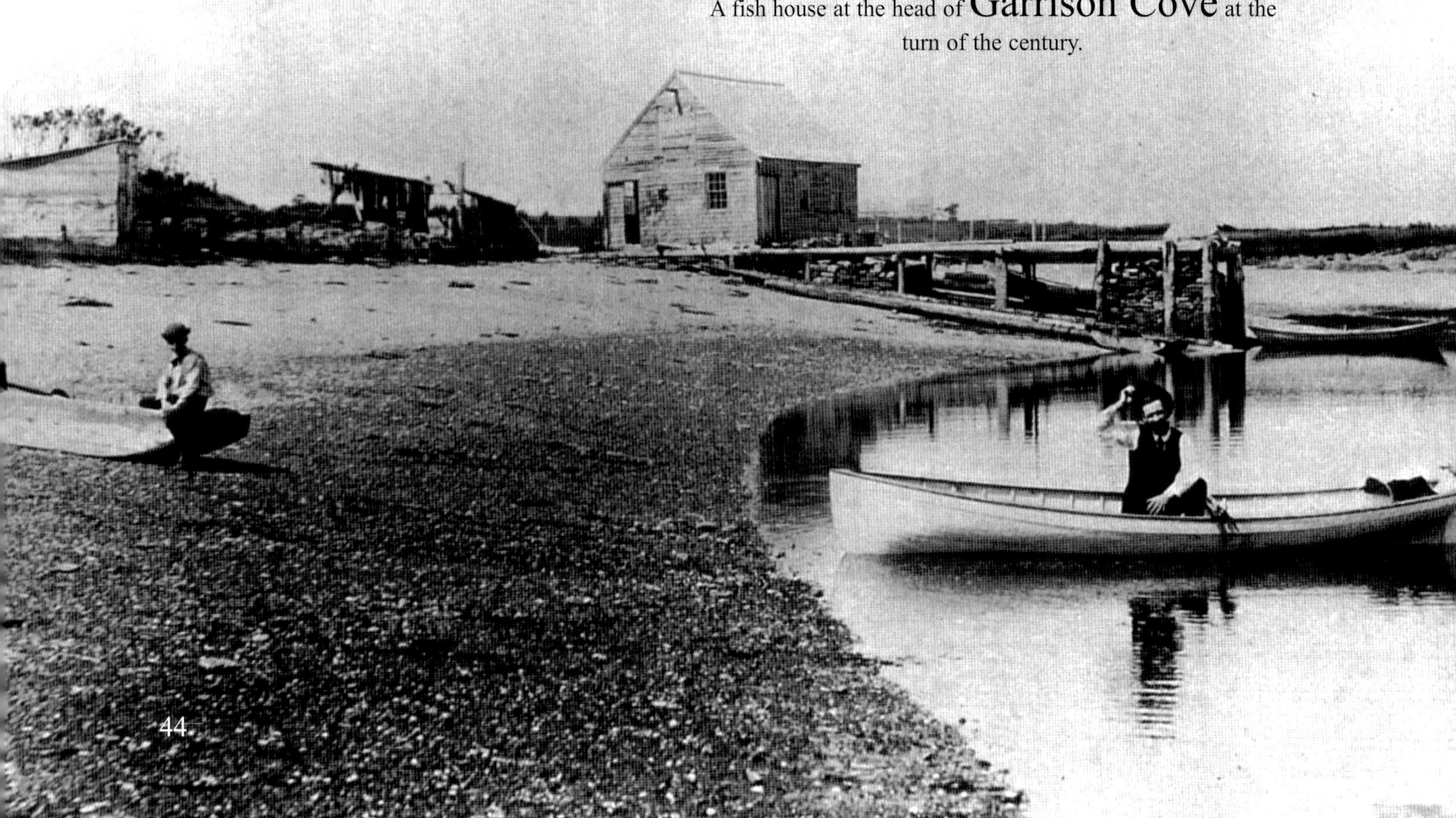

The Controversy

The building of a bridge to connect Bailey and Orr's Island was a controversial subject. It was not approved by the Harpswell voters until 1923, after forty years of strong and bitter debate.

In 1883 the state passed an act giving authority to the inhabitants of Harpswell to construct a bridge between Bailey Island and Orr's Island. In 1921 an additional act was passed. In 1922 a way was laid out and accepted at a town meeting.

The Highway Commission presented the cost to the voters in the fall of 1922, and another town meeting was held to accept those costs. According to the *Brunswick Times Record* voters were "rushed in by automobile from all quarters, and hurriedly registered while the meeting was in progress." The proponents won, but in the recount the opponents won. It was then discovered that 515 ballots were cast when only 512 voters were eligible.

Later that September two town meetings were called for the same day and time, one on Orr's Island and one at Harpswell Center, "both purporting to be the regular meeting." While the legality of these meetings was being decided in court, "the town then had a hearing in the State House on the proposal of the citizens of Harpswell Neck and Great Island be separated from the citizens of Orr's and Bailey Island, and for the latter two islands to be known as the town of St. Thomas."

The heated arguments continued until the Supreme Court finally settled the dispute and the bridge was begun.

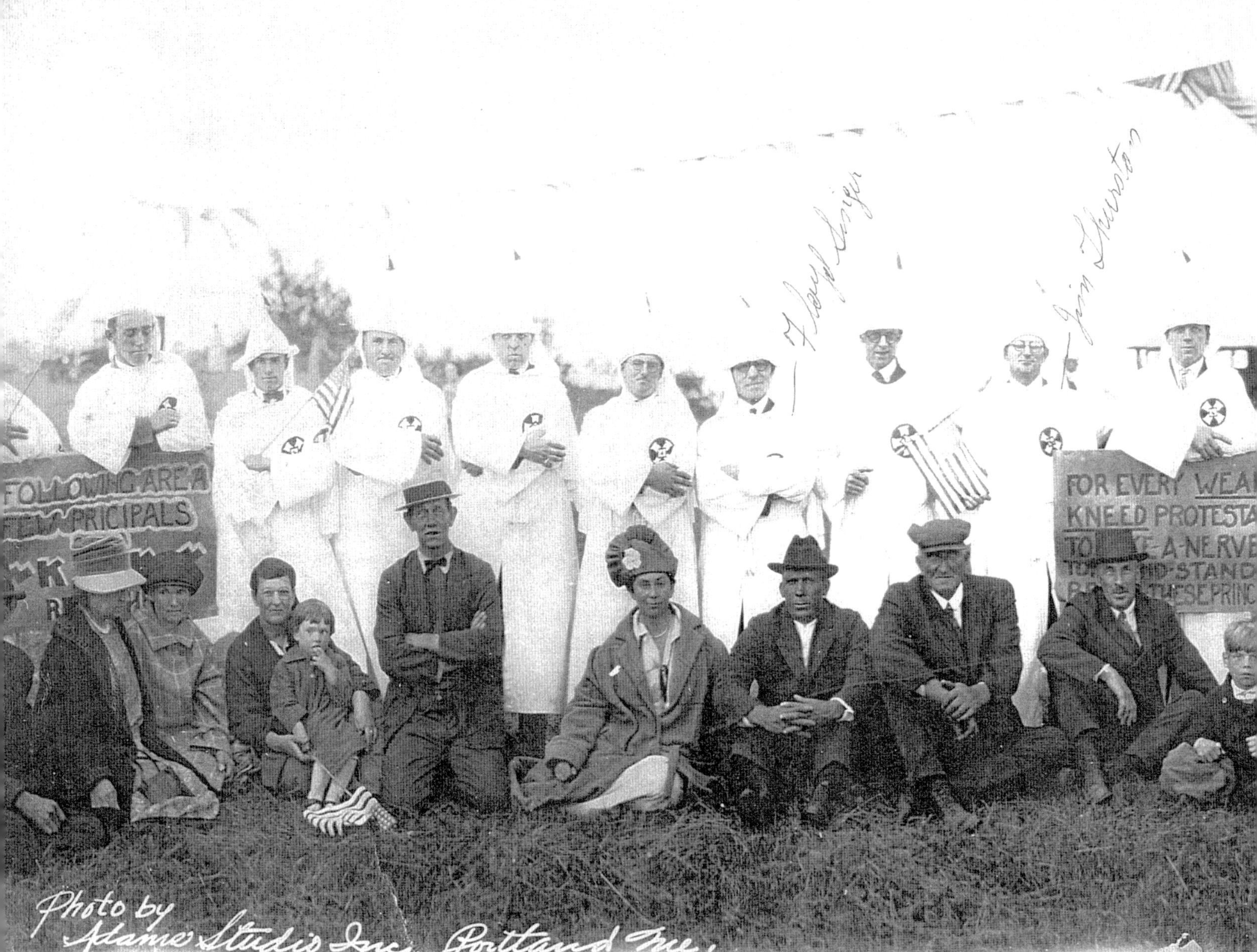
FOLLOWING ARE A
FEW PRICIPALS
FOR EVERY
KNEED
Photo by
Adams Studio Inc. Portland Me.

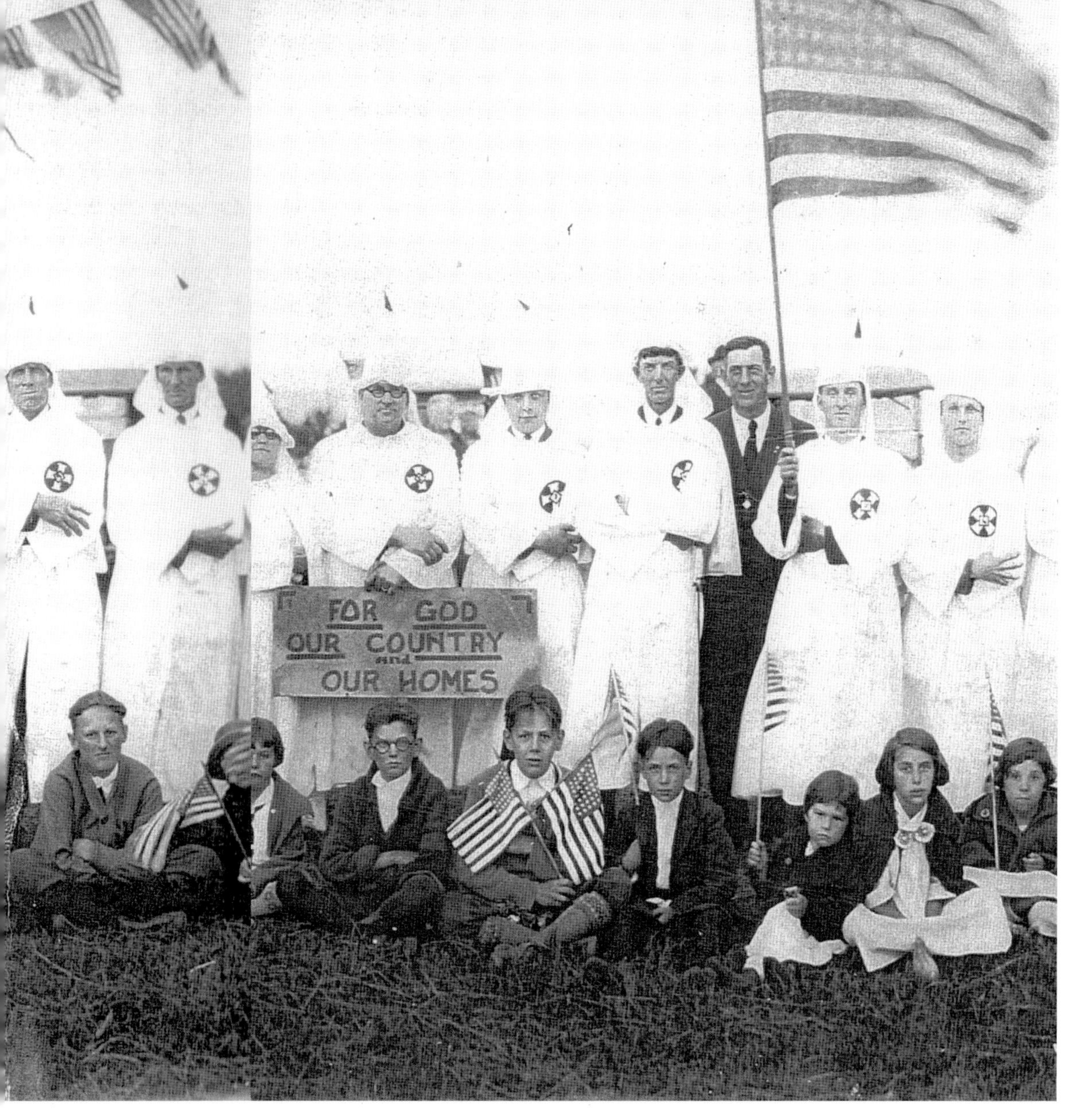

KU **K**LUX **K**LAN

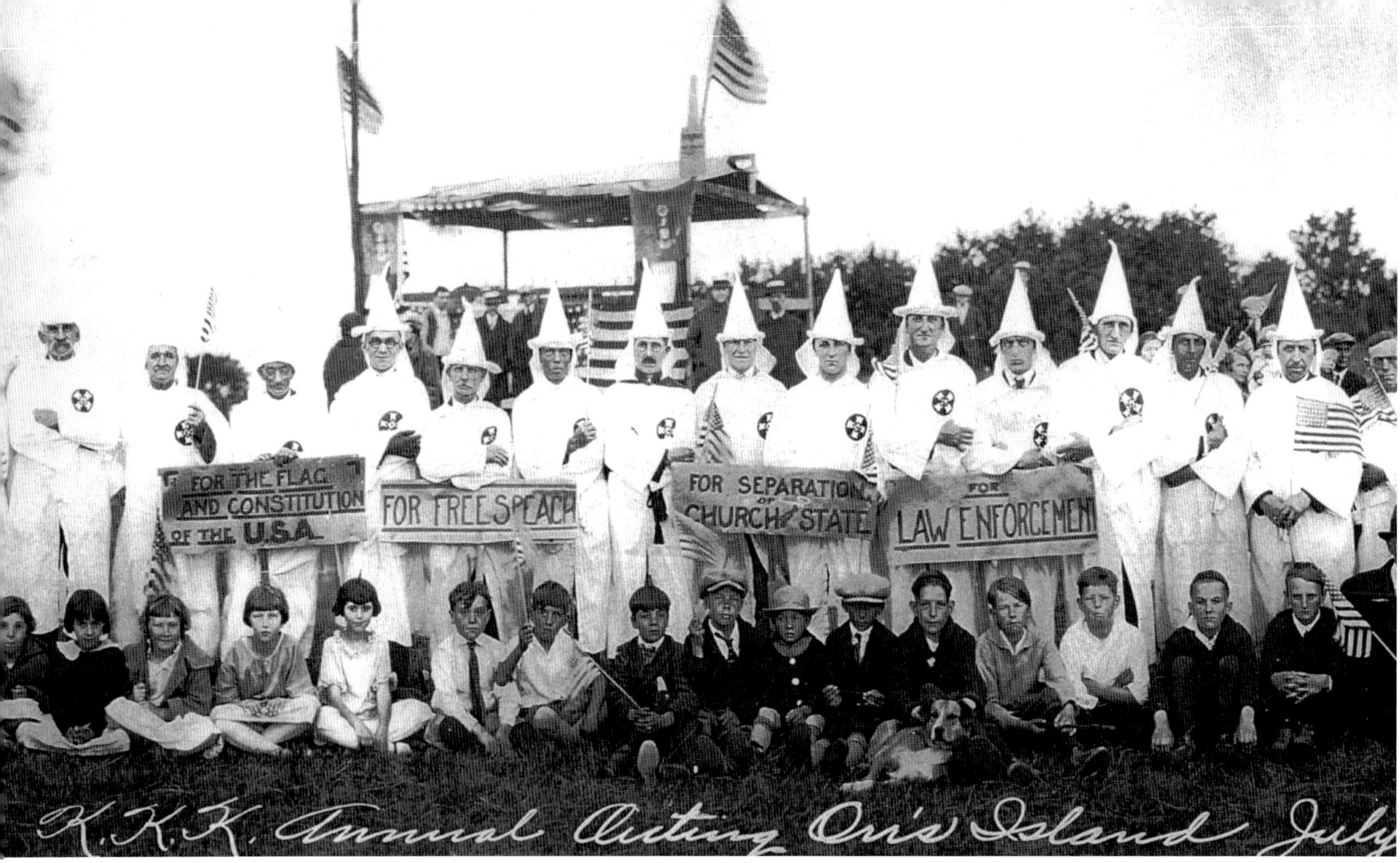

It was only a few years ago that I first heard about the KKK's connection to the islands. It came up in conversation after my brother, Steve, found this picture of the group taken by Adams Studio, Inc. of Portland, Maine. The picture was taken at Johnson's Point on Orr's Island after a parade and clam bake at a July 4th celebration in 1925. When I asked Mother, she said, "Oh, you never knew that?" Perhaps it wasn't anything to be proud of and so was never talked about.

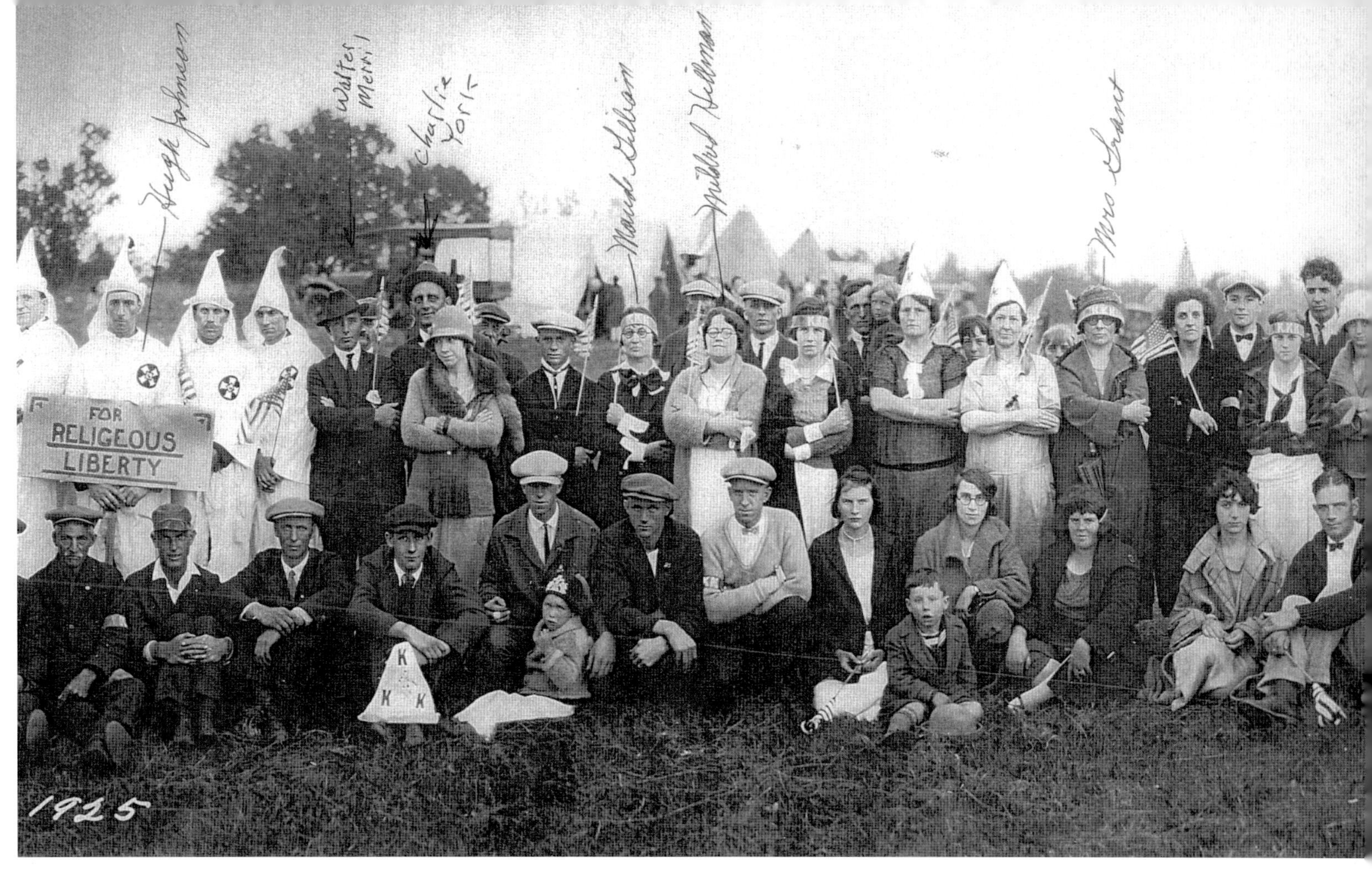

In the early 1920's the Ku Klux Klan was gaining popularity in Maine, particularly in Portland. At that time the steamboat came from Portland to Bailey Island four times a day. It didn't take long to recruit a large number of island men to the Klan. The Klan's motto was, "Service for humanity, home, country and God."

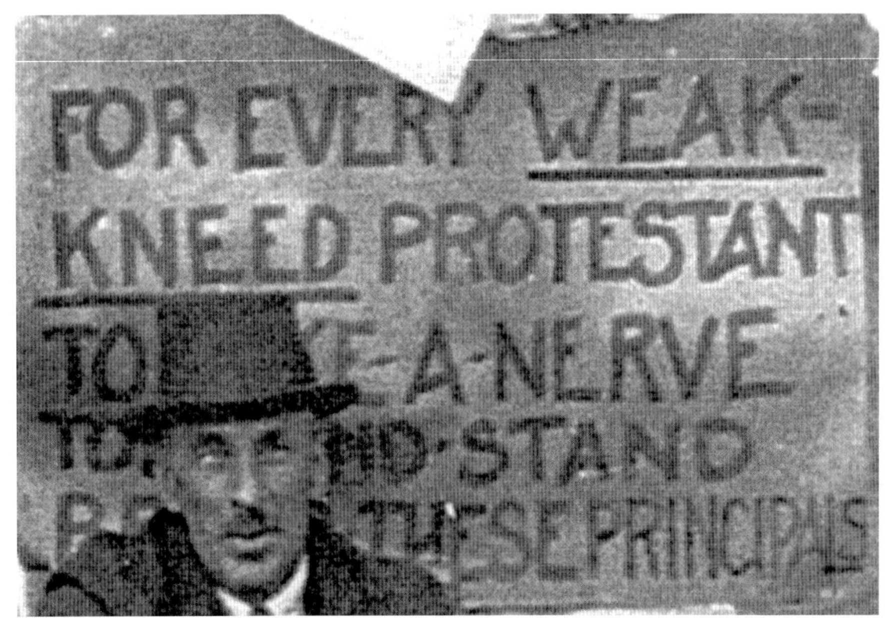

In the book *Charlie York: Maine Coast Fisherman* by Harold Clifford, Charlie is quoted: "The Ku Klux Klan come to our town in 1924. I joined that. I never enjoyed any Lodge so much as I did the Klan at first. It had the principle of brotherly love for feller members and they was a high moral tone to it...."*

The organization strongly favored the building of the Bailey Island Bridge and they made their feelings known. After a stay of nearly two years, the Klansmen left town around 1926. According to some of the islanders who remembered the KKK, they probably were forced out because the islanders became suspicious of their presence and didn't like being told how they should vote in political matters.

Grandmother was opposed to building a bridge from Bailey Island to Orr's Island and I'm sure she was vocal about her feelings. My father told me stories of harassment from the KKK, and these were confirmed by the islanders I interviewed.

When I asked Clayt Johnson, a longtime resident of the island, if he knew anything about a wheel being rolled down the hill to Grandmother's house, he replied with a twinkle in his eye and a grin, "Sure do. It was a huge wagon wheel and we gave that thing a shove. It got rolling and it began picking up speed. Just as it got to the house, it veered off to the side and went into the bushes." My father claimed that the wheel hit the house with great force.

***Charlie York: Maine Coast Fisherman* by Harold B. Clifford. International Maine Publishing Co. Camden, ME. 1974. Reprinted by permission of the McGraw-Hill Companies.

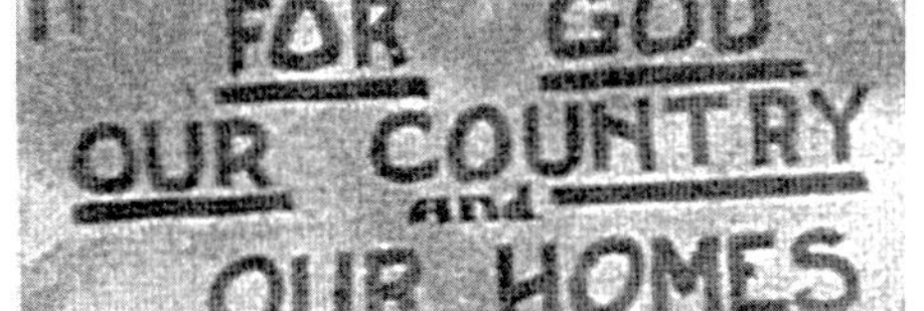

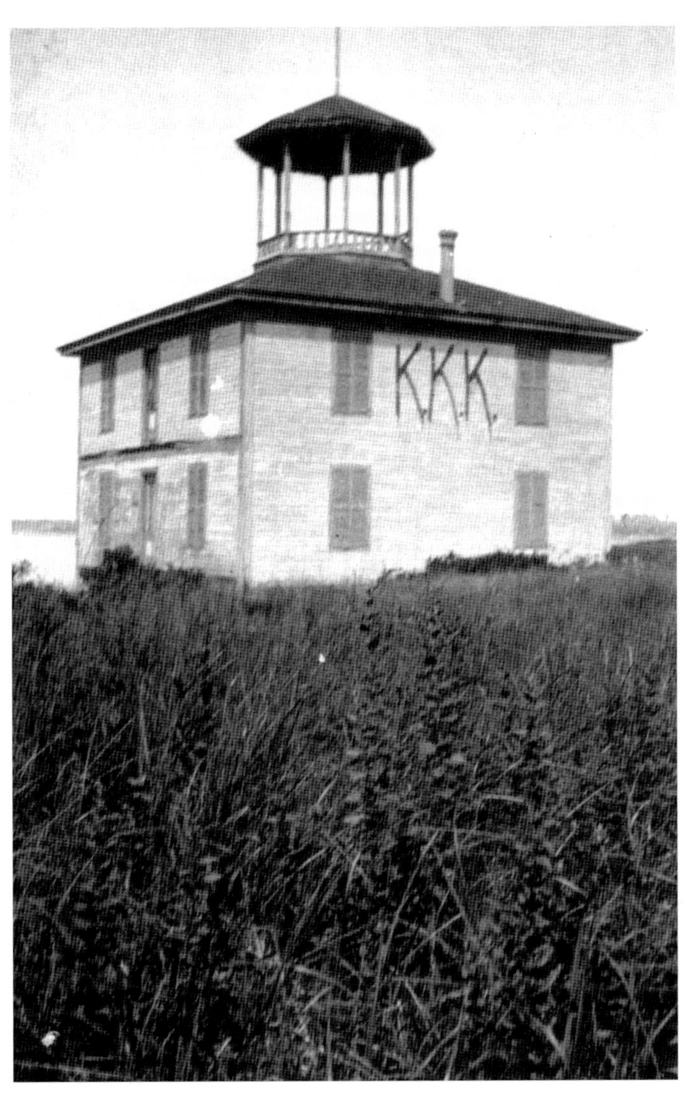

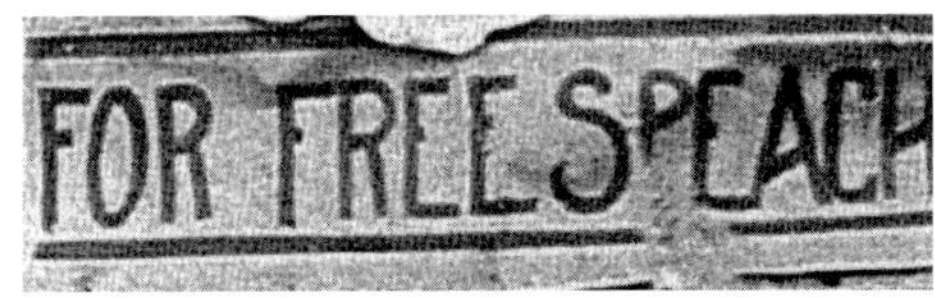

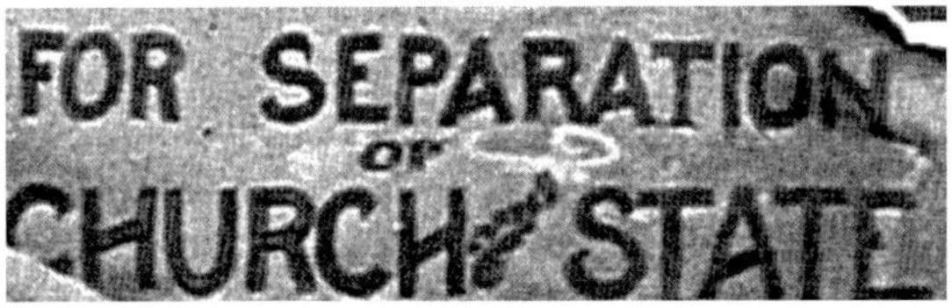

Although the Spring House was torn down about the time I was born, the building always came up in conversation because it was partially owned by Grandmother Ethel. Local lore suggests it was a boarding house as well as a spring water bottling company, but nowhere could I find information about guests staying there.

This picture of the Spring House shows evidence of the KKK's presence by the letters painted on the side. I've been told that Rip Black, a teenager at the time, admitted doing the work. He said he was asked by the KKK because he was young and strong.

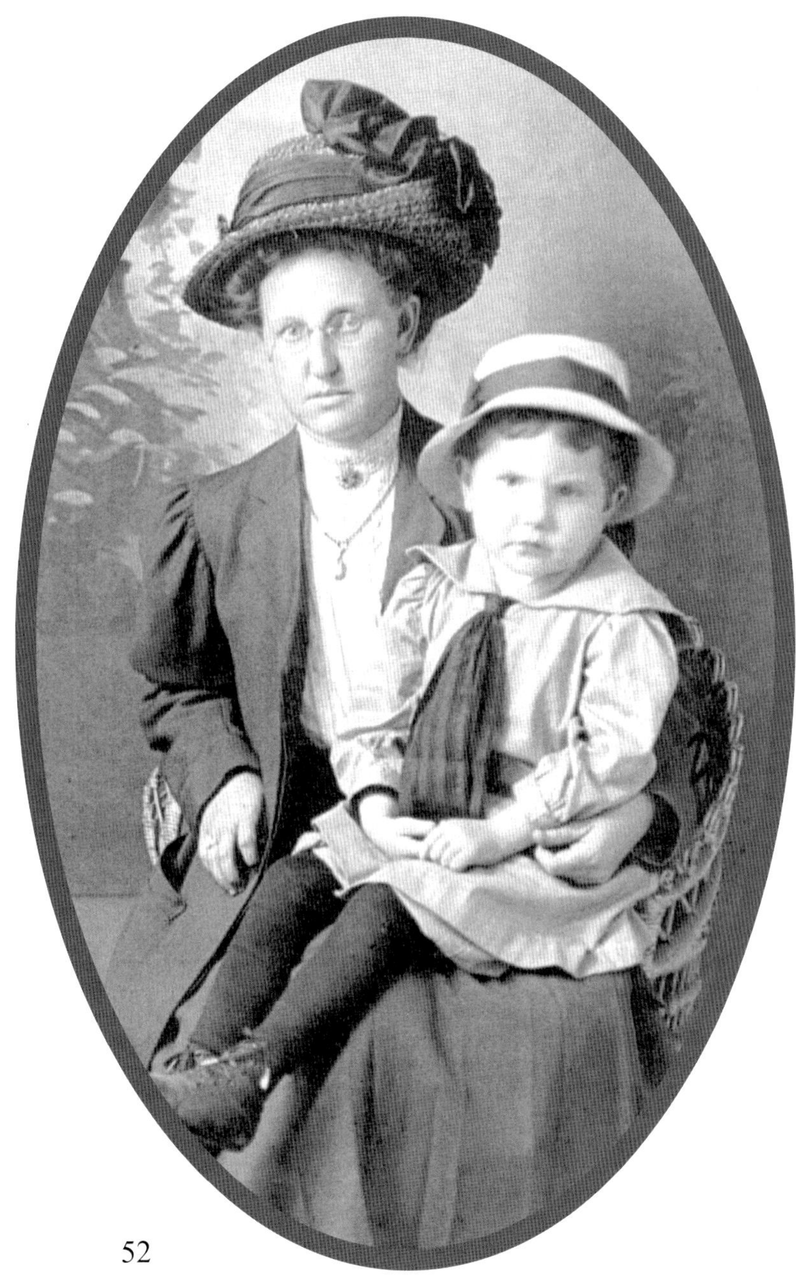

My family was musical. Grammy Ethel played hymns on the piano for church services and jigs and reels for dances on Bailey and Orr's Islands, along with Grampy on the fiddle and Dad on the drums. She also played piano for silent movies in Brunswick. Grammy also had strong views. When she received the following letter it was evident her feelings about the bridge were not appreciated.

At left: Grammy Ethel Johnson and Dad—Linwood Johnson—about 1912.

To whom it may concern: —

Please take notice to whom this is addressed, you may take it as you like, but if it concerns you, take it!

Some people remind us of a cat that is always sticking her nose where she has no business to, but watch out, some-day, you'll get caught, for remember; "With charming ease the quick black fox jumps over the lazy dog".

Have you learned how to play Jazz yet? What is that stuff you pound out on the piano and call that? Perhaps you can name it, no-one else can, it sounds most like a hurdy-gurdy, or a monkey with a hand organ.

Are you playing for dances much nowdays, did you ever play for a real dance? We hear that by your conversion you lost your job and since then have not been able to regain it. Do you play in church any now, or have you lost that job. It must be kind of tough on you to loose both. I'll say you're out of luck. Did you play Jazz in church, it is little wonder that you were the only soloist there for who could keep up to such a tune?

We wonder if it is the style nowdays to stand while you sing, leaving the congregation and minister sitting, are you trying to introduce that to Bailey Island? Have you found out about church affairs yet?

Dont you remember how so much excitement was created when you fell down in church? If it is remembered correctly it was when the presiding elder, Rev. Aitaw was here, the night you so kindly passed him the lamps, Poor Man, the situation must have been rather embarassing for him, when he had just blown out. It was too bad to lay the cause off your falling on someone else tho; never mind if you have got big feet and you are clumsy, always shoulder your own faults, don't throw it on to some one else.

How about voting? Did you vote against the bridge? You must have found it rather tough when you had you're wires cut down, especially when you wanted to do a little gossiping over the line. Did the boys serenade you a little bit? You seemed to have got, in dutch, when you cast that vote against you're native town and her citizens.

We heard that you were going to play for graduation, but the teacher said, "She really didn't intend to have you, + felt quite pleased whe you said, you wouldn't be able to play.

Well, cheer up, it will soon be time for blueberries, and then you can pick from sunrise until sunset, possibly you could get Mr. Ward to help you, but remember there will be two boats a day so you must plan your blueberrying, work, etc and govern yourself accordingly, for it is doubtful if the boat could land if you wasn't there, so don't fail to be there, for some poor soul may want to stop off here.

Always shoulder your own troubles, don't put the blame on someone else, it makes you look as tho' you had a "Yellow Streak", its only a coward that shirks his own responsibilities & duty.

Remember how nervous you were when the Home Brew fuss started!

We trust this summer may be prosperous and enjoyable for you & yours, hope your jazz holds out & you secure some new positions.

We also hope you will receive this in the spirit it is intended, & it will make you very happy, for why shouldn't it, isn't it every word true?

Yours in regret
"Those who Know".

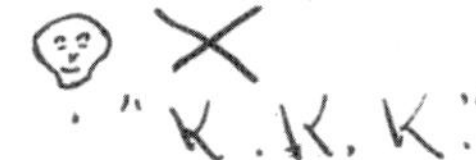

"K.K.K."

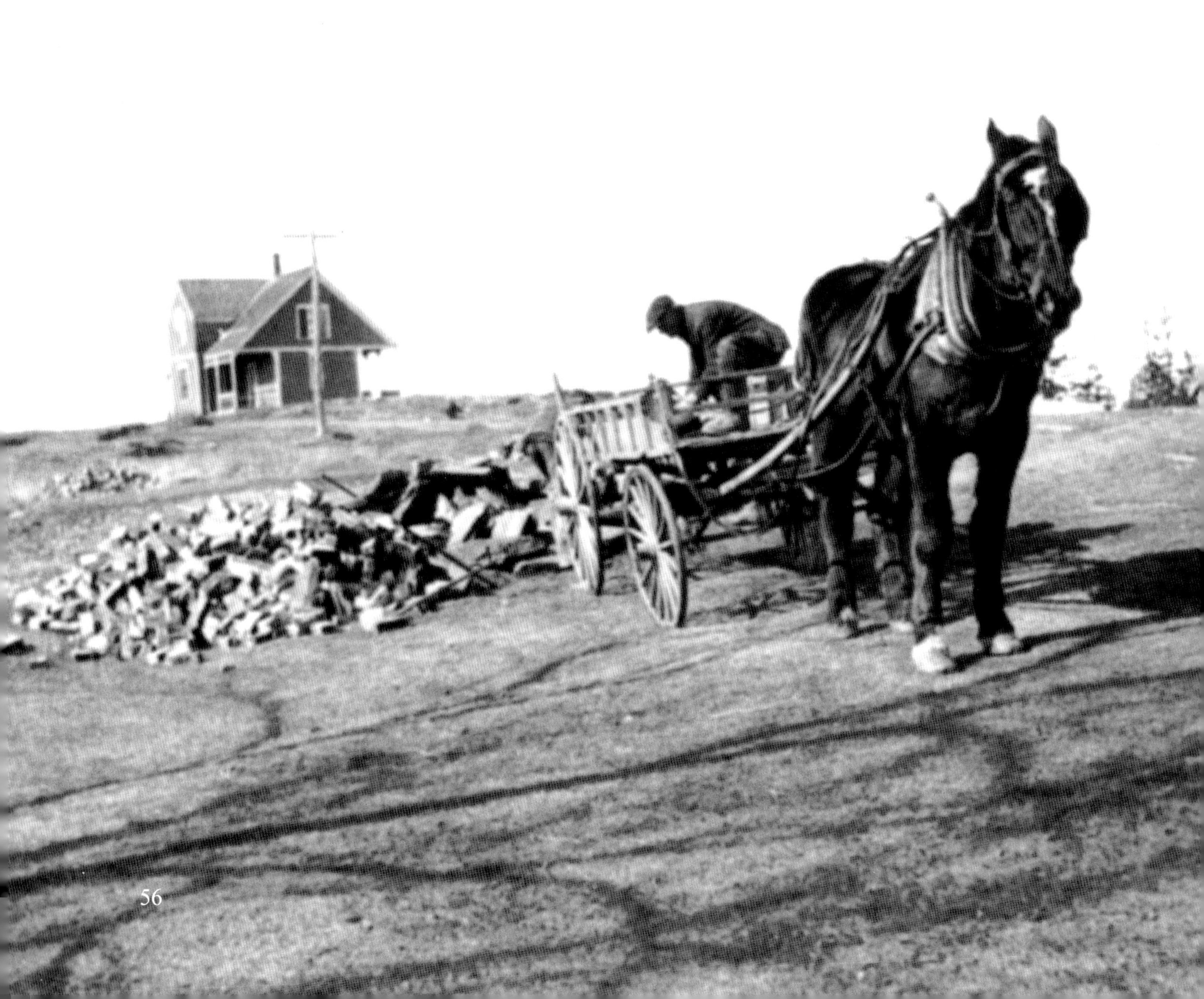

Building the Cribstone Bridge

Llewelyn Edwards, the state bridge engineer who was in charge of the bridge project, realized the problems of constructing a bridge over Will's Gut. The bridge would have to go over ledges, and there were strong currents, tides and ice floes to deal with. He finally decided to go with a plan for a cribstone bridge knowing there was plenty of granite nearby. Construction started in 1926 and was completed in 1928.

The granite was quarried in Yarmouth and Pownal, Maine, and brought to the site on a barge. A railway was used to bring a crane out onto the bridge as it was being built. No mortar or cement, no steel girders, no suspension cables, and no base pillars of concrete were needed. Only the weight of 10,000 tons and the positioning of the granite slabs, laid crosswise and then lengthwise, was necessary to hold the bridge together. The cribstone fashion allowed the rushing tides to flow through. The bridge cost a total of $112,400. The state paid $56,200, the county paid $33,720, and the Town of Harpswell paid $22,480. It was dedicated as a National Historic Civil Engineering Landmark in 1984, and remains the only bridge like it in the world.

My father took many of the Bailey Island Cribstone Bridge photos as it was being built. He was very proud of the fact that he was one of the first to cross the bridge. He was 18 when he drove his 1925 Dodge across the span.

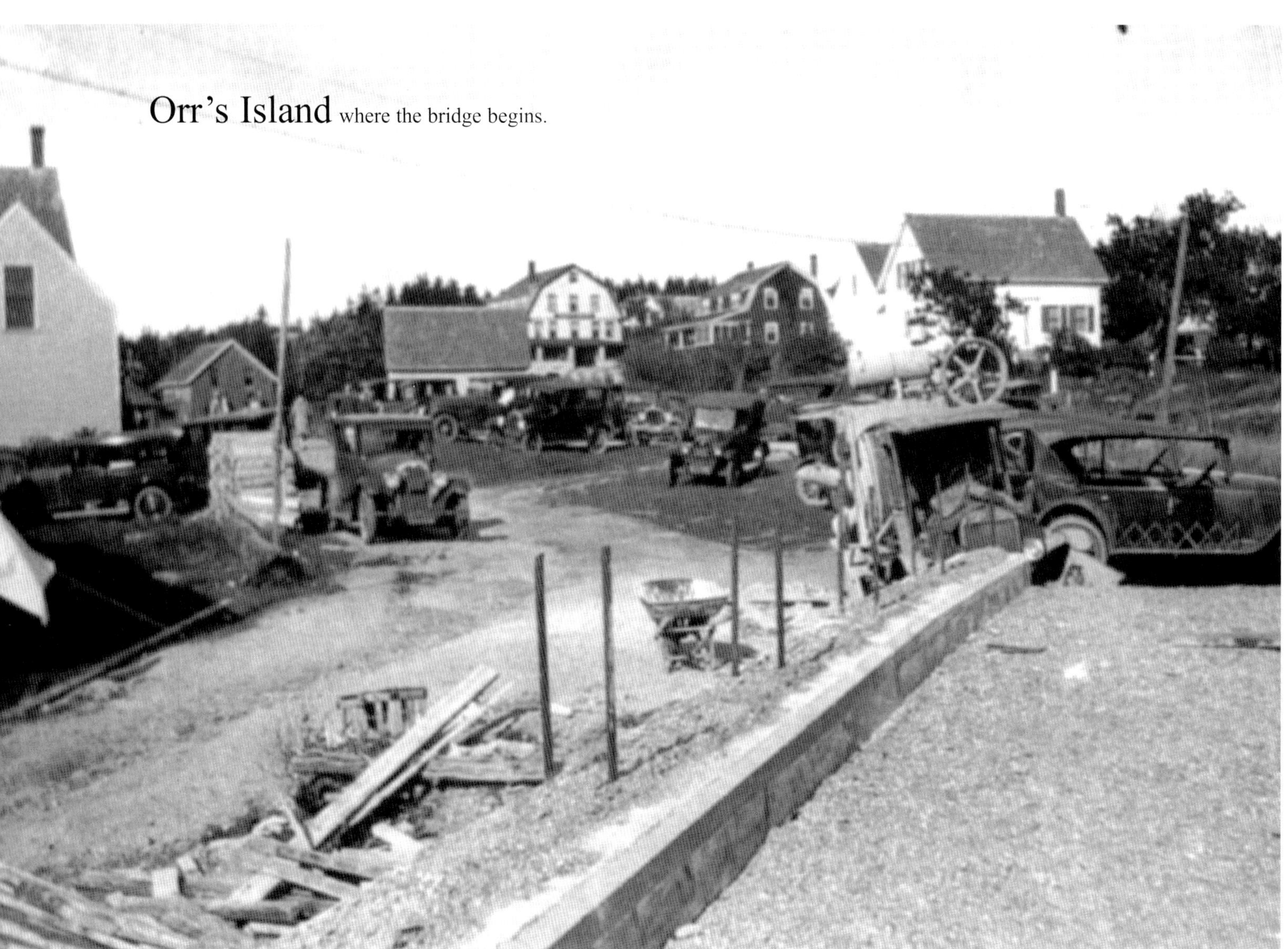

Orr's Island where the bridge begins.

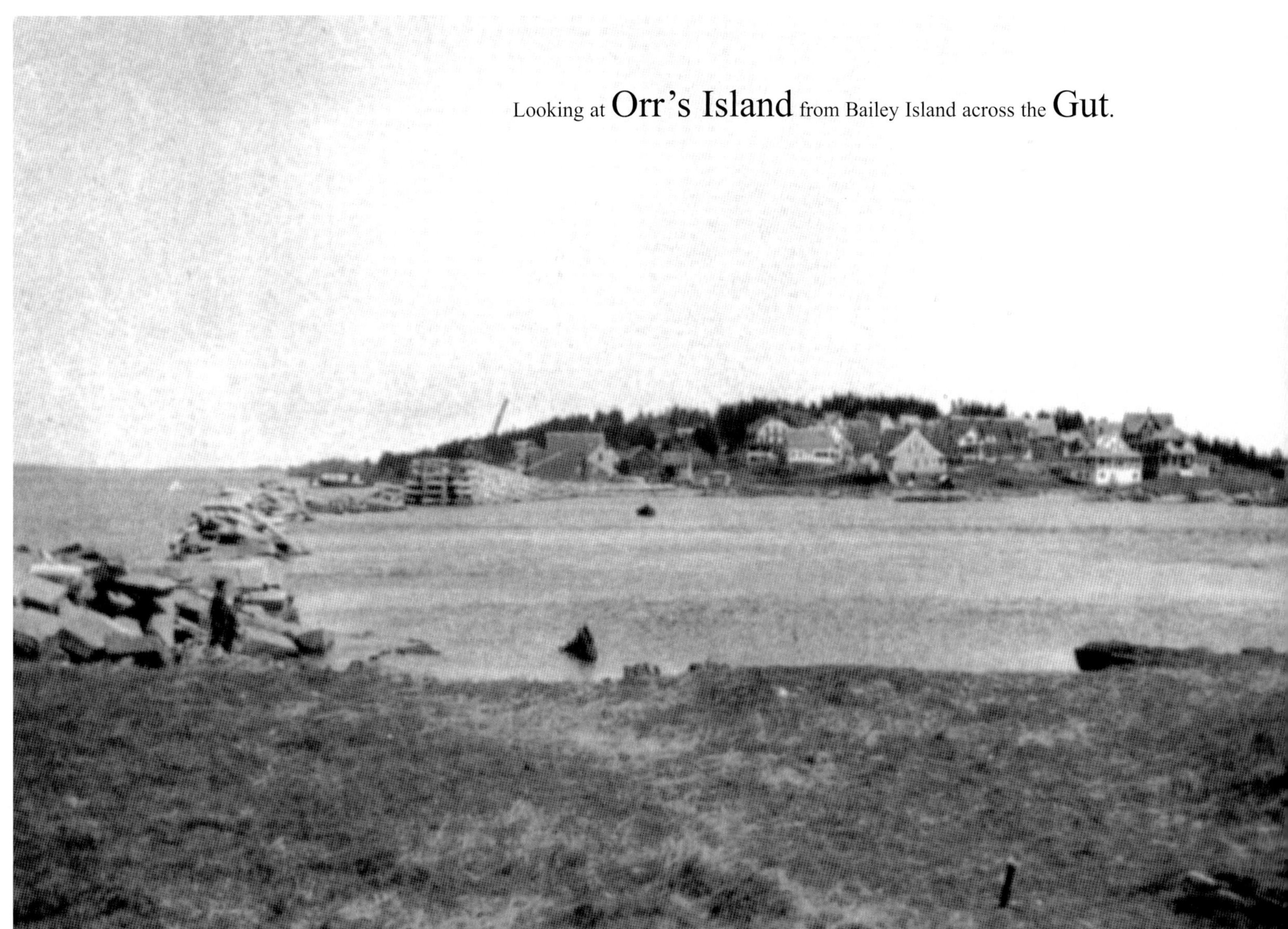

Looking at Orr's Island from Bailey Island across the Gut.

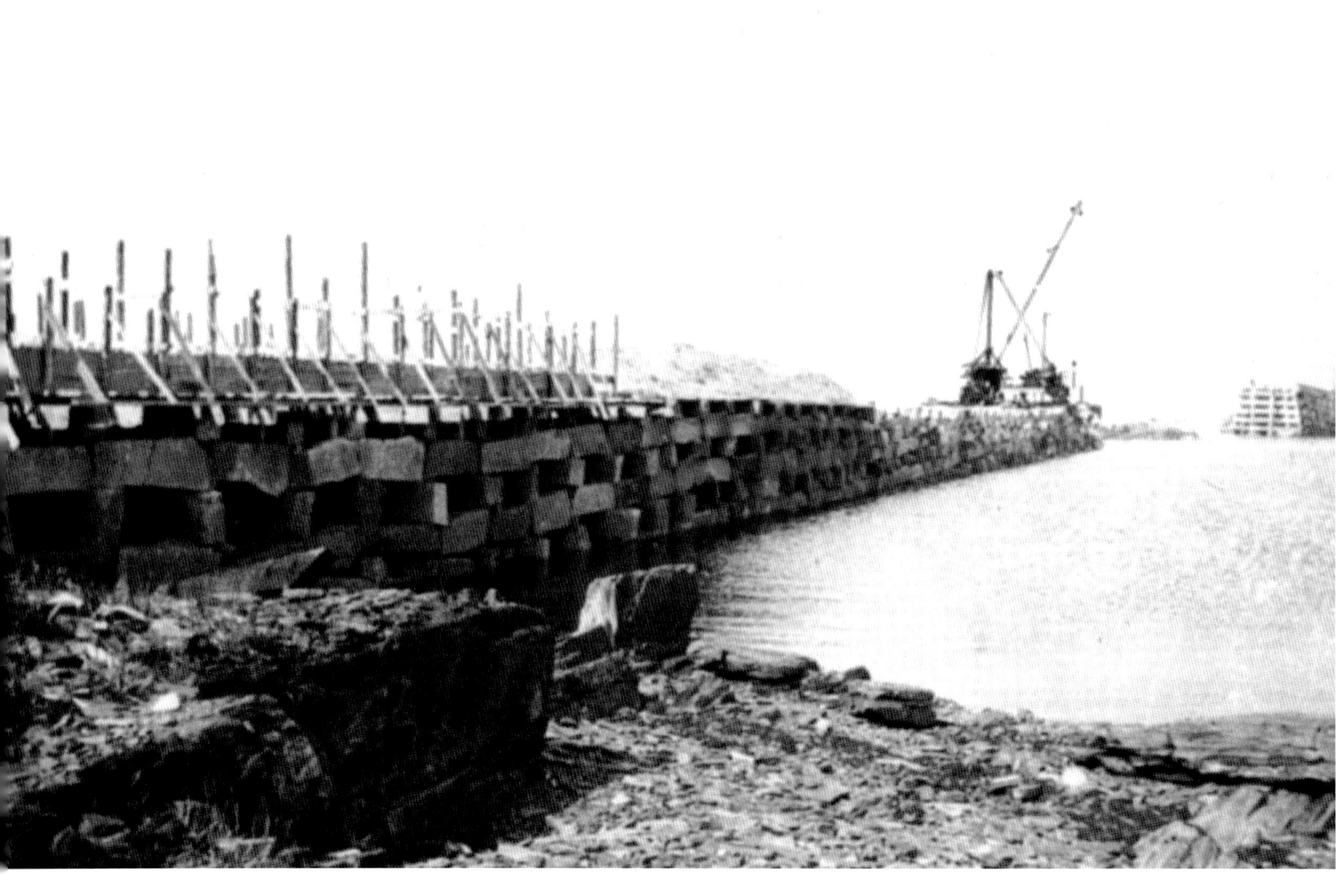

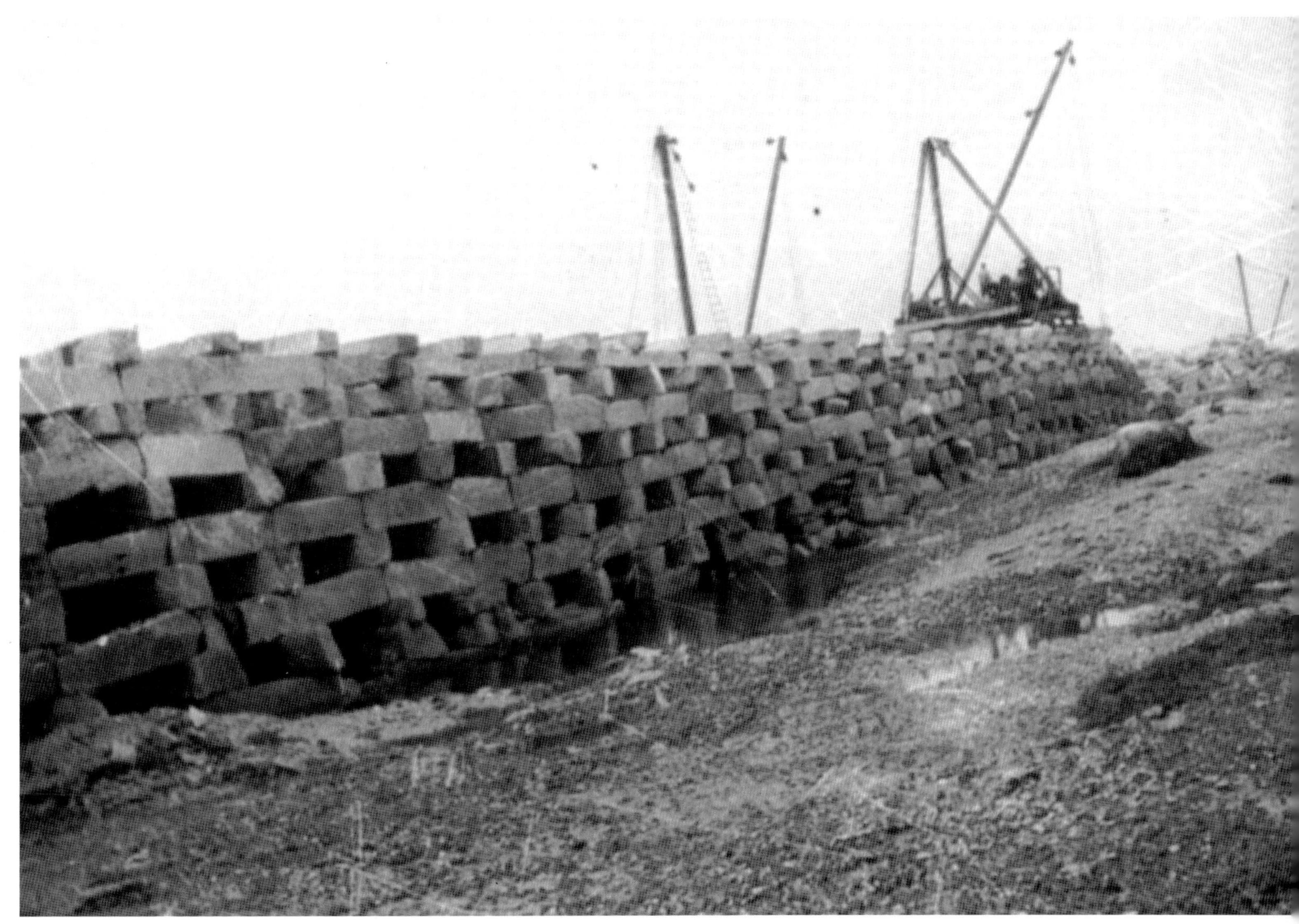

Phyllis Boyce clowning around on the Bailey Island Bridge.

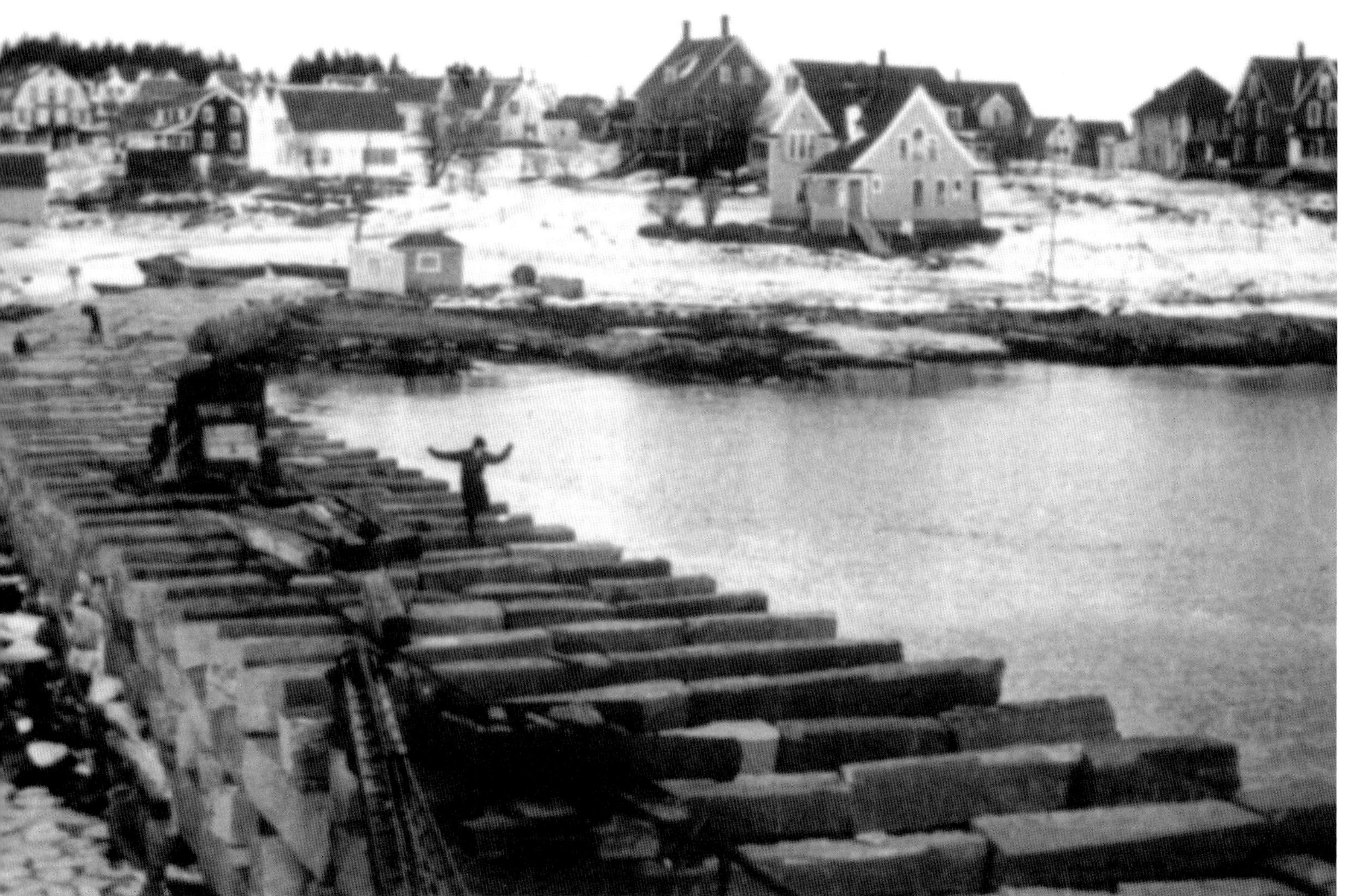

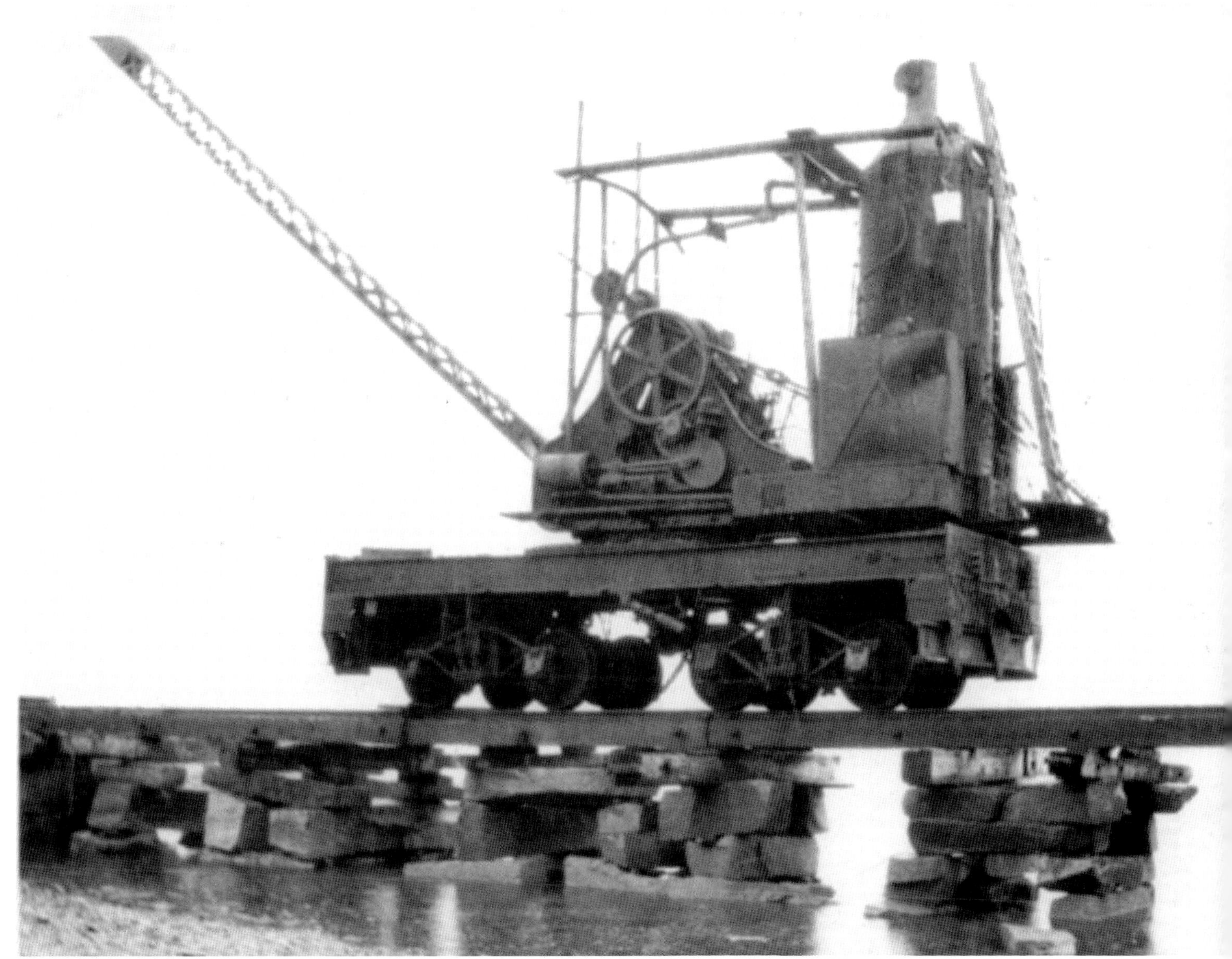

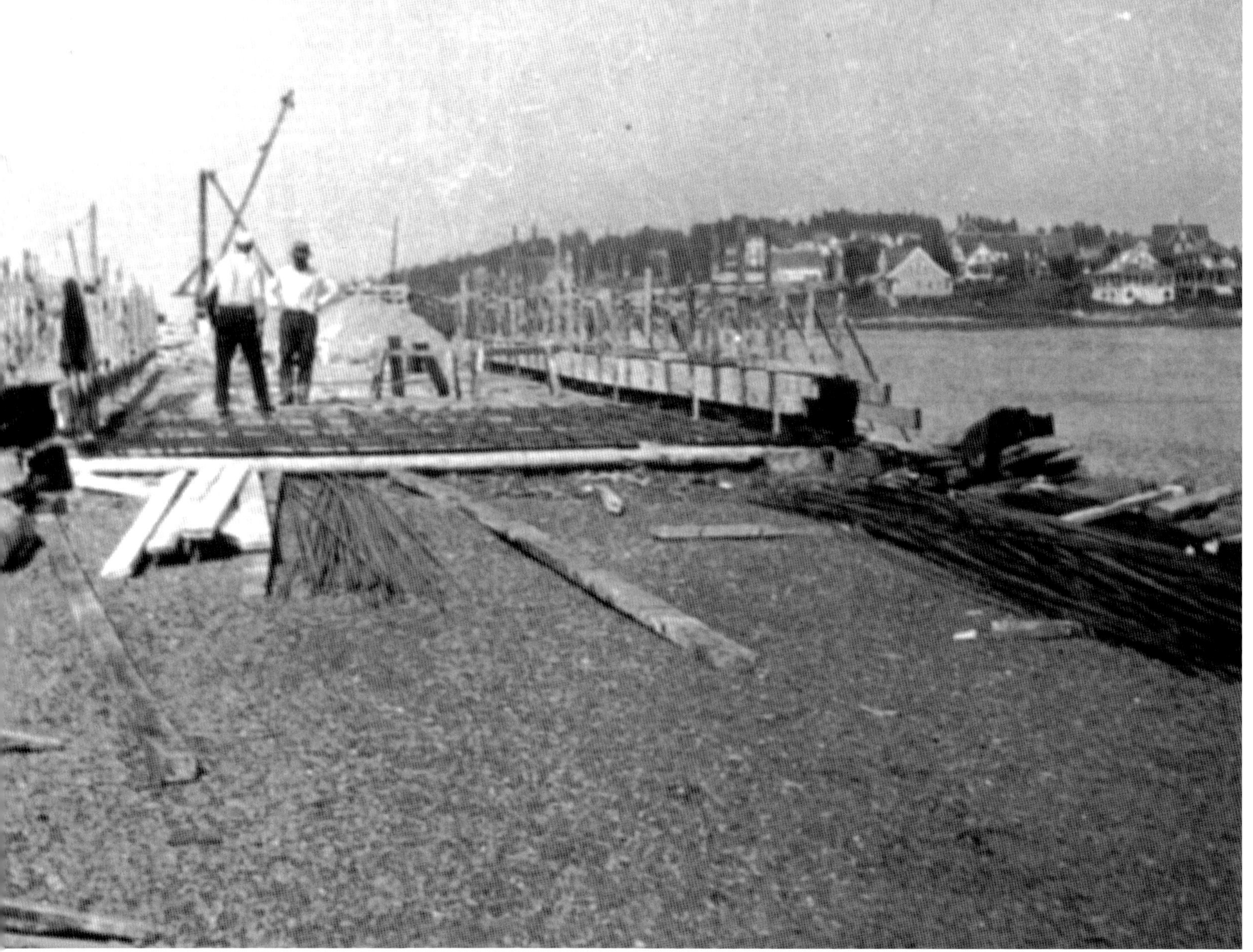

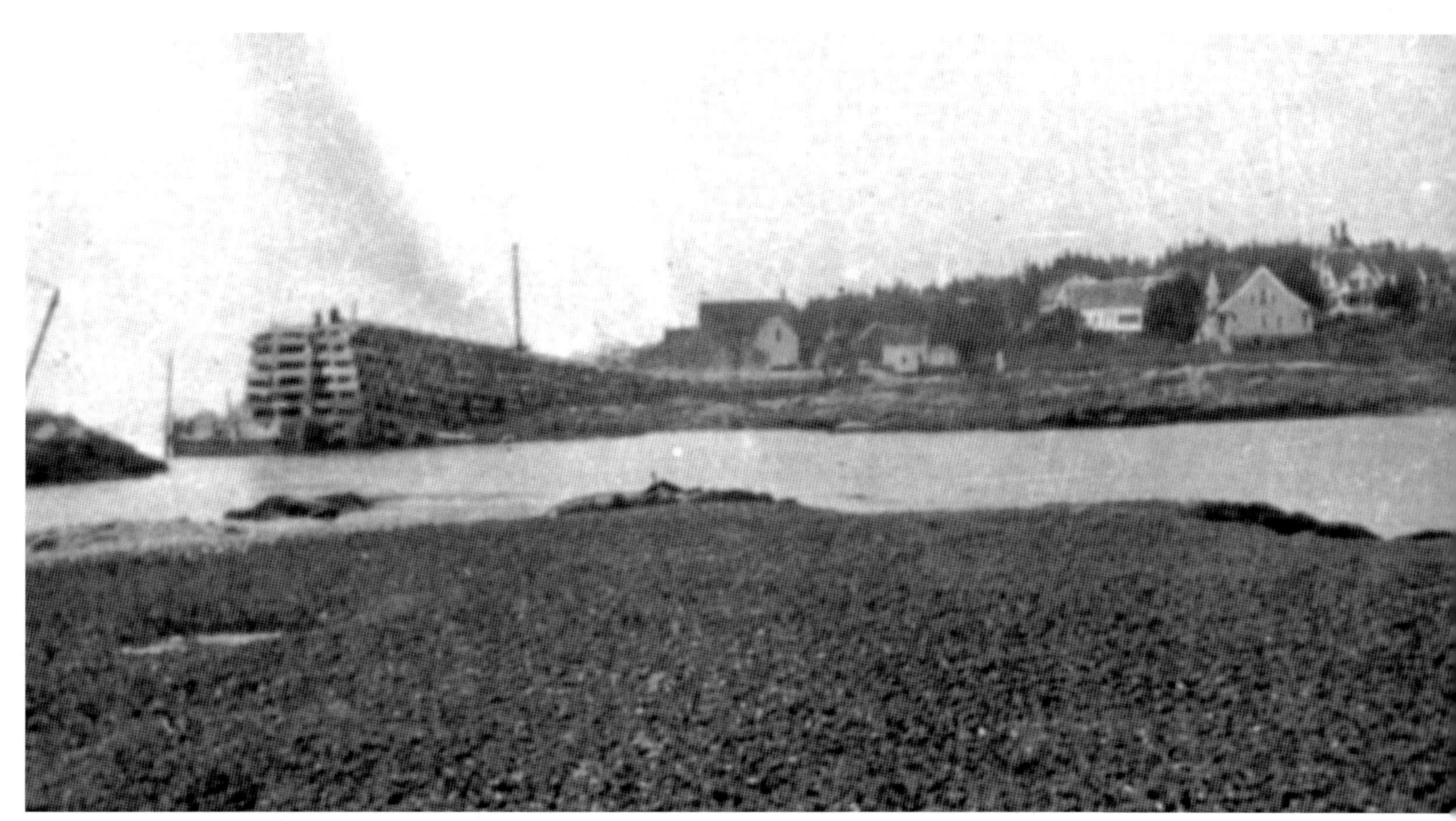

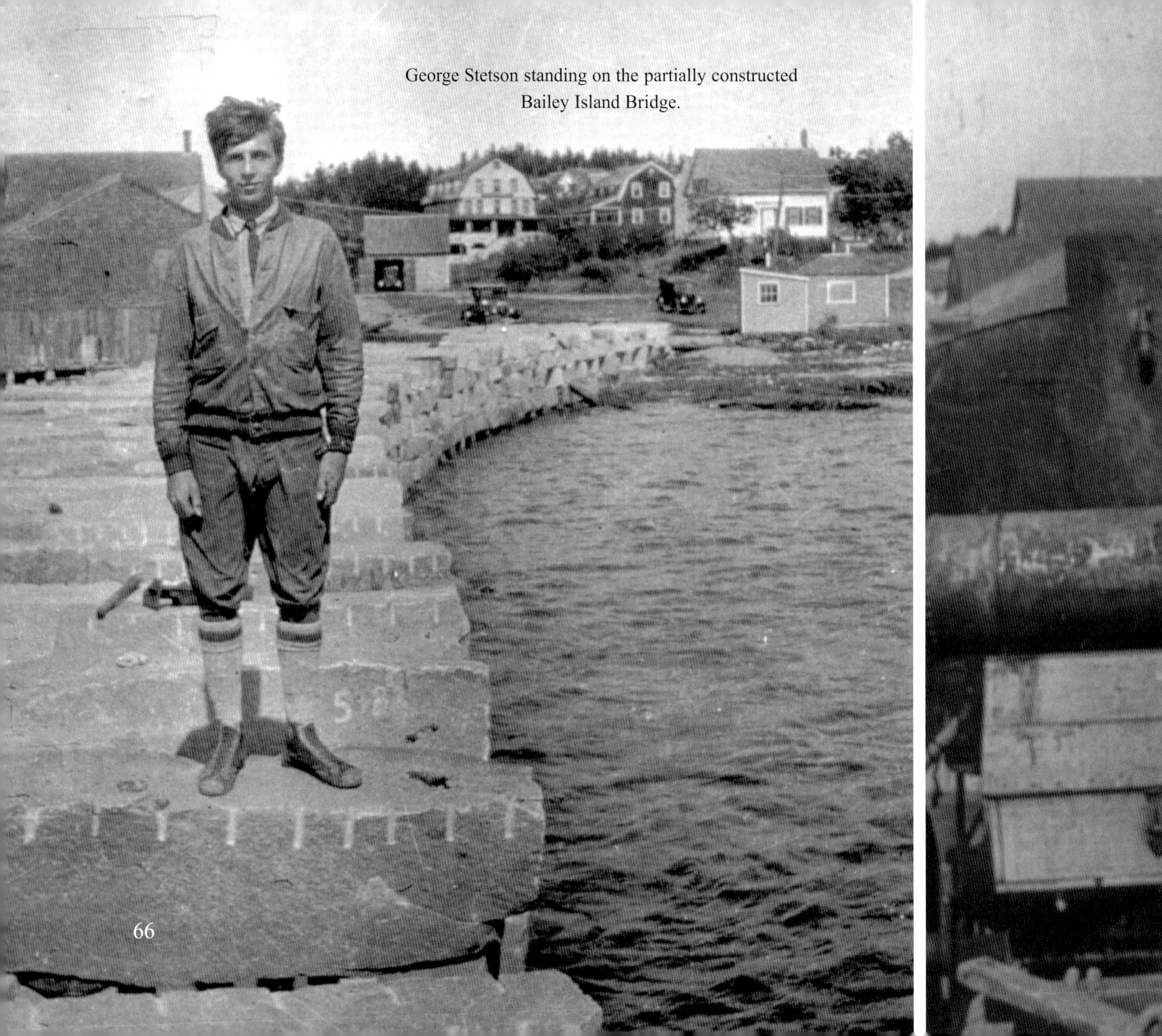

George Stetson standing on the partially constructed Bailey Island Bridge.

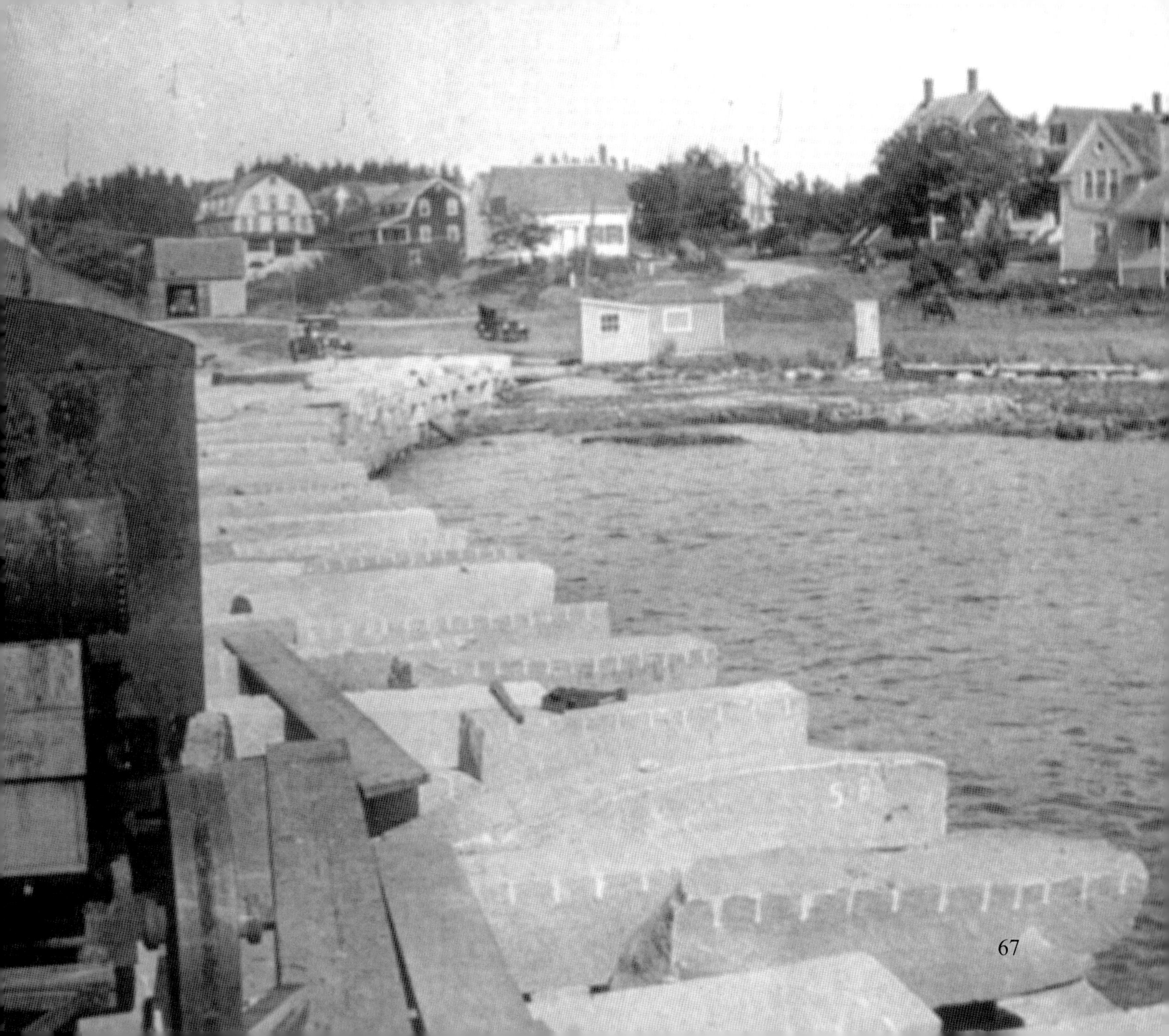

ORR'S ISLAND FROM BAILEY ISLAND BRIDGE, MAINE 3693

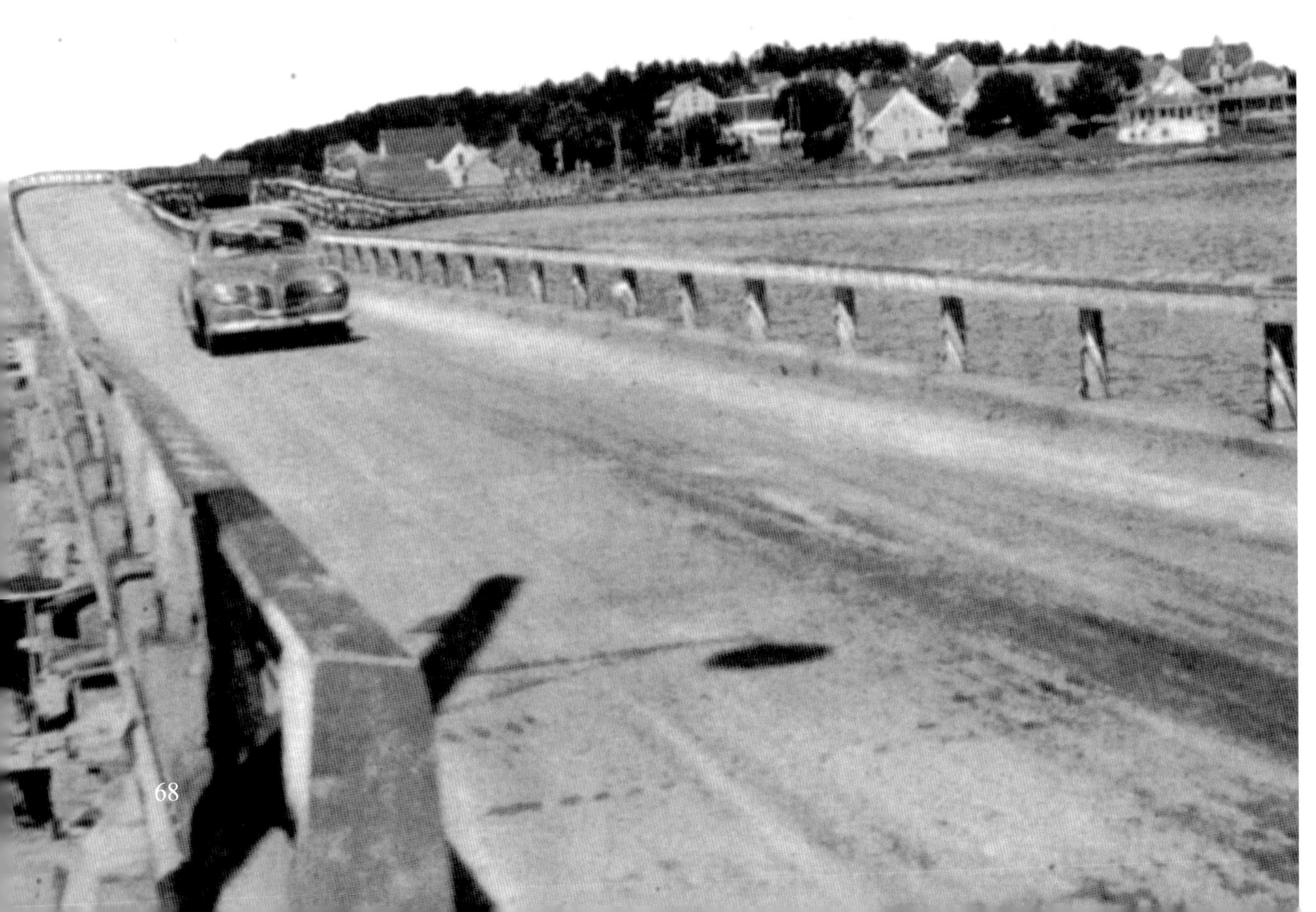

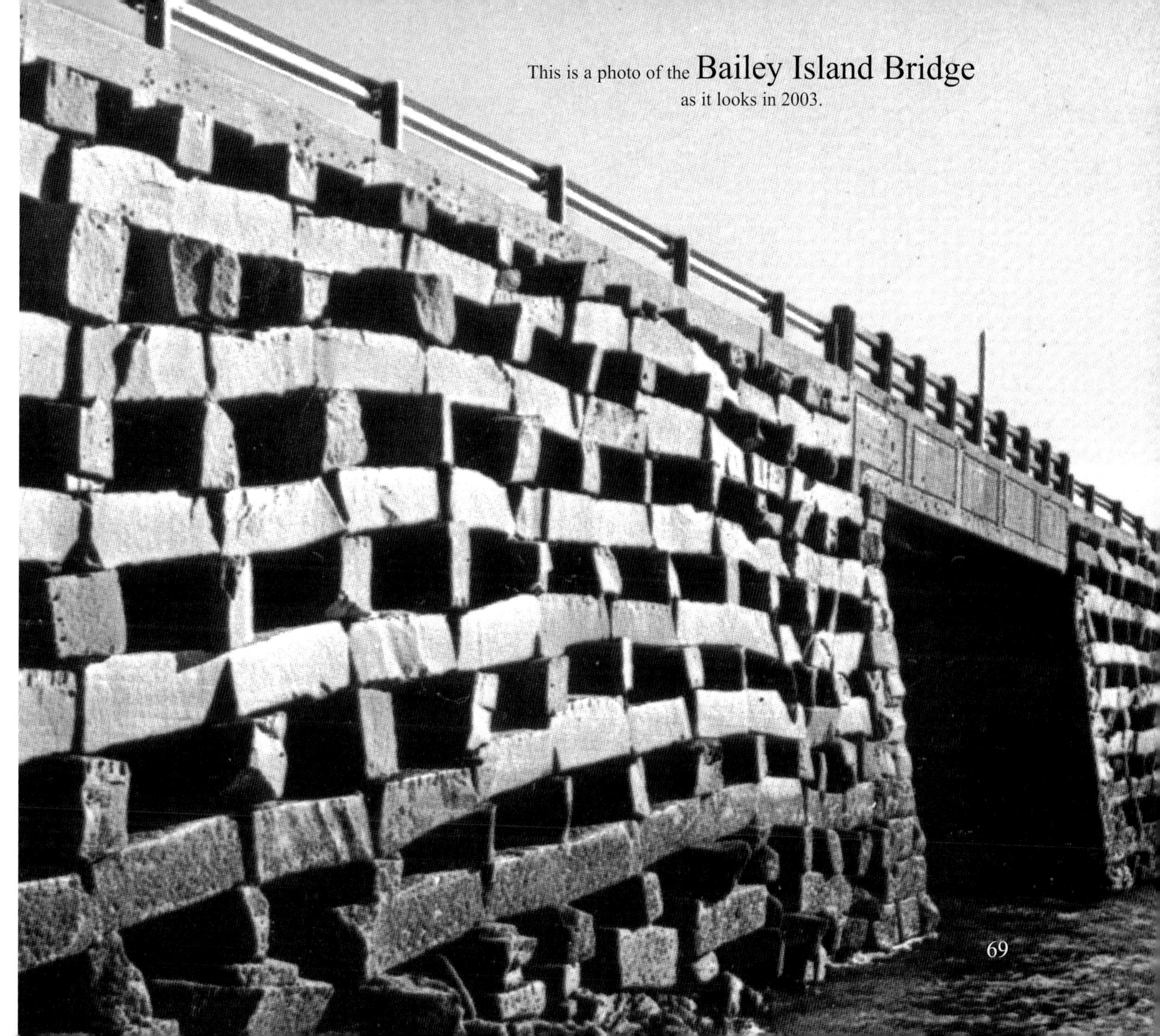

This is a photo of the Bailey Island Bridge
as it looks in 2003.

Cedar Ledges Treasure

This story about a legendary Bailey Island resident is found in many sources.

In the winter of 1840, John Wilson was out duck hunting on Cedar Ledges, located between Ram and Elm Islands, nearly two miles east of Bailey Island Bridge. The tide was low and with his mind on the ducks he was about to fire upon, he lost his balance on the slippery seaweed-covered ledges and got his foot stuck in a deep hole. After getting his foot free he dug around and felt something round and metal. With a piece of driftwood he dug some more and pulled out a copper kettle. He pried it open and found it filled with gold coins.

Several island folks saw John, a day or so later, heading to the north end of the island carrying a heavy suitcase. He went to Boston where he sold his treasure of Spanish gold. Much to the amazement of his neighbors he came home in a brand new sloop and soon bought one of the most desirable farms on the island. John Wilson had found what many had believed to be Captain Kidd's treasure—at Cedar Ledges. The hole at Cedar Ledges is still known as the "Pirate's Gold Pot" and is said to be easily found at low tide.

Homerus Americus
The Maine Lobster

Lobster fishing is a common occupation on Bailey Island. My brothers, like many others, are lobstermen. Not too many years ago lobstermen made their own traps using wooden lathes. Often, during the long winter months, wives of fishermen helped knit heads for the traps by using strong twine and a shuttle to make the knots. Heads are the funnel-like nets inside the trap through which the lobster crawls to reach the bait. Once inside the trap, the lobster can't get out. The traps are usually attached in a string of 5 to 10, with a buoy placed on one end. Every lobsterman has his own color buoy with his license number painted on it. Wooden traps are a thing of the past. Wire traps have replaced them. Bricks or rocks are used as weights to keep the traps upright on the ocean floor.

At right: Grampy Orrin Johnson 1923.

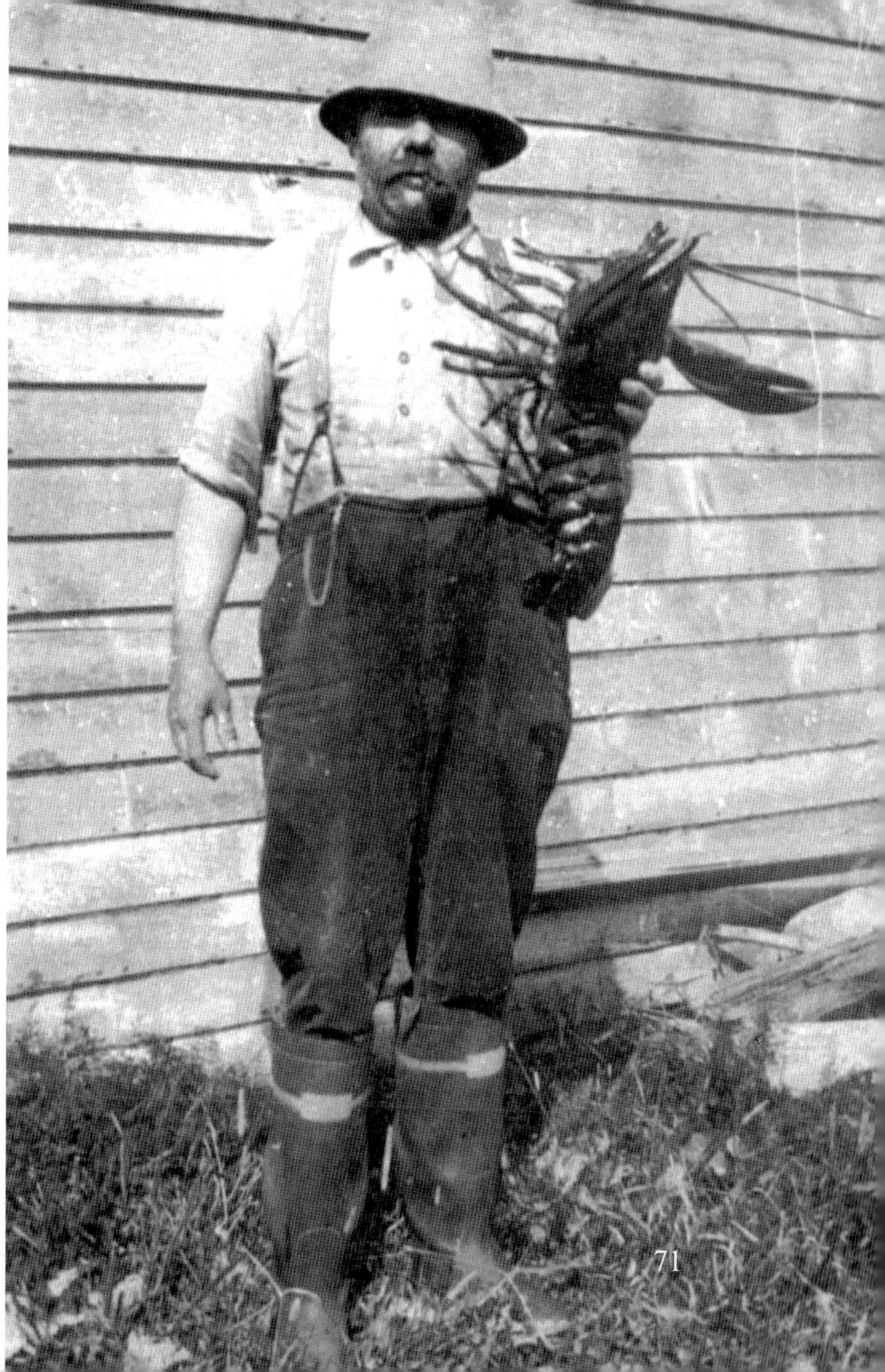

Lobsters eat plants, scallops, mussels, snails, clams, fish, sea urchins, crabs and other lobsters. Most of the lobsters sold on the market are 5-11 years old. They will have molted 25 times before they are 6-7 years old.

Lobsters weigh an average of one to two pounds each. Right after they're caught they are measured and must fit within a certain guideline, 3 1/8" to 5" from the eye to the back of the body shell. A female lobster bearing eggs cannot be sold. A lobsterman who catches one must notch it in the tail and throw it back. After lobsters are caught their claws must be banded so they won't damage the other lobsters.

Lobsters thrive in the cold waters off the coast of Maine. The season when most hard-shelled lobsters are caught is July to November. However, some lobstermen continue to go out all year. In some areas on the coast the season is only during the winter months. Pulling lobster traps on Sunday is illegal in June, July and August.

Lobsters molt, or shed, as their bodies grow and they continue to do so throughout their lives. After shedding, their bodies are soft and don't become hard until six or eight weeks later. When a lobster loses a claw or appendage to fighting, it can grow back to normal size within 3-4 sheddings.

When alive, lobsters are dark green. They turn red as they are being cooked. A blue lobster is rare but occasionally caught.

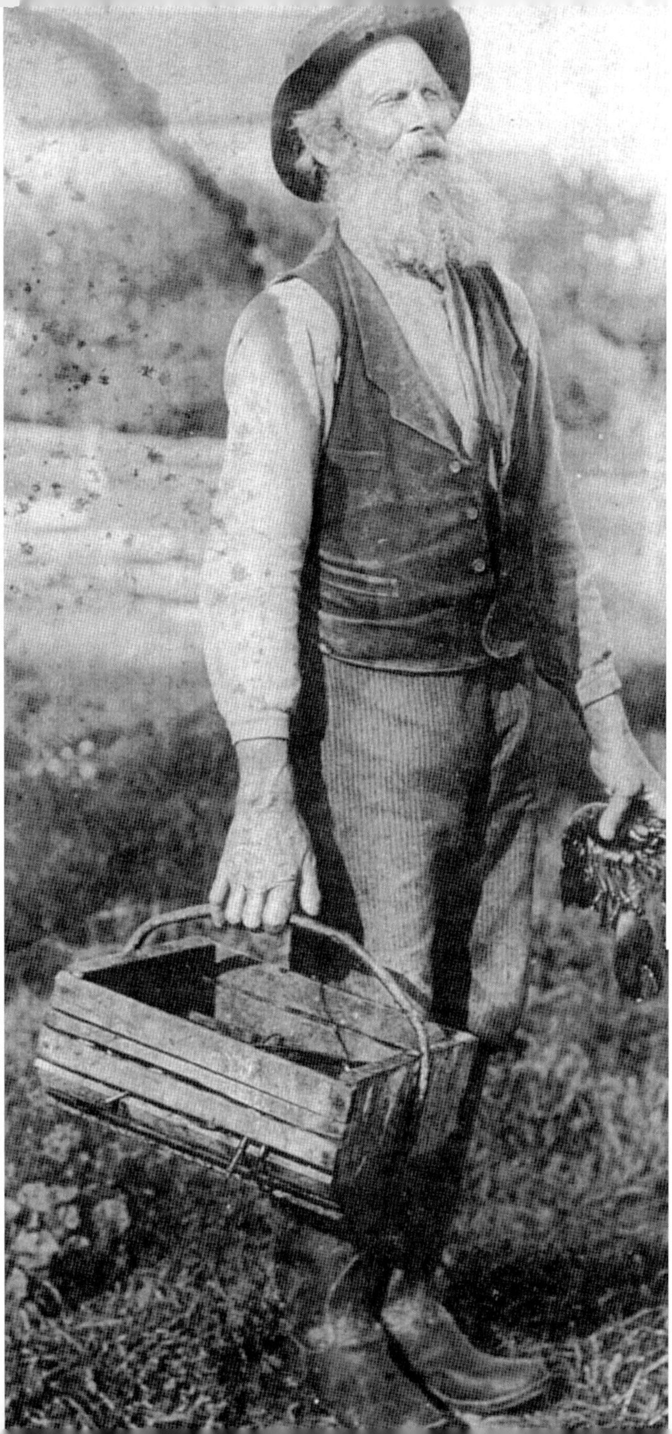

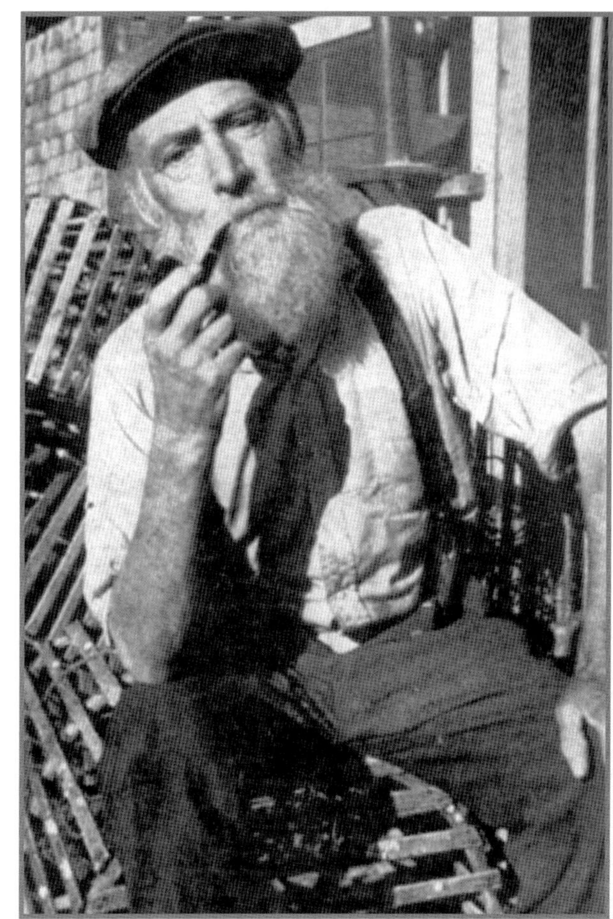

At left is Charles Black, from Orr's Island, carrying his lobsters. Above, Bert Sinnett, maybe the most photographed man on Bailey Island, takes a moment to smoke his pipe.

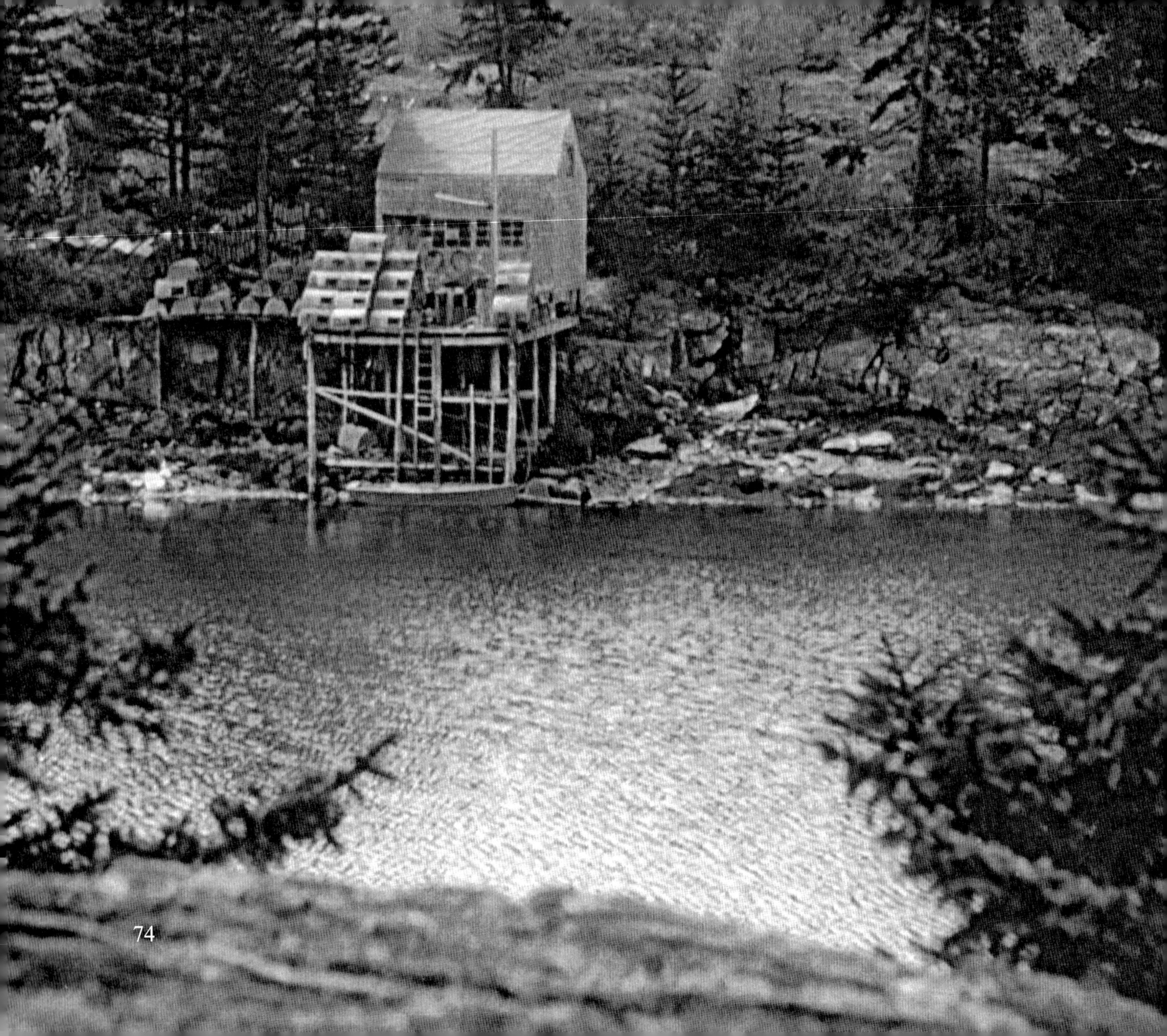

The Old Fish House at Harpswell

Frank L. Bailey

Old gray fish house by the shore,
I see you sitting there,
Snug-fitted to the ledge-banked score
With scanty shingles bare;
Your rusty stove-pipe stands atilt
While weather-beaten sides
Are etched and eaten by the silt
Of many pounding tides.

Your dingy window 'gainst the light,
And scant of glassy pane
Is stuffed with cloth that once was white,
To keep out snow and rain.
Beneath your sills the rising tide
Bears drifting things afloat
While at the nearby moorings ride
Full many a lapstreak boat.

Within your walls repose the gear
Of the seafarer's art—
Those implements so near and dear
To every fisher's heart.
The air is scented with the tar
Of lobster-warp and trawl,
An oar, a gaft, a broken spar
Are resting on the wall.

A rusty can sits on the stove,
A hogshead tub imposes
Its porgy-sliver smell above
The tallest upturned noses.
The gray gull's cry faint greets the ears,
The wash of waves about it
As Memory's hand turns back the years
For those who know and love it.
Old fish house, I know not your end
Now that you are no more,
Maybe I'll see you sometime, friend—
Upon another shore.

Frank Bailey grew up in Harpswell in the late 1800's. He later moved to Plymouth, Massachusetts. His poetry describes his feelings and memories of his childhood. He exchanged poetry with Grandmother Ethel.

Note at left: Elisha Leeman's fish house on Water Cove. Although his granddaughter, Janet Freeman, was a good friend, I rarely went to the north end of the island.

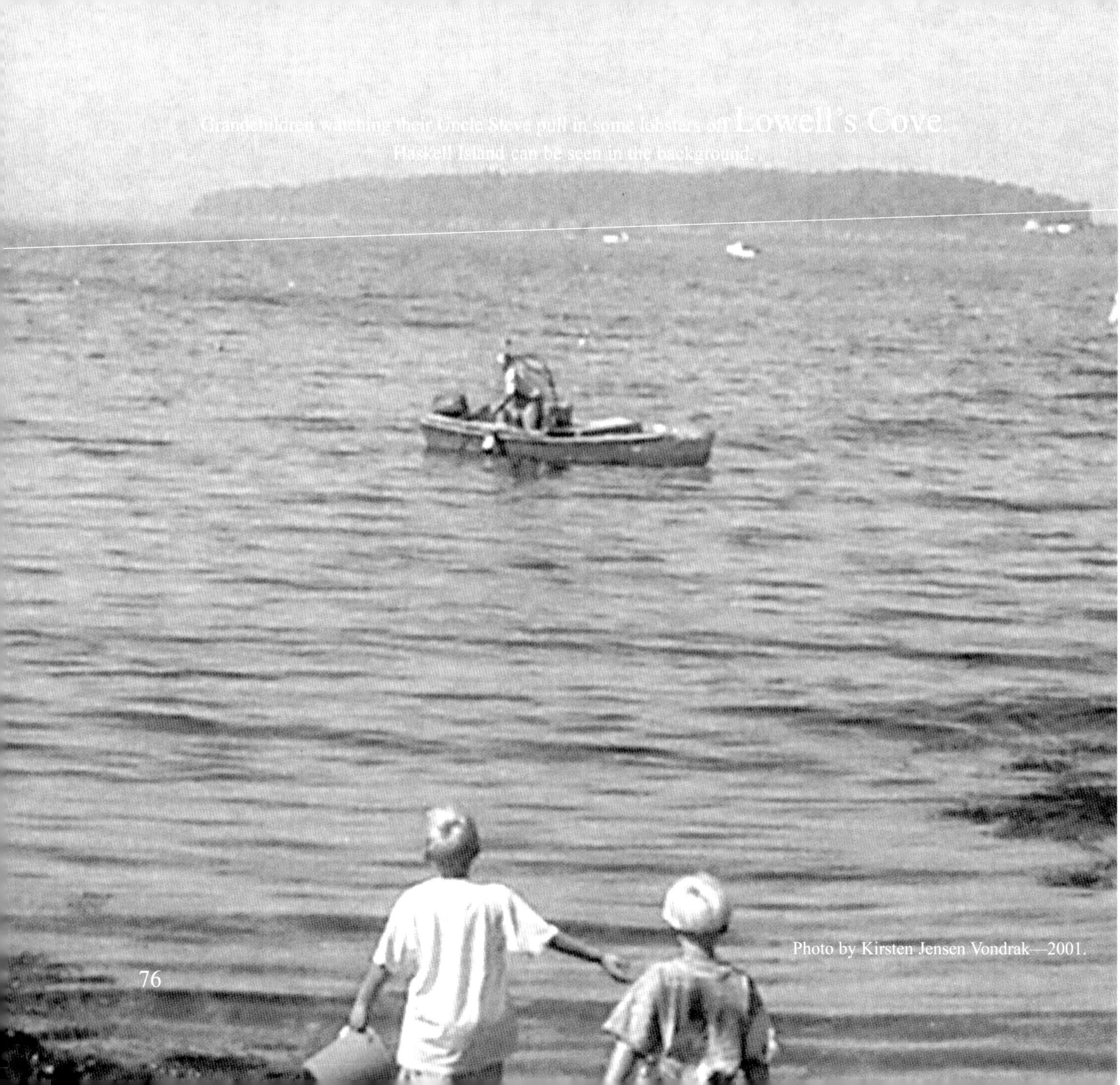

Grandchildren watching their Uncle Steve pull in some lobsters off Lowell's Cove.
Haskell Island can be seen in the background.

Photo by Kirsten Jensen Vondrak—2001.

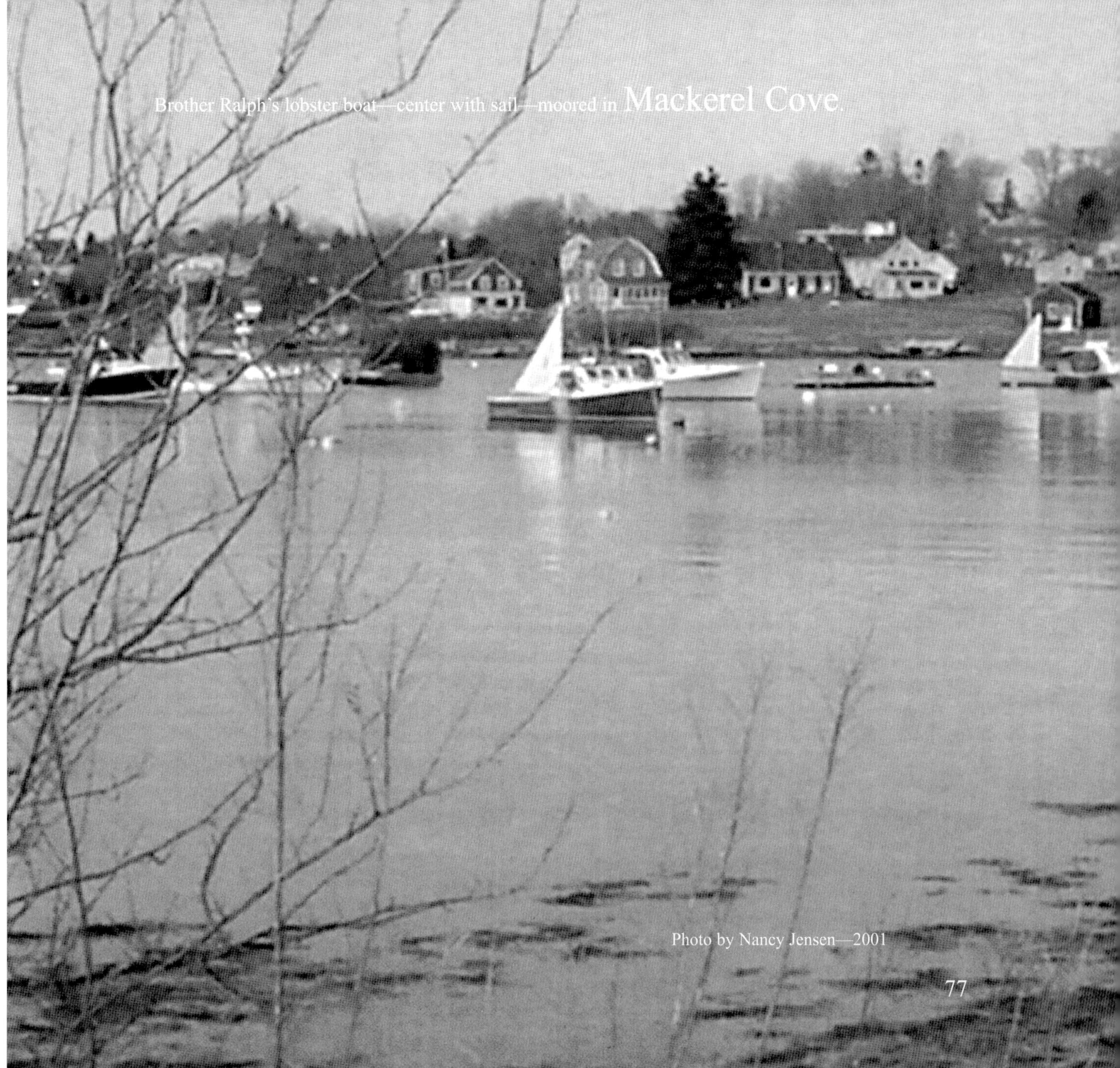

Brother Ralph's lobster boat—center with sail—moored in Mackerel Cove.

Photo by Nancy Jensen—2001

I found this unidentified calendar picture of (left to right): Walter Toothaker, Frank Bichrest, Clayton Drake, Clayton Baker and Phil Baker pulling in nets from a dory. It reminds me of early days on the island when many of the men went seine fishing. I can still picture their nets drying in the field above Mackerel Cove. When the dories weren't in use, they were turned over on the banks of Mackerel Cove. As kids we spent hours hiding under those dories or rocking on top of them.

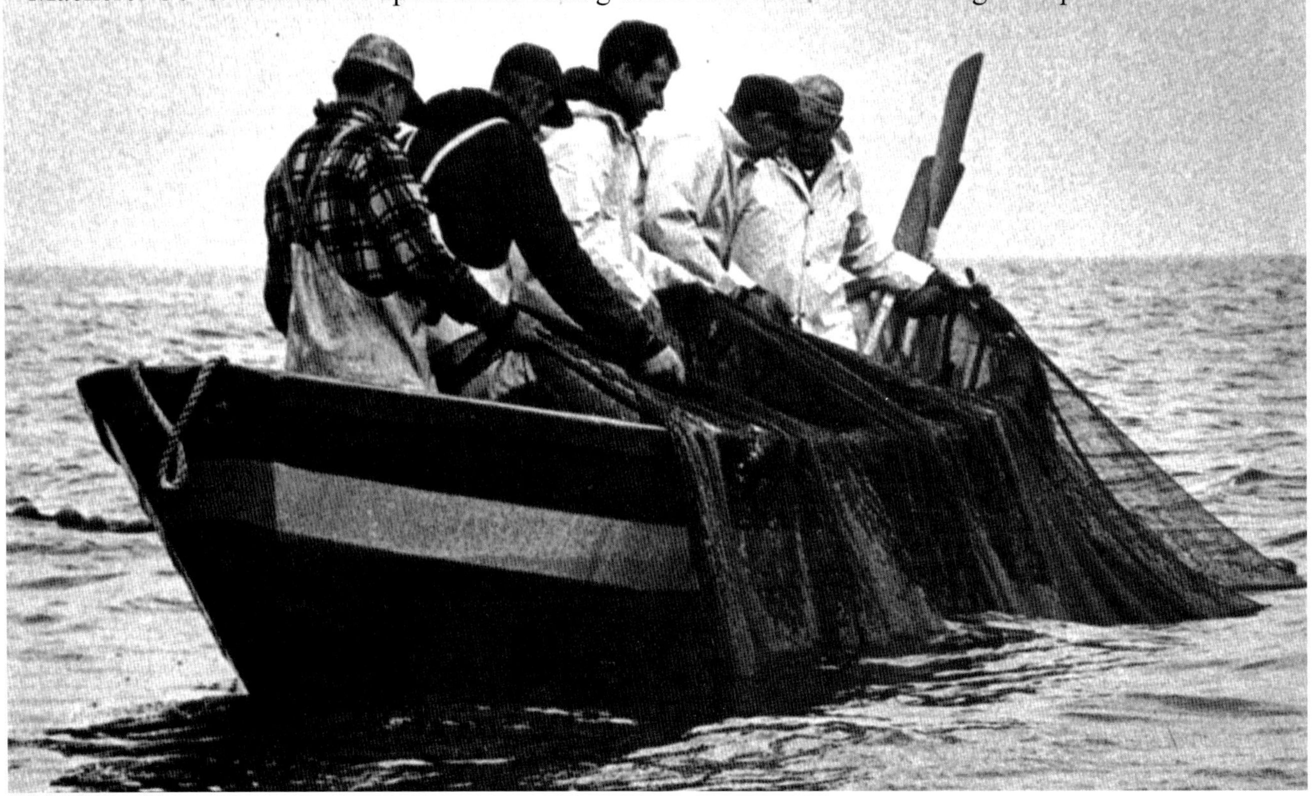

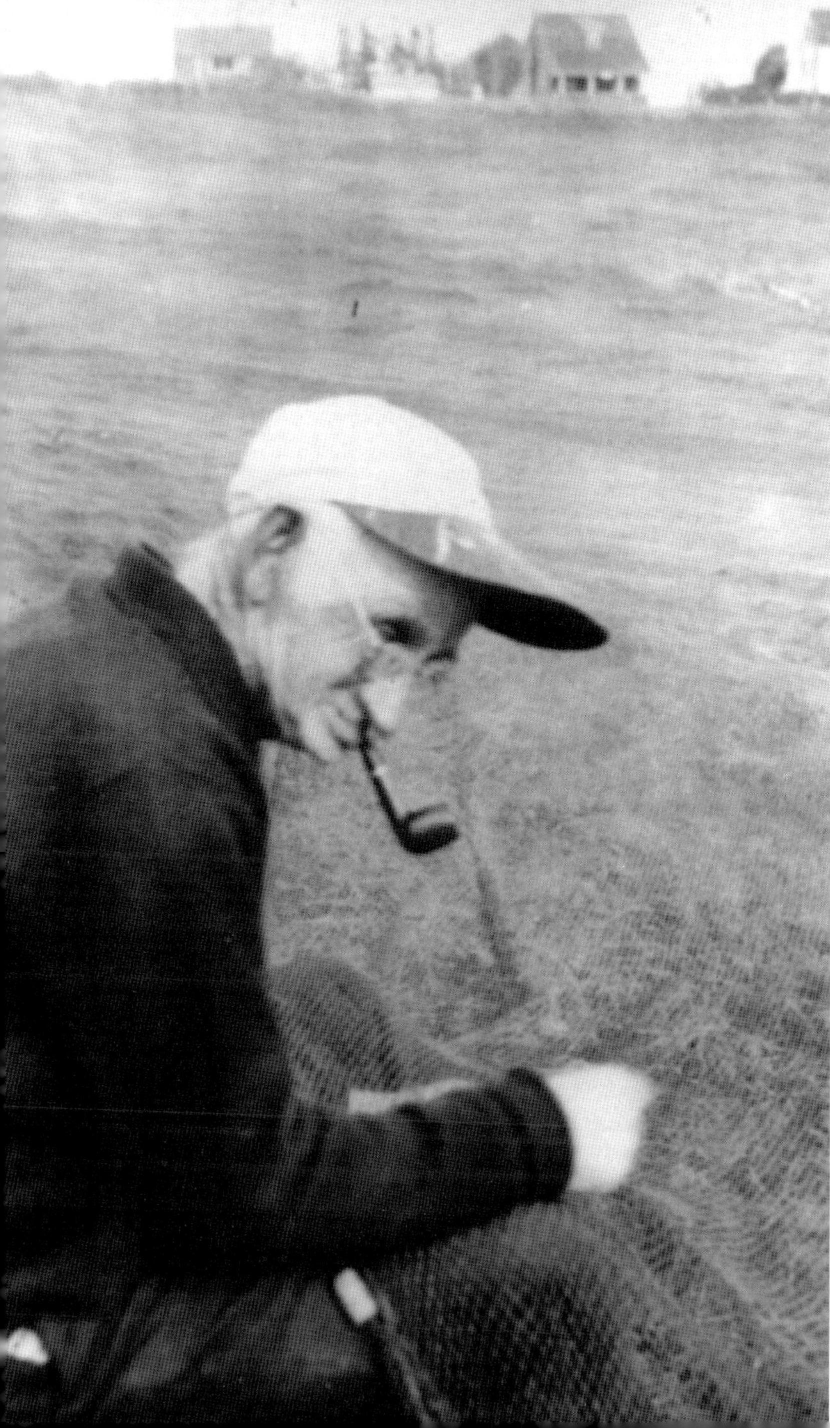

At left: "Bish" (Sinnett Winfield Orr) mending nets at the head of Mackerel Cove.

Bishy was a very kind man who lived alone in a shingled shack at the head of Mackerel Cove. He kept his many cats overhead in the loft. He spoke few words and always had a pipe in his mouth. When his shack burned my folks took him in, even though they barely had room for themselves and certainly no money to feed another mouth. But he was a good friend and they wanted to help.

Bish chats from his boat with my father on the beach at Mackerel Cove.

I grew up never knowing most of the island men's real names. As a matter of fact, I had to go around asking about their real names to put in this book.

Another one of these island characters was "Dicer" who lived alone in a flat-roofed shack by Abner's Wharf in Mackerel Cove. He had a gruff voice, a loud laugh, and a gnarled face. Dicer was one of a number of island folks who put salt-cod on lines to dry. We often went over after dark and helped ourselves to a fish or two.

The only way to get any money for candy was to either be lucky enough to find a coin by the side of the road or hunt for returnable bottles. Dicer always had milk bottles that he would give us to return for a nickel apiece. It was daring to enter his place, go past his big black dog and hear him shout out in that gruff voice, "Argh, argh, argh!" He got such a kick out of scaring us, but he loved kids and was always kind to us.

Nicknames of Islanders From the Past

Bishy	Sinnett Winfield Orr, son of Hudson Bishop Merriman Orr (Hut)
Washie	George Washington Doughty
Boog	Royston Leeman
Muffin	Charles Sinnett
Wink	Elroy Doughty
Newey	Ernest Johnson
Bunker	Olin Johnson
Snood	H. Elroy Johnson
Dicer	Archibald Doughty
Bim	Alonzo Doughty
Rip	Edmund F. Black
Link	Ernest Gardner
Gilly	Henry Durant
Lish	Elisha Leeman
Teddy Bear	Orrin Johnson
Cootie	George W. Johnson
Bub	Ellis Leeman
Hymie	Alton Leeman
Tykie	Alton Leeman11
Peter Hadlock	Harold Rogers
Bill Guzzick	Bill Johnson
Scup	Irving Dexter
Prout	Clarence Doughty
Spence	Charles Leeman

In the early 1800's, David Johnson's son drowned near Bailey Island. David buried him on his land, which was in the area of the present-day cemetery. He invited others to use this land for the same purpose, establishing the Bailey Island Cemetery. Later the cemetery was enlarged by a land gift from Captain James Sinnett. In 1927 the Stover, Merriman and Orr families, my ancestors, donated more land for the cemetery with the stipulation that only natives (defined as one whose grandfather had been born on Bailey Island) were to be buried there.

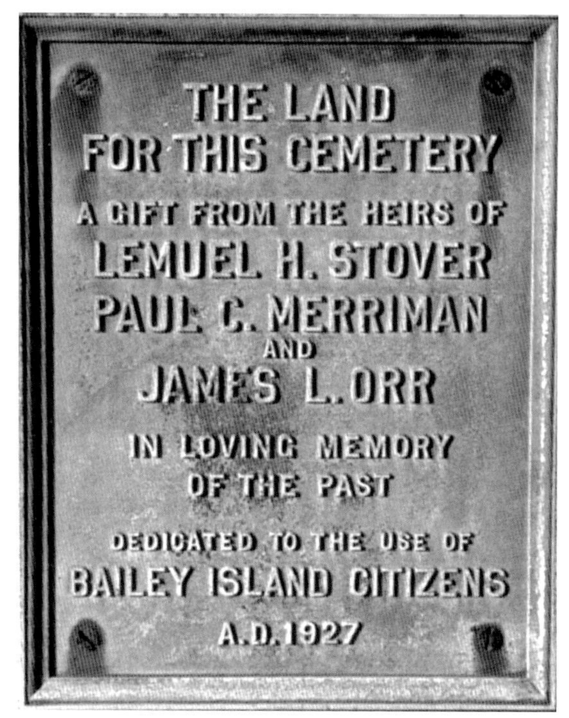

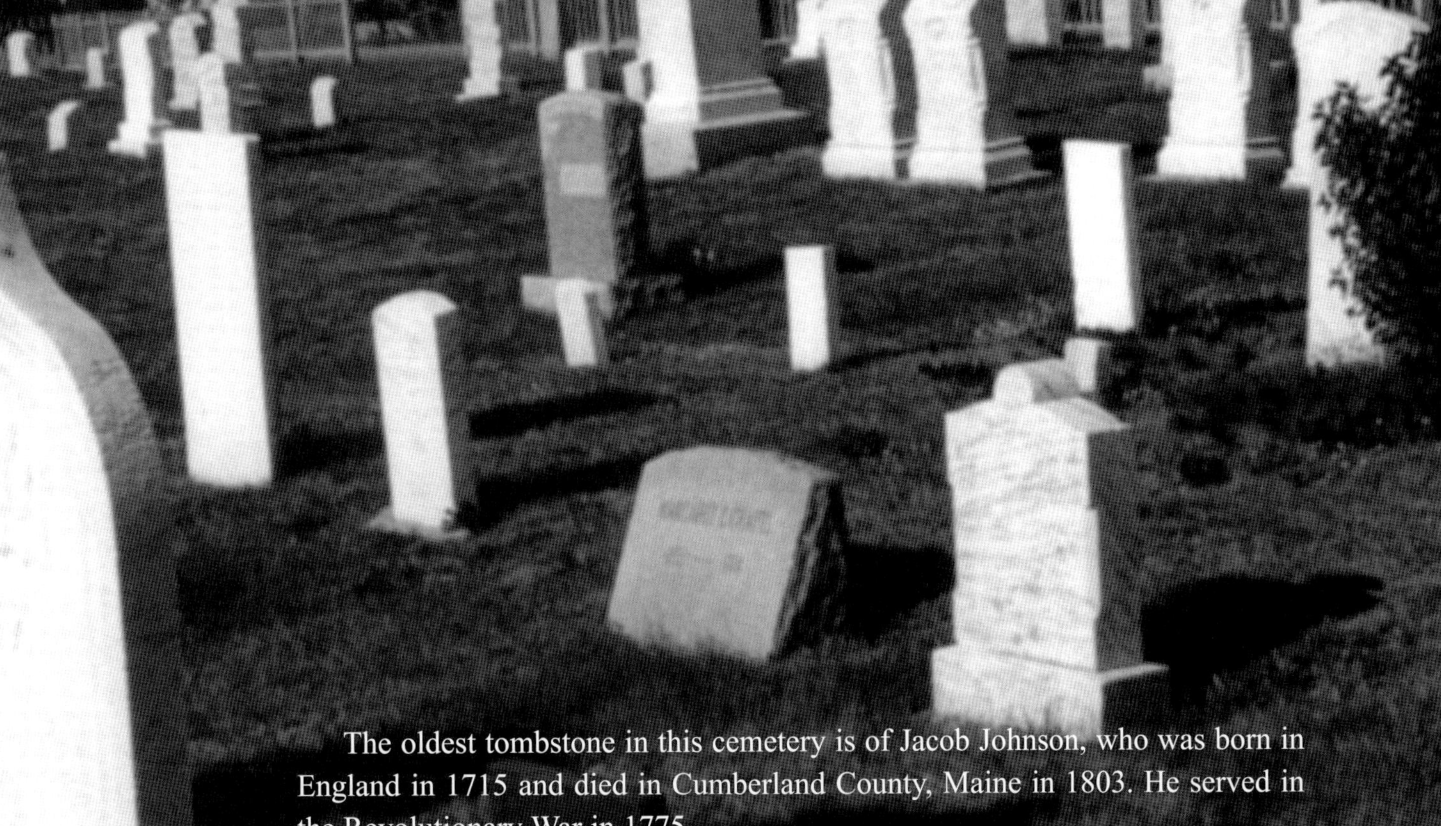

The oldest tombstone in this cemetery is of Jacob Johnson, who was born in England in 1715 and died in Cumberland County, Maine in 1803. He served in the Revolutionary War in 1775.

The most interesting epitaphs are those of Harvey (d. 1868) and Emery Sinnett (d. 1871), sons of David Sinnett. They were both lost at sea at age 22.

Harvey
Not in the churchyard shall he sleep
Amid the silent gloom:
His home was on the mighty deep,
And there shall be his tomb.

Emery
Break not for him the grassy turf
Nor turn the dewy soil
His dust shall rest beneath the surf
His spirit with its God.

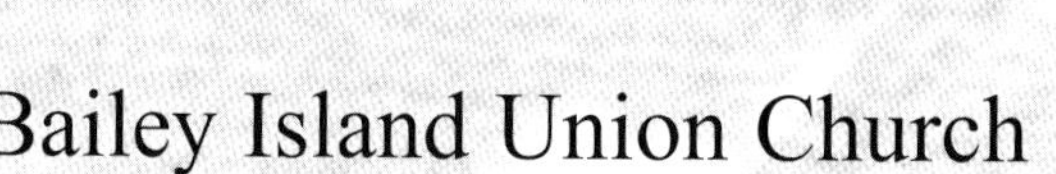

Bailey Island Union Church

The Bailey Island Union Church was one of many favorite places to play. Sandra Stevens, Donna Leeman and I went in the church many times during the week and pretended to perform a church service. Since I could read music I was usually at the pump organ playing hymns. Sandra and Donna would go up to the pulpit to give the sermon and read a Psalm and an Old or New Testament verse. We loved to sing as loud as we could and shout out the sermons and readings. The church was always open and no one ever bothered us when we were there.

Sunday School was an important part of the lives of island children growing up in the 1940's. We were rewarded at the end of the school year by a pin which had a bar added for each year of perfect attendance. The competition was strong to see who got the most bars over the years. My sister Ruth was always in the lead.

The plaque below is a memorial to the island men who served in World War I and II.

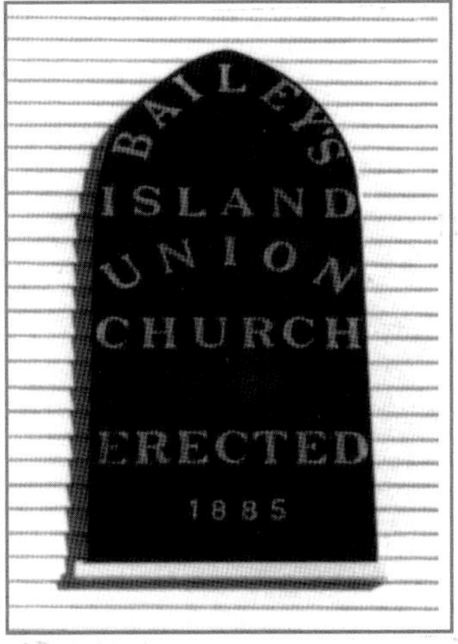

Wednesday evening was sing-along night at the church. Many islanders gathered in the church and sang hymns, mostly by request. One of my favorites was *Let the Lower Lights Be Burning*. I always thought it was a hymn written only for island people because it was about the ocean and lighthouses. I was an adult before I realized it was a popular hymn in many Protestant churches. We always liked *Stand Up, Stand Up For Jesus,* too, because as soon as we got to the chorus everyone stood up. *Whispering Hope* brought out the talent we had for singing parts. I always sang the counter part. *Onward, Christian Soldiers* was always sung with great spirit as though we were marching as we sang.

The Christmas concert was held every year on Christmas Eve. The church was always filled on that occasion. We were all given poems or Bible verses to memorize for that night. Santa Claus came at the end of the evening to distribute gifts spread under the huge tree standing up front.

My sister Ruth's Perfect Attendance pin.

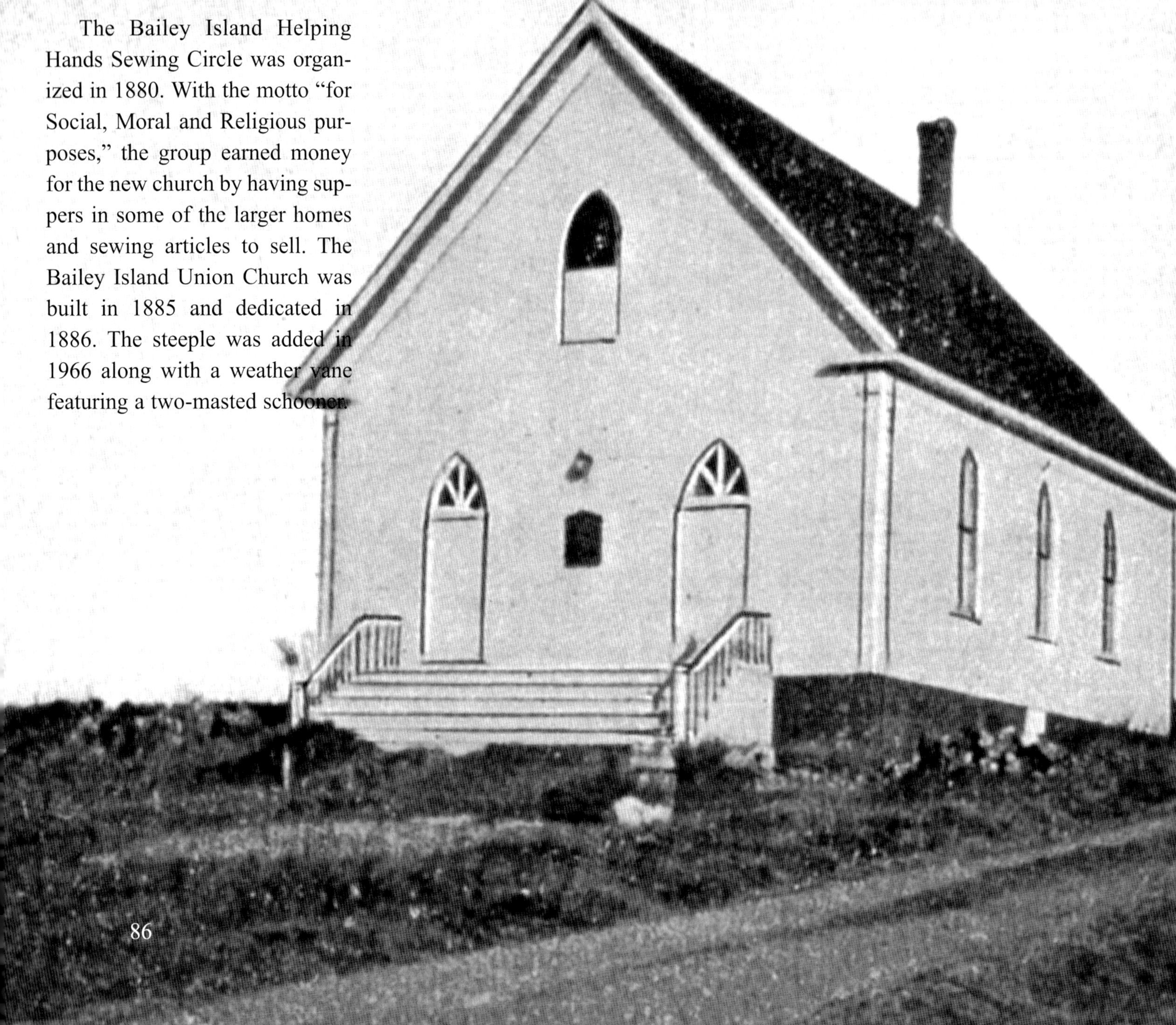

The Bailey Island Helping Hands Sewing Circle was organized in 1880. With the motto "for Social, Moral and Religious purposes," the group earned money for the new church by having suppers in some of the larger homes and sewing articles to sell. The Bailey Island Union Church was built in 1885 and dedicated in 1886. The steeple was added in 1966 along with a weather vane featuring a two-masted schooner.

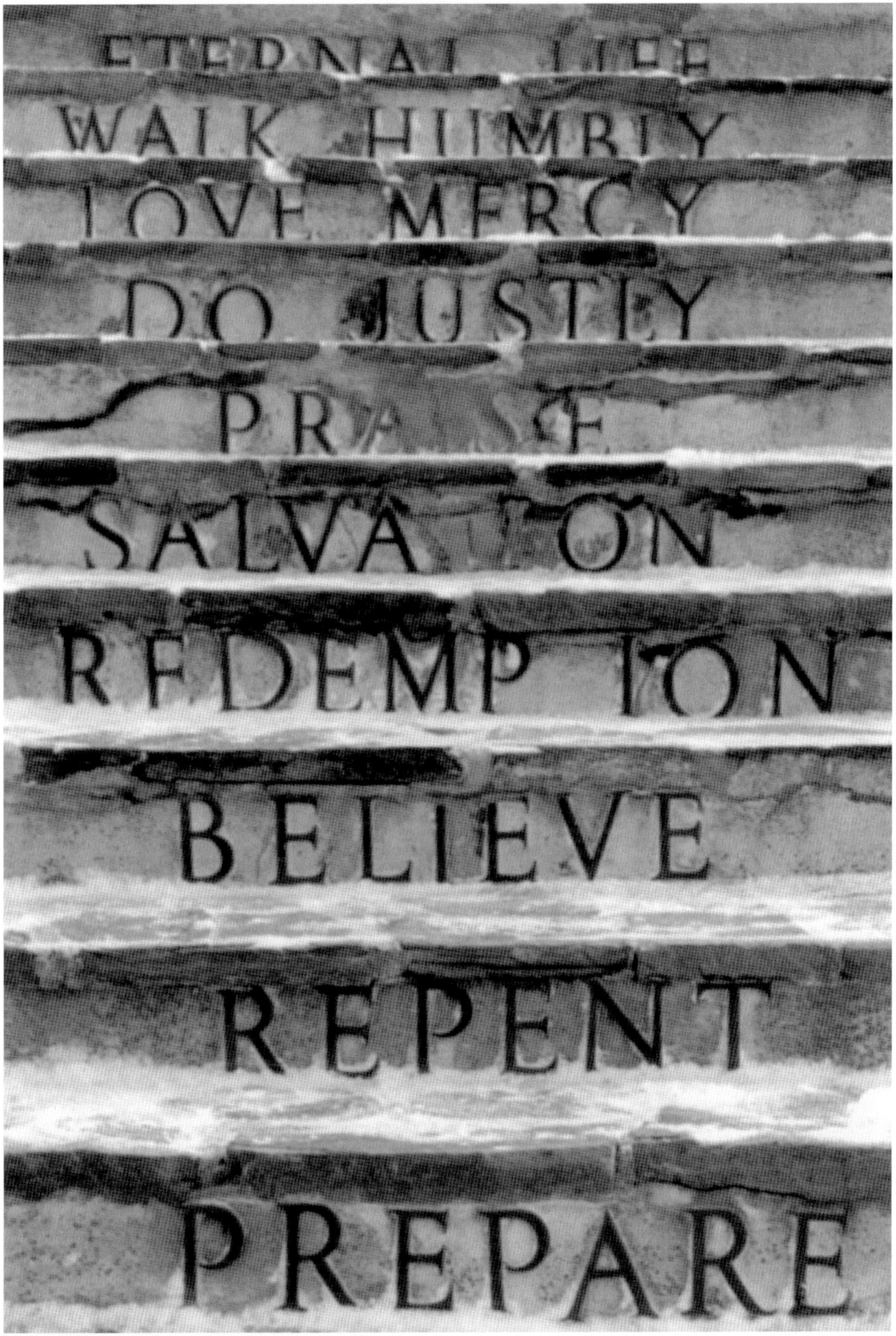

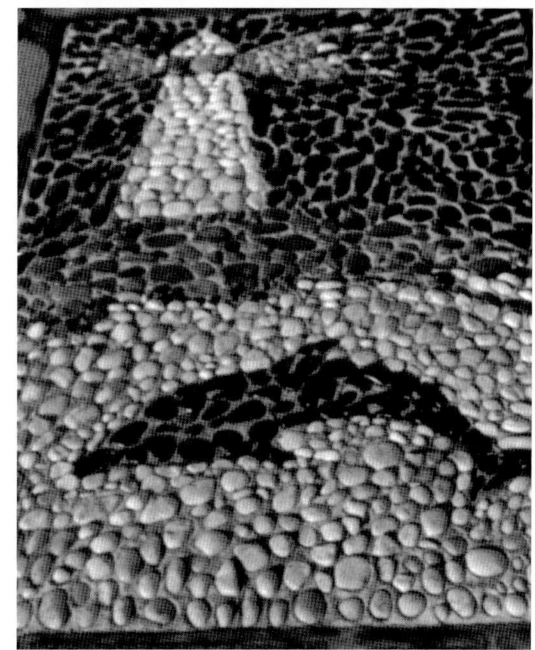

Above: In 1999 the church contracted Bailey Island resident Jerry Leeman to design and create a step made of area stones on the south side entrance of the church.

At left: Each of the ten steps leading into the church has a word of wisdom: *Prepare, Repent, Believe, Redemption, Salvation, Praise, Do Justly, Love Mercy, Walk Humbly, Eternal Life*.

The Bailey Island School

I couldn't wait to go to school. Before I was old enough to attend I often went to the schoolhouse with a friend and sat on the bottom step of the wrought iron fire escape by the downstairs window, hoping Mrs. Leeman, the teacher, would invite us in. One day she did, but only for a few minutes. The following year, 1943, I started school.

We looked forward to the day when we could go to the upstairs room where Mrs. Skillings taught grades four through eight. By the time we were in fourth grade, though, we were bused to the school on Orr's Island. In the 1950's, a centralized school was built on Great Island and the Orr's and Bailey Island schools were closed.

The Bailey Island School sat across the road from the Bailey Island Union Church. The school was built in 1891. The upper floor was added in 1902. A combination coal and wood stove heated each floor of the building. There was no plumbing in the school, and although the bathrooms were inside the building, they were essentially outhouses. There was a water cooler in the room for drinks, and the children walked home for lunch. The building is now a private residence.

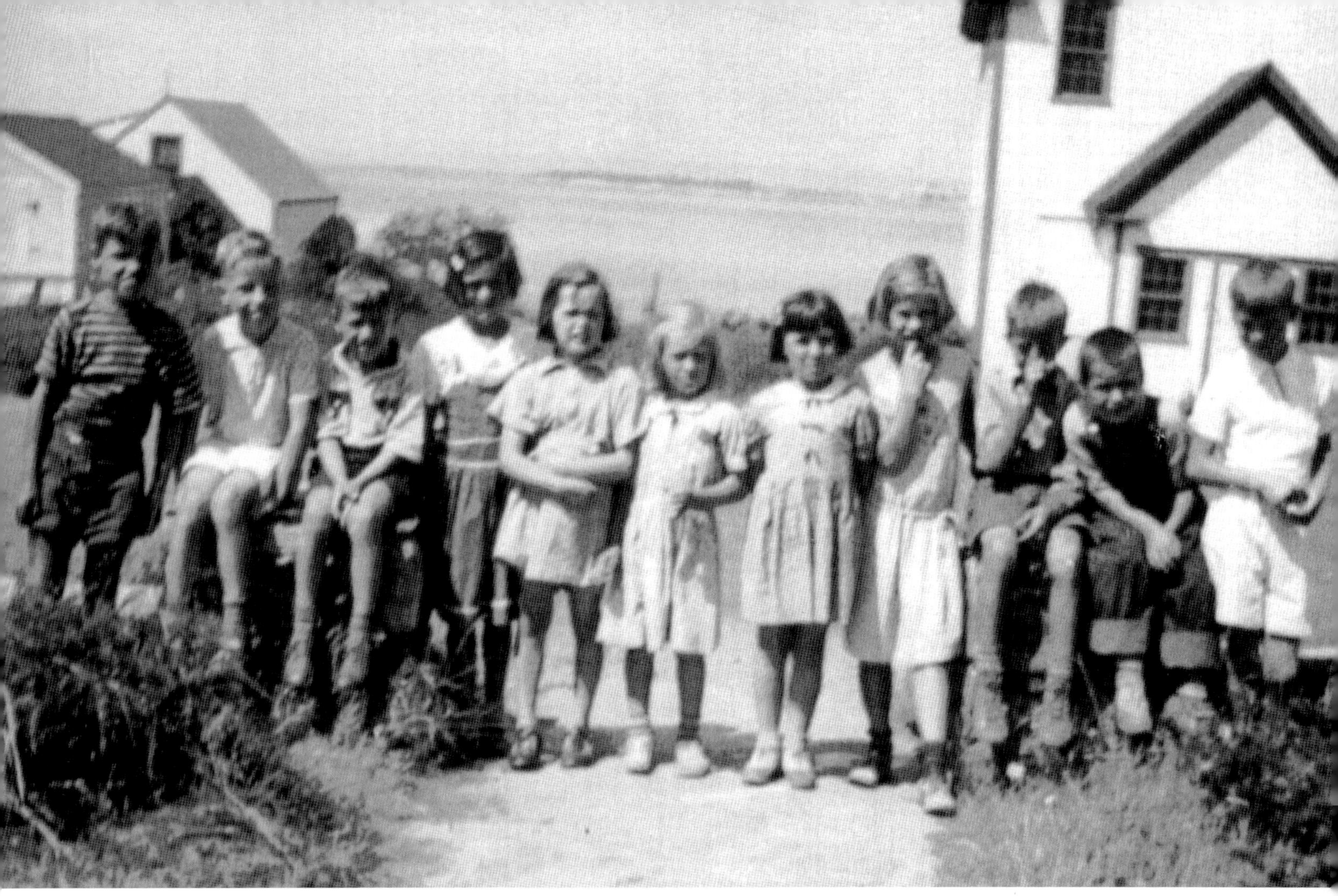

Students attending Bailey Island Vacation Bible School—1939. Left to right: Jack Huff, Bobby Leeman, Bruce Doughty, Connie Johnson, Helen Herrick, Madelyn Baker, Jeanine Doughty, Barbara Doughty, Eugene Keiffer, Fred Stilphen, Bo McMacken. In the background is the Bailey Island School.

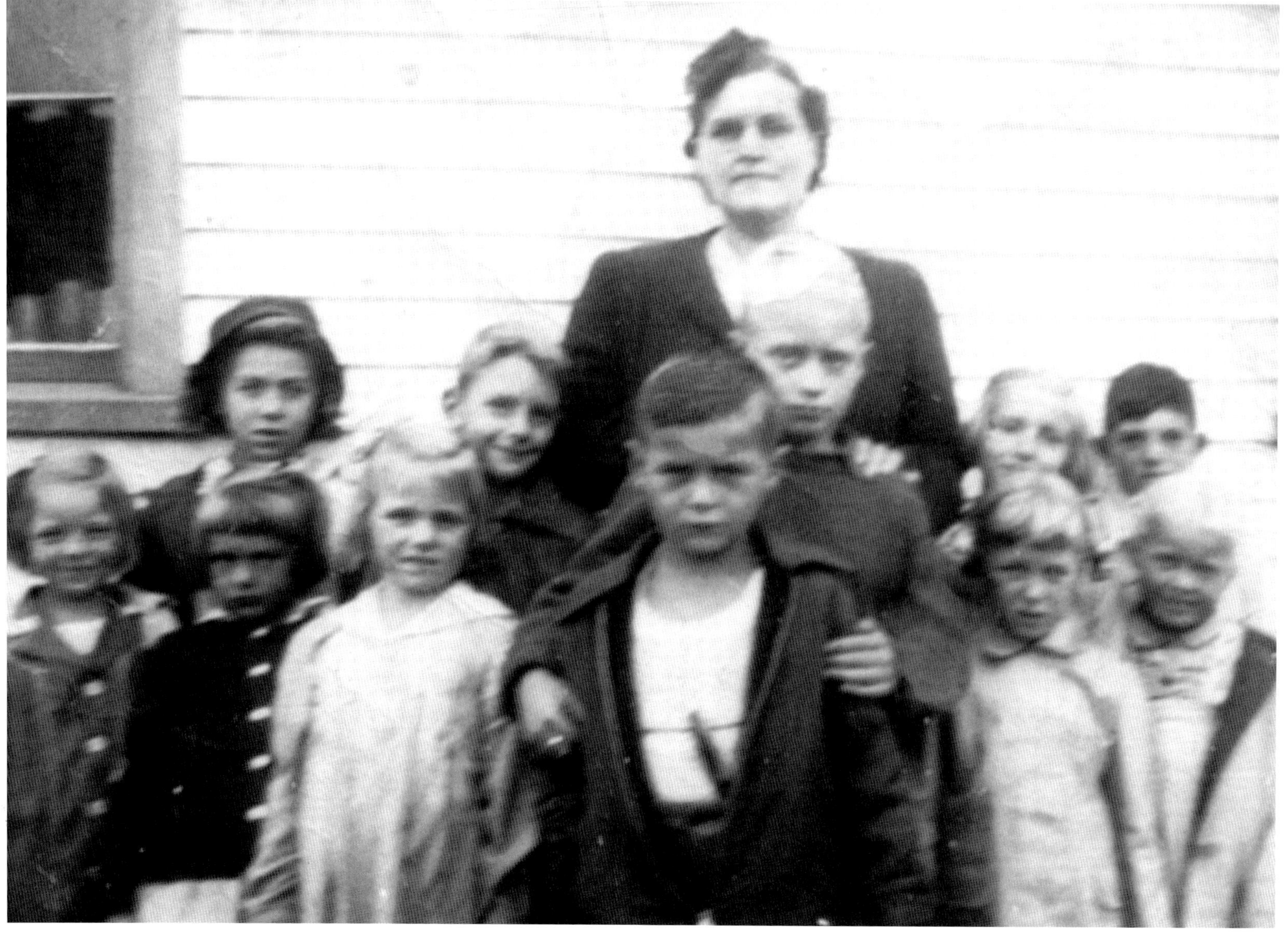

Vara Leeman's Bailey Island Class (K-4): Front row: Sandra Stevens, Sally Murray, me, Jerry Leeman, Donna Leeman, Janet Freeman. Second row: Corrine Johnson, Bump Orr, Gordon Freeman, Ruth Johnson, Don Rogers.

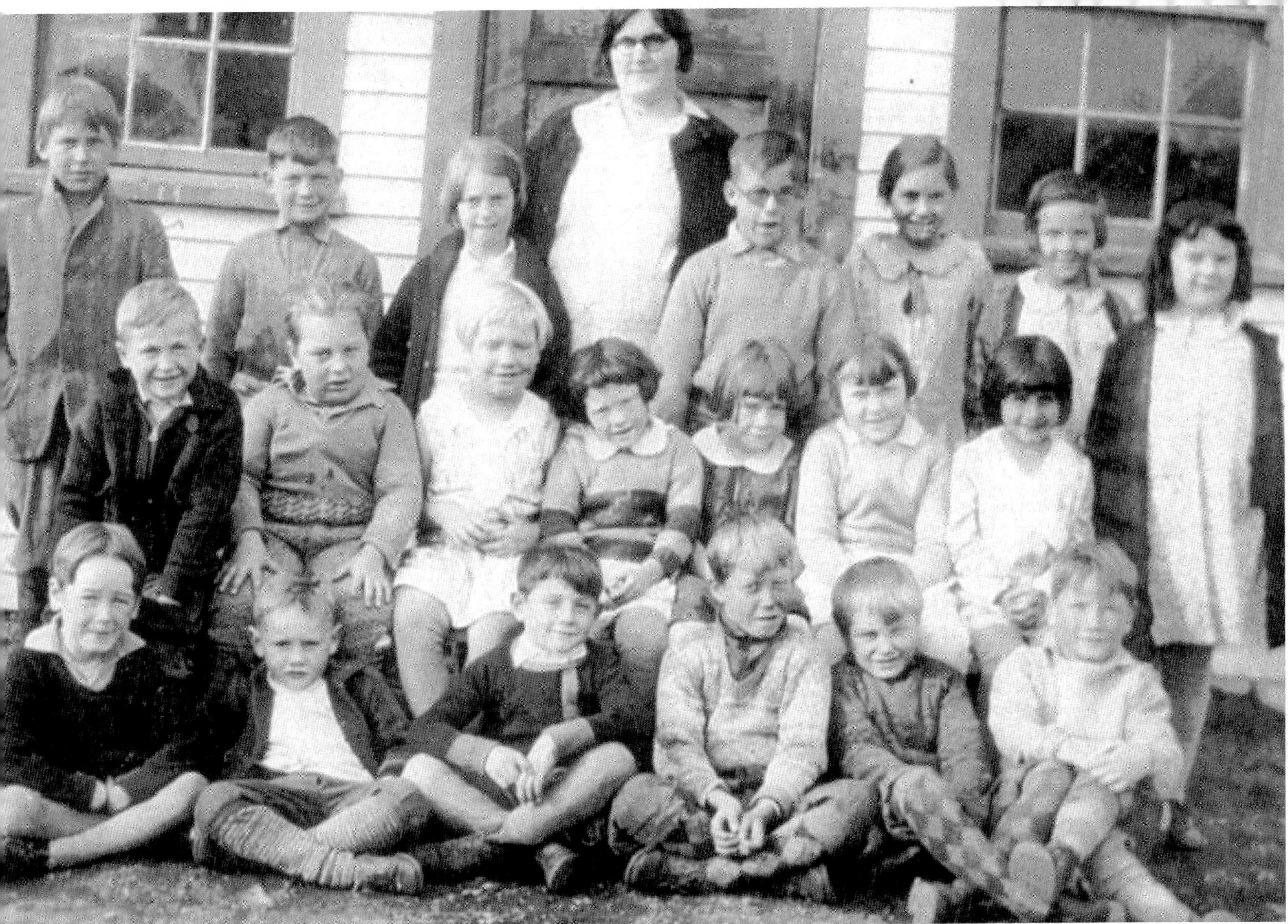

Students in Vara Leeman's Primary Class 1931-32. Back row: Paul Doughty, Charles Dexter, Barbara Doughty, teacher Vara Leeman, Donald Mathieson, Inez York, Marion Munsey, Patricia Smith. Middle row: Granville Johnson, Harold Leeman, Hazel Dexter, Lorraine Clark, Virginia G. Johnson, Drucilla Doughty, Sylvia Strout. Front row: John Skillings, Reginald Johnson, Adelbert Richardson, Phil Baker, Clayton Baker, Russell Lord.

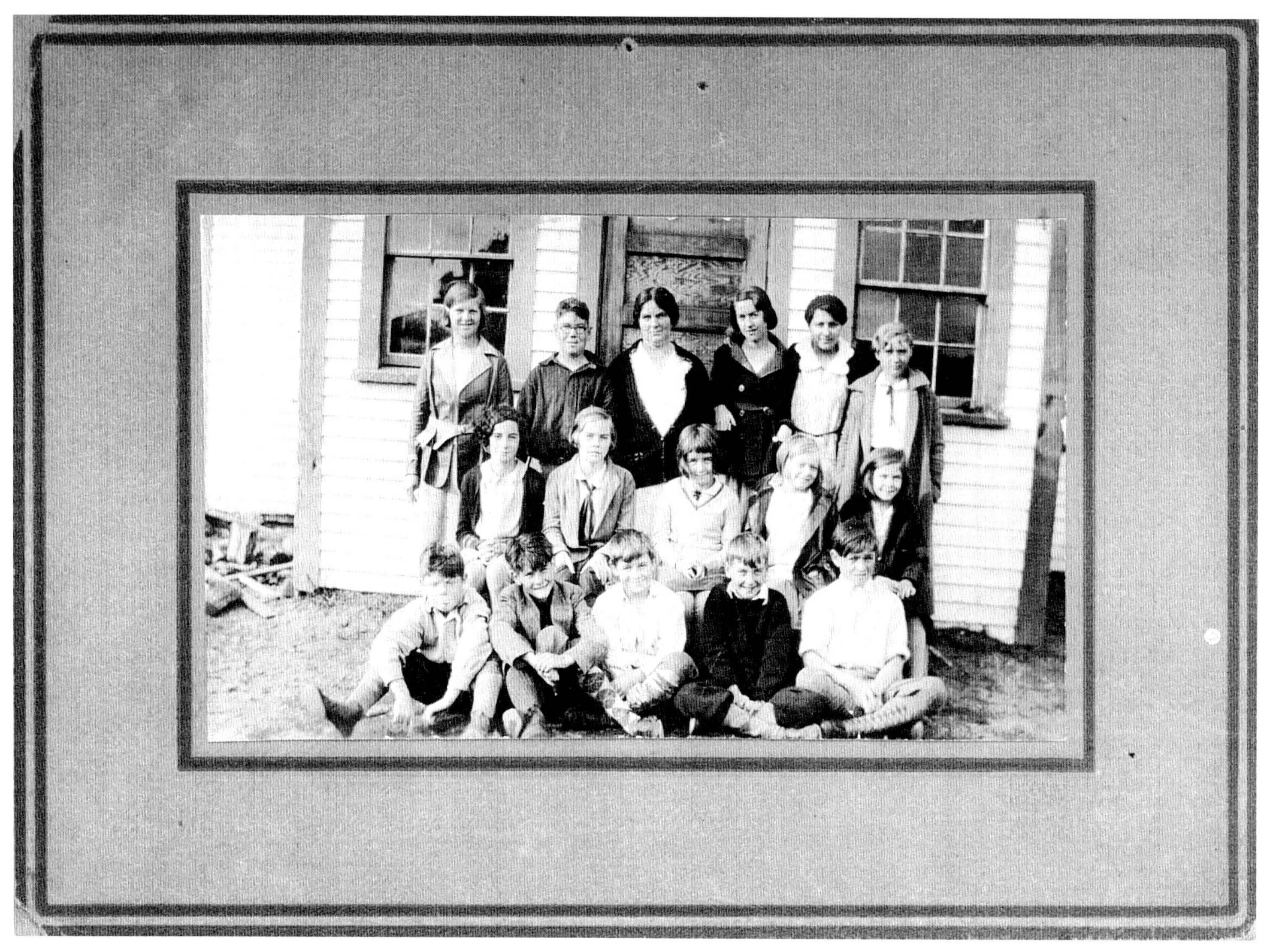

Bailey Island Grammar School Class 1930-31. Back row: Geraldine Johnson, Raymond Johnson, teacher Margaret Black Skillings, Dorothy Doughty, Mabel Clary, Celina Shea. Middle row: Georgie Smith, Ernestine Lubee, Dorothea Skillings, Lila Baker, Jeanette Johnson. Front row: Franklin Lord, Elroy Doughty, John Murray, Paul Skillings, Jim Shea.

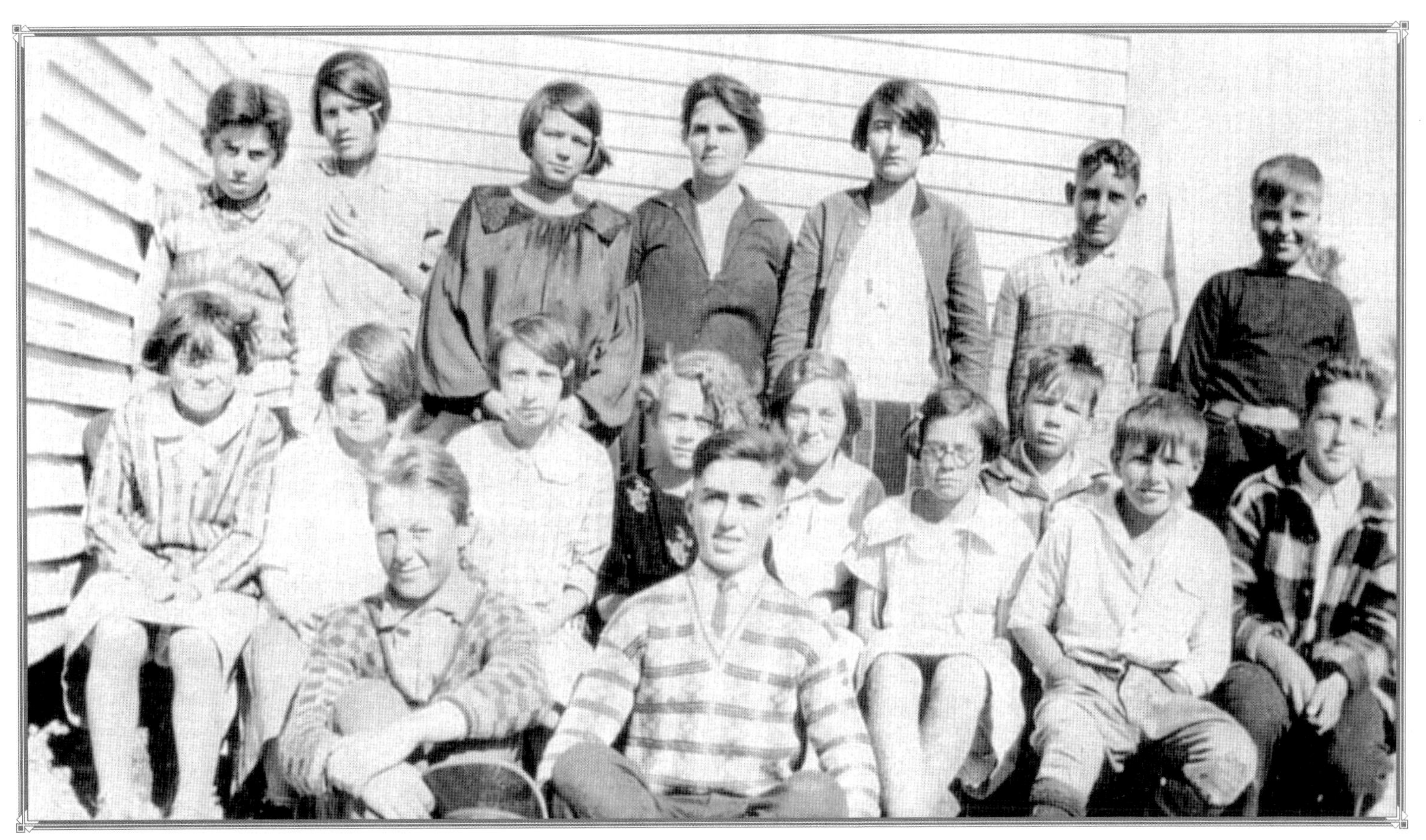

Bailey Island Grammar School Class, 1926. Back row: Nelson Lubee, Leona Doughty, Harriet Murray, teacher Margaret Skillings, Vera Smith, Herbert Leeman, William Skillings. Middle row: Grace Murray, Charlotte Colby, Elfreda Clary, June York, Marie Shea, Louise Murray, Cecil Griffin, Carleton Skillings, Herbert Griffin. Front row: Arnold Perry, Warren Lubee.

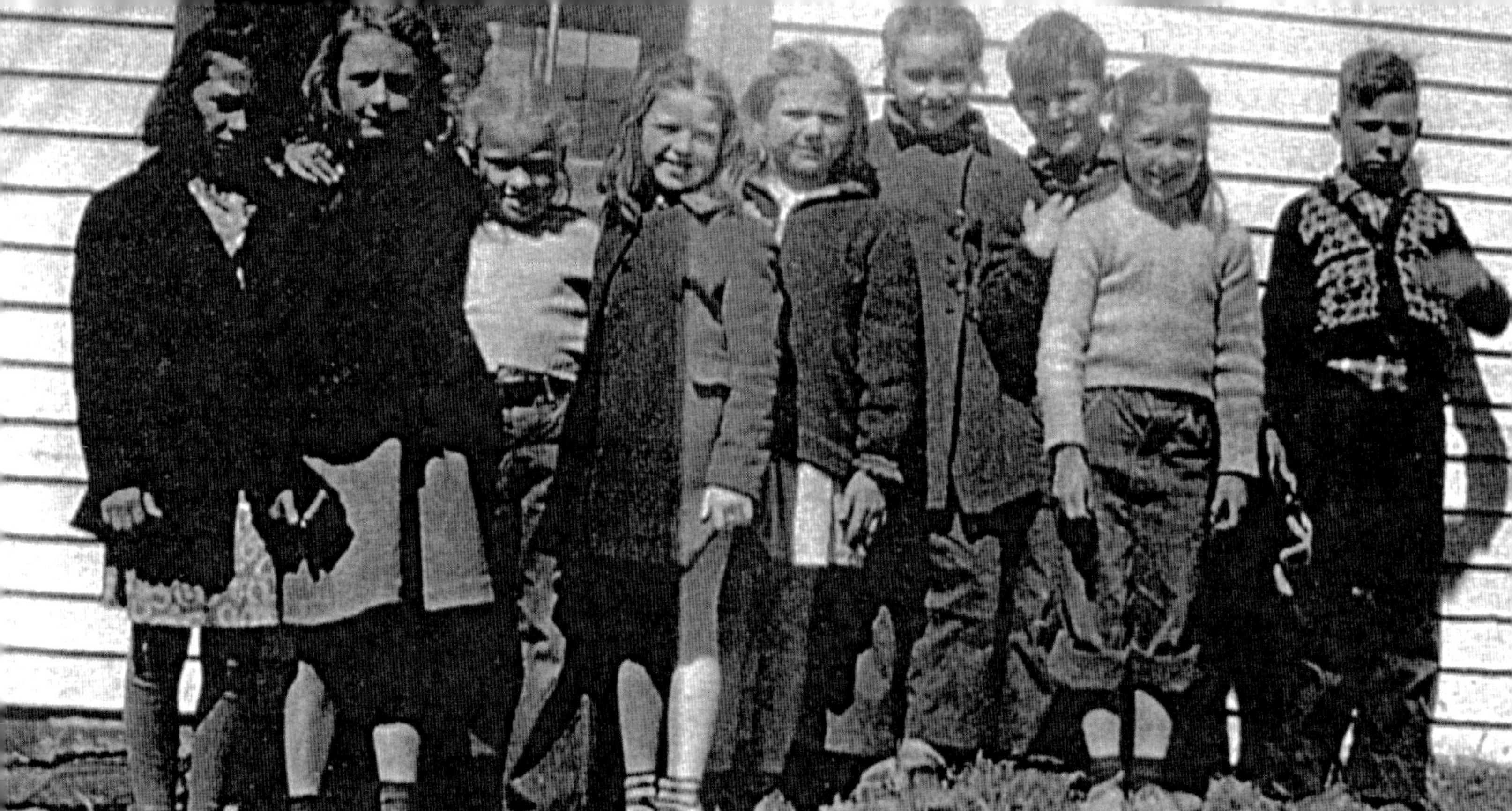

Left: Sandra Williams, Shirley Shea, Janet Freeman, Sandra Stevens, me, Judy Harris, Jerry Leeman, Donna Leeman, Richard Crowe, early 40's.

Some of my favorite school memories include the games we played: *Red Light, Green Light*; *Giant Steps*; *Go In and Out the Window*; *Button, Button, Who's Got the Button?*; *Eraser Tag*; and *Black Magic*.

May Day was my favorite holiday. We decorated empty matchboxes with colored crepe paper and filled them with grass and flowers. After school we went to the store to buy some penny candy to put in the baskets, then we'd head first to our teacher's house to hang the May Basket. We'd put the handle of the May Basket on the doorknob and call out, "May basket for Mrs. Leeman." You had to be prepared to run. If you were caught, you got a big kiss!

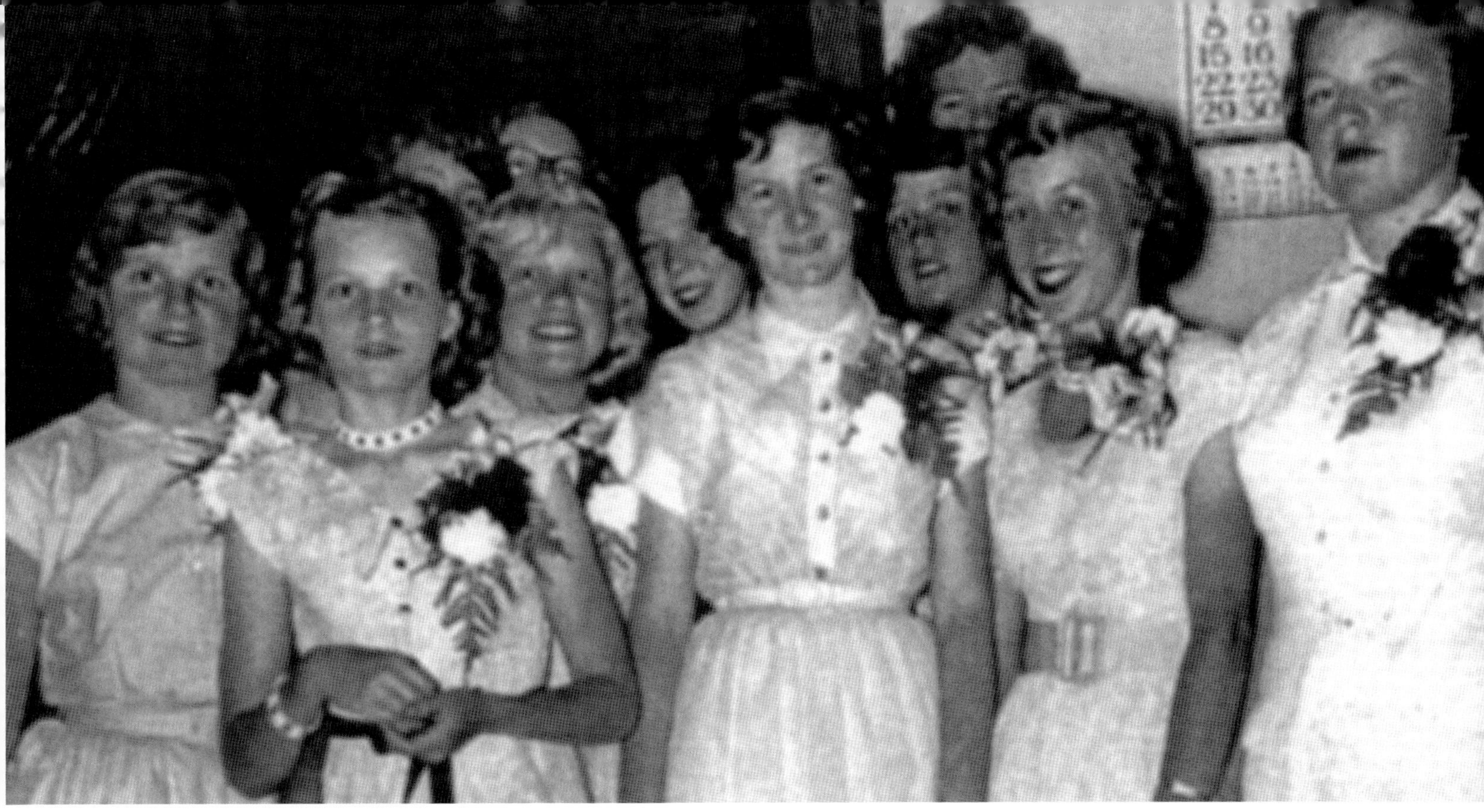

Left: Me, Shirley Dodge, Janet Freeman, Mabel Dunning, Melinda Bradley, Judy Harris, Donna Leeman, Sandra Stevens.

Eighth-grade graduates. I was at the Bailey Island School five years. By the time I graduated from eighth grade in 1952 I had been going to the Orr's Island School for four years. The Town of Harpswell included three islands—Great, Orr's and Bailey—and the peninsula of Harpswell. The graduation ceremony included all eighth graders from the town. Until that time we had never met the kids from other parts of town. The graduation ceremony was a recital of sorts. I played the piano. Others recited poetry or prose.

In 1887 the main road on Bailey Island was two lanes of gravel with a wide, grass divider. One lane was for walkers and the other was for carriages. This picture was taken looking north from Starr's Field in the center of the island.

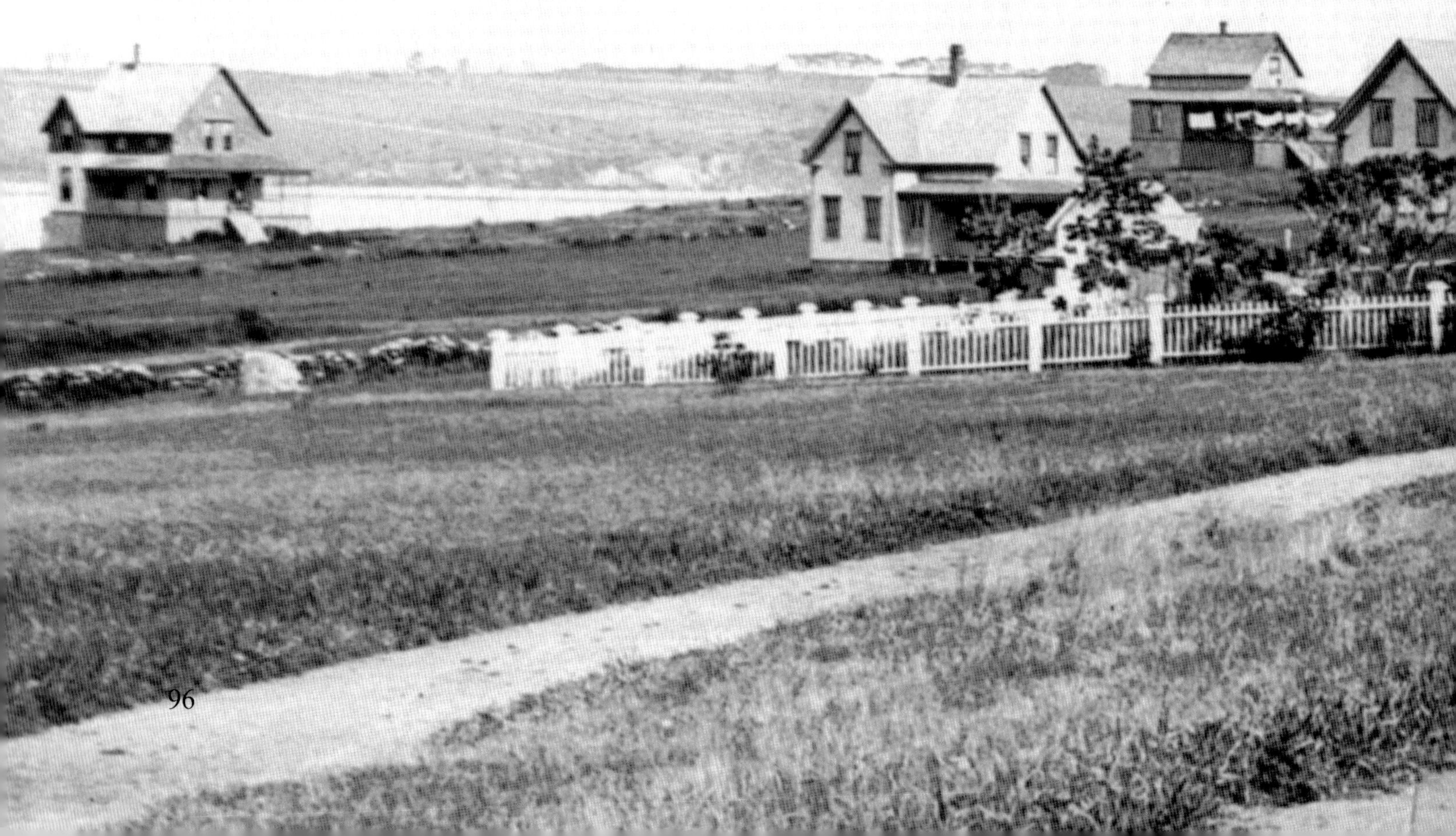

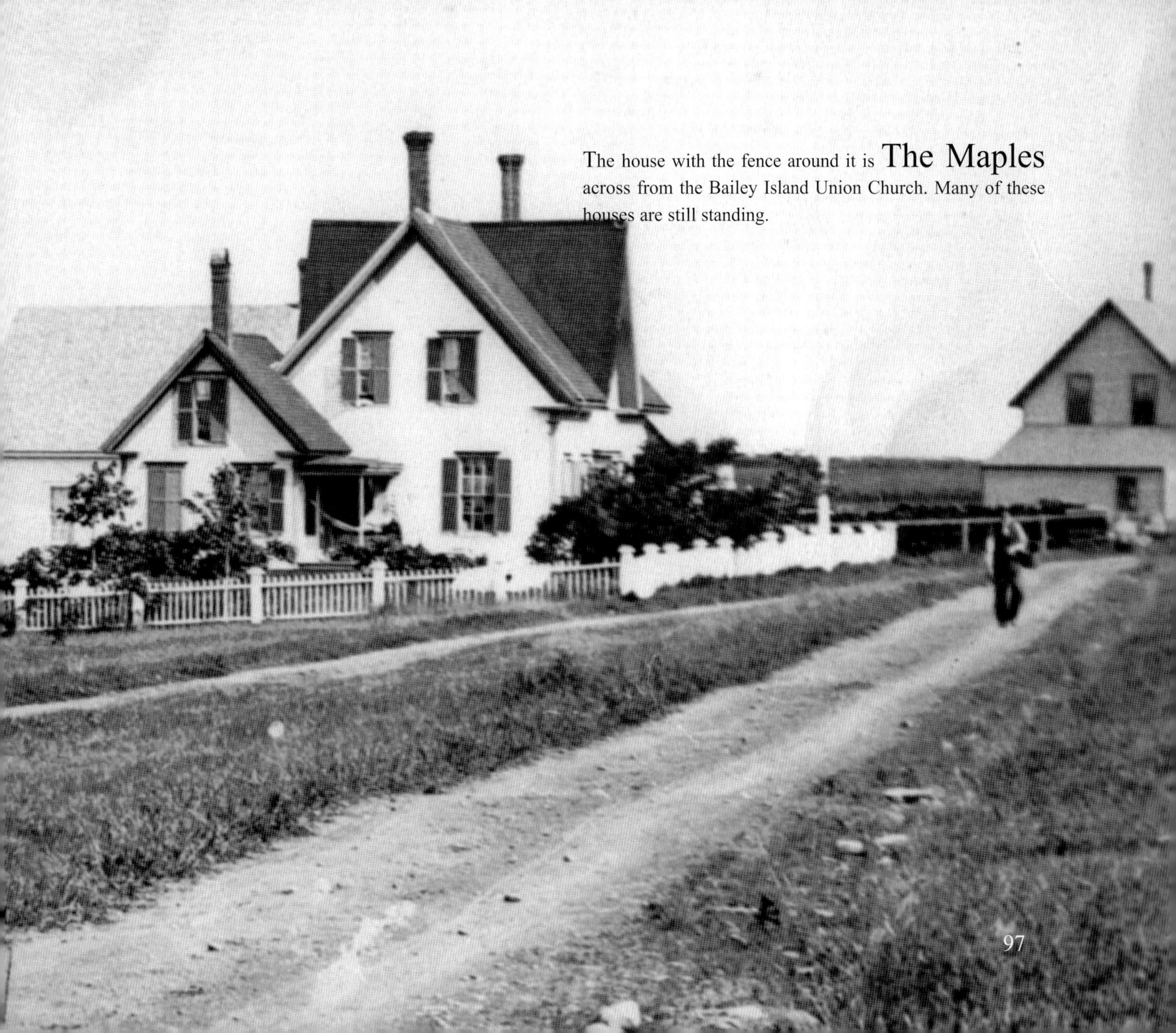

The house with the fence around it is The Maples across from the Bailey Island Union Church. Many of these houses are still standing.

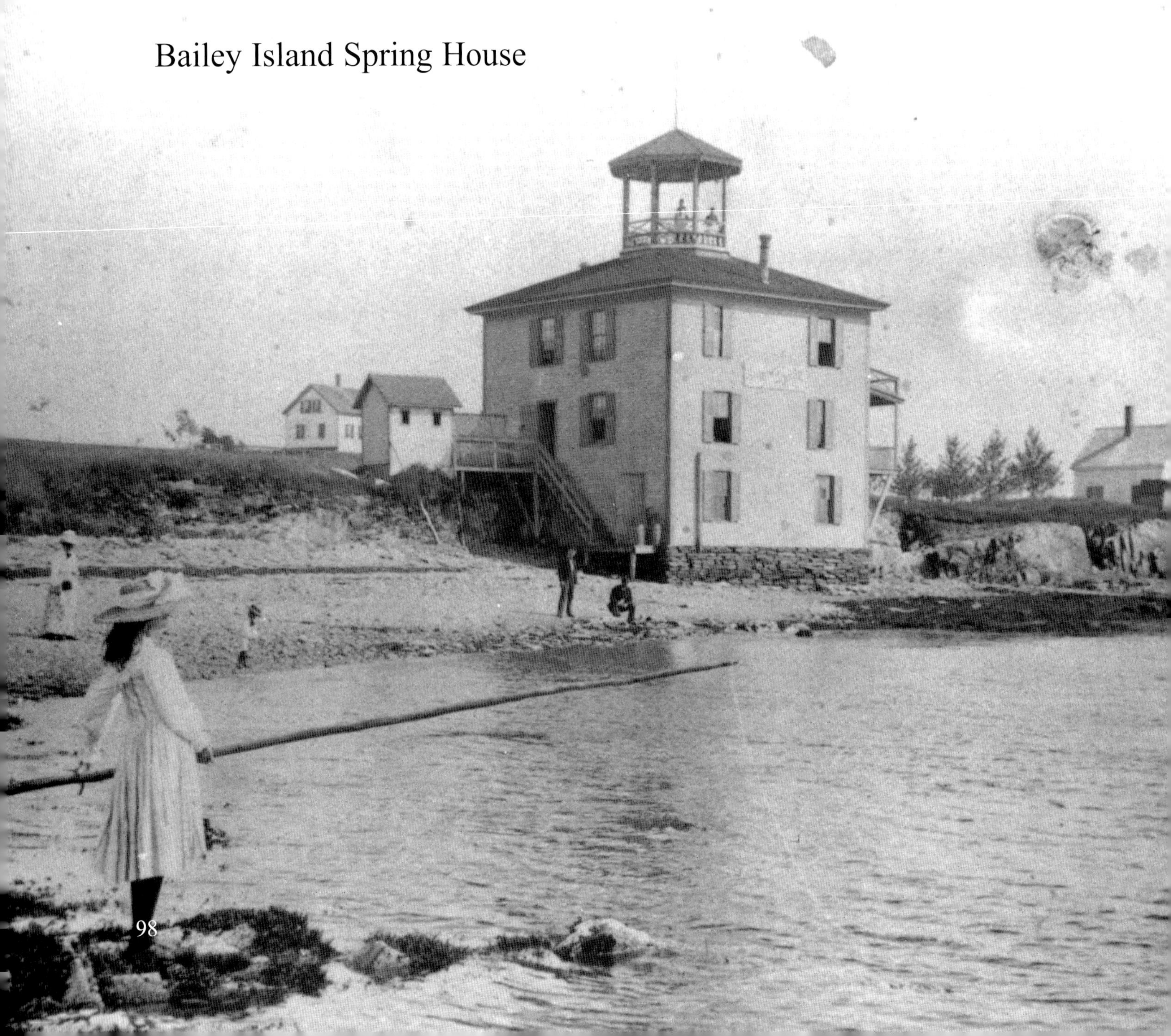
Bailey Island Spring House

Near our house, on the east shore of Lowell's Cove, was the site of what was once the Bailey Island Spring House, owned in part by Grandmother Ethel Johnson. (This is the same house that wore the KKK graffiti). It is uncertain when it was built, but records show that in 1881 a spring water bottling service was started there. It is believed the lower level was the bottling area and the upper level was a boarding house. Sometime between 1936 and 1938 the building was torn down and the wood was used to build Bub Leeman's house.

Barbara Munsey, a childhood resident of Bailey Island, remembers the Spring House being boarded up during the 1920's and 1930's. She said students from the Bailey Island School would run down there at recess and go into the building. Only the boys went in because the girls were afraid it was haunted.

The label on the Spring House bottle reads as follows:

Bailey's Island
Chalybeate Spring Water,
Aerated to hold valuable Medicinal
elements in solution.
TO BE USED MEDICINALLY or as a beverage.
For a mild Cathartic take freely in the morning before breakfast.
To produce an alternative effect use as a table water with the food.
For the various forms of Kidney and Liver diseases it has no equal.
Bottled in the Bailey's Island Chalybeate Spring Co.
Bailey's Island, Harpswell, ME

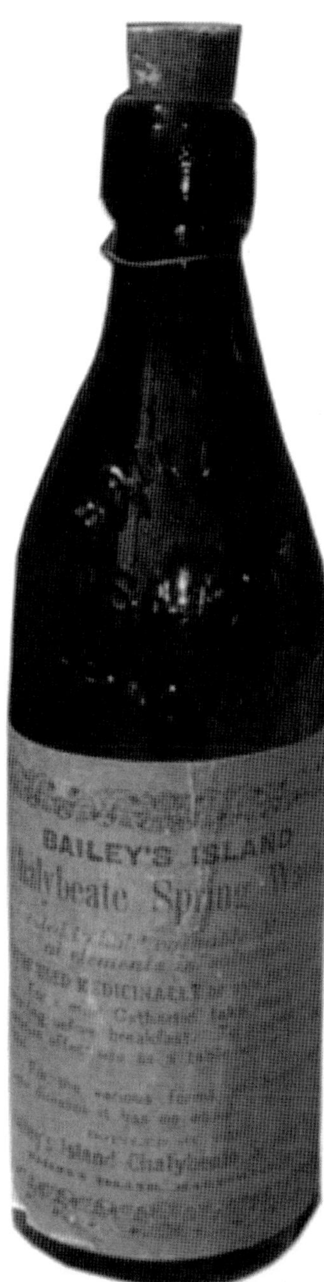

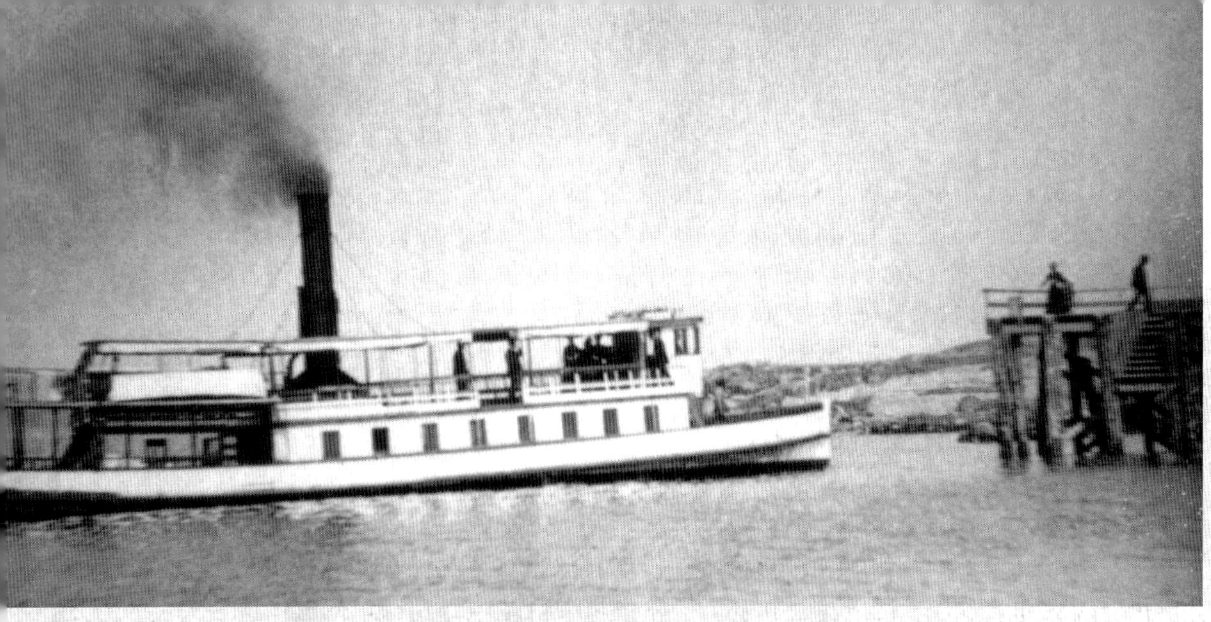

At left, the Steamer *Gordon*, the first steamboat at York's Landing.

York's Landing in Lowell's Cove was also called **Old Wharf** in the early days. Lendall York ran a coal and lumber business there in the late 1800's. He also had a store and post office at the top of the hill. Len would meet the steamboat, load up his wagon, and deliver the mail and dry goods to his store.

In 1895 the steamboat landing was changed from York's Landing in Lowell's Cove to the Steamboat Wharf on the east side of Mackerel Cove.

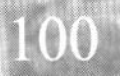

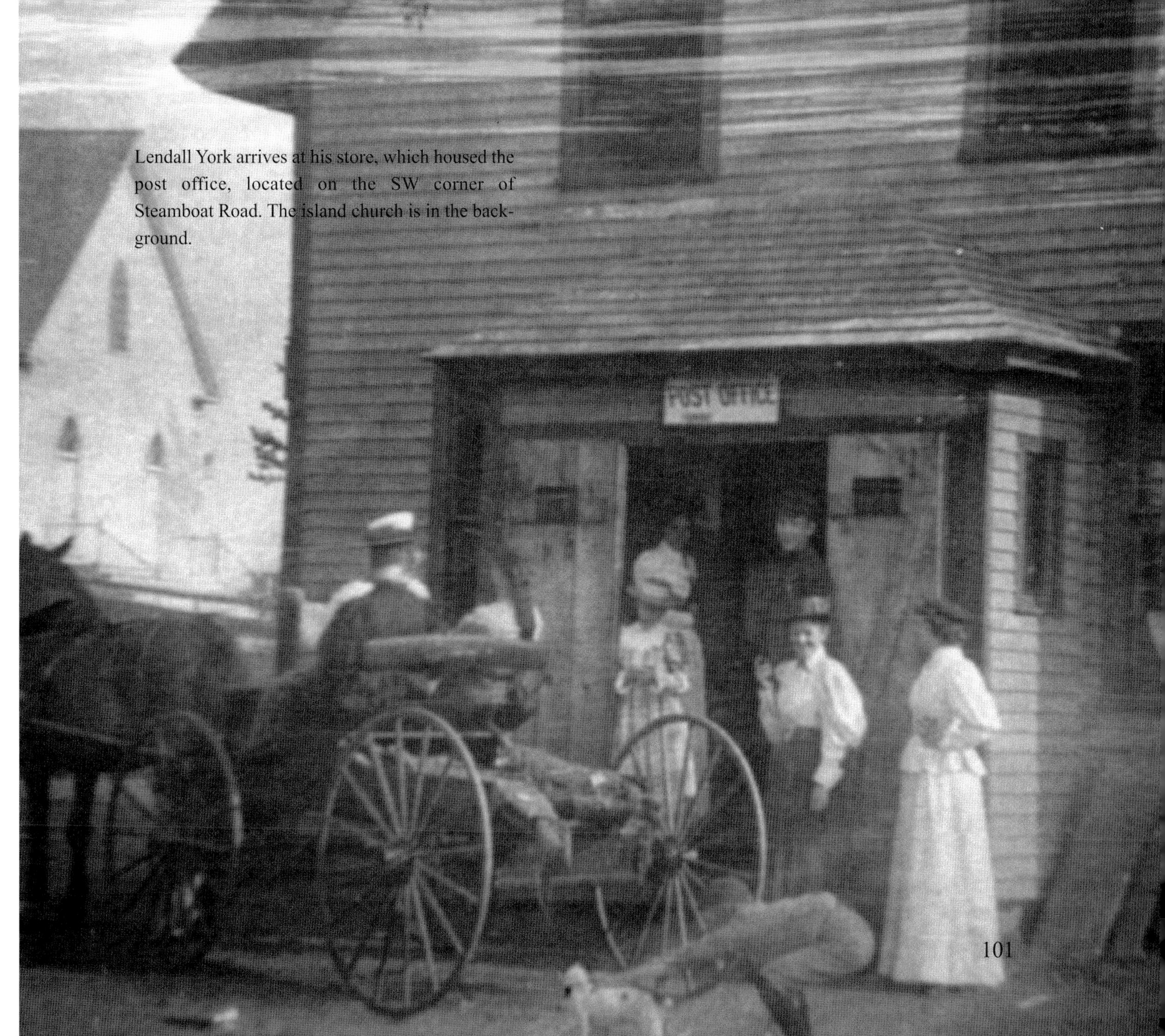

Lendall York arrives at his store, which housed the post office, located on the SW corner of Steamboat Road. The island church is in the background.

BAILEY'S ISLAND

E. S. LEEMAN

Expressing, Trucking and Carriages to meet all boats. Have your baggage marked care of Leeman's Express, Bailey's Island.

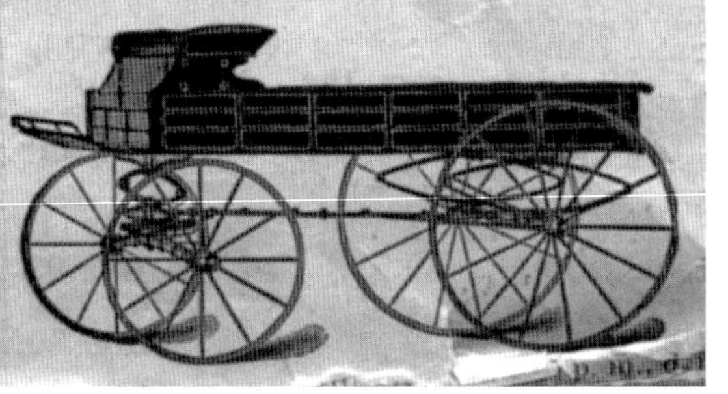

Elisha Leeman's delivery ad.

In the early 1900's land on the southeastern part of the island was broken up and sold as cottage lots. Hotels and boarding houses sprung up and flourished. Livery businesses were started and their drivers with horse-drawn carriages would meet the boat each day and transport tourists with their heavy trunks to the cottage, boarding house or hotel where they would spend a few weeks or the entire summer. Elisha Leeman had a livery business, which he advertised in the *1904-05 Casco Bay Directory*. He once commented on how he dreaded the summer's end when he'd deliver these same folks back to the boat for their return home. "Their trunks would be heavy with all the rocks they'd collected from Pebbly Beach."

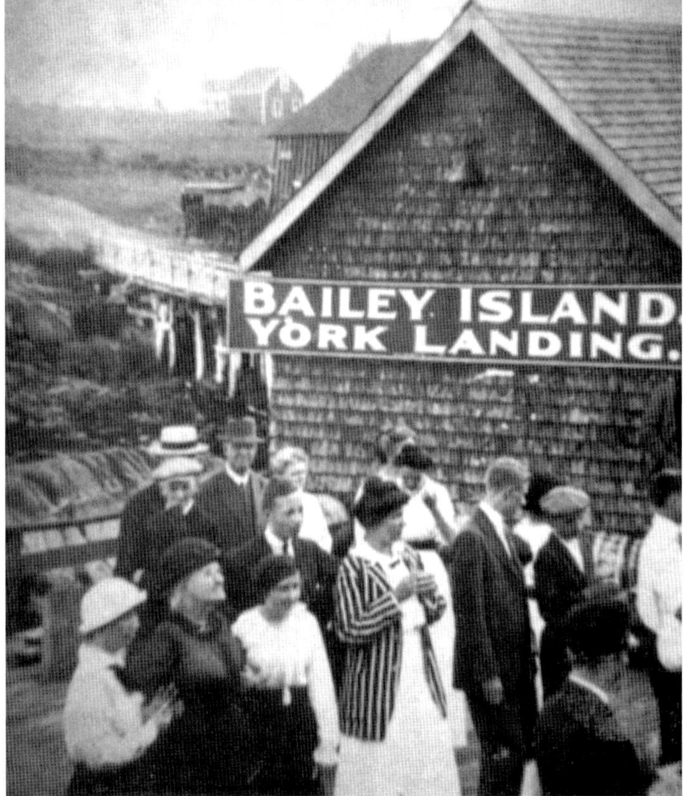

Orrin L. Johnson

BAILEY ISLAND, ME.

SAILING PARTIES

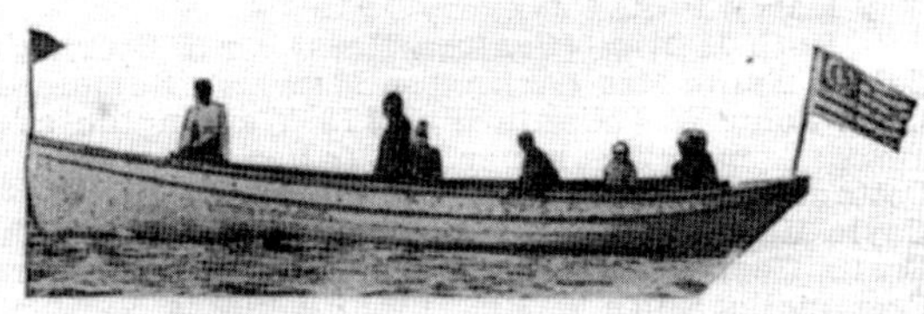

Trips to any point of interest in the Bay. Experienced boatman in charge. Rates Reasonable.

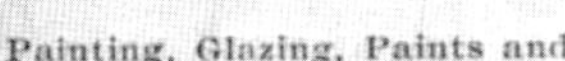

Painting, Glazing, Paints and Oils for Sale. All work in this line promptly and carefully done. Res. Tel Harpswell, 6-5

Grandfather Orrin Johnson took sailing parties out in the early 1900's. My father, Linwood, usually accompanied him. Grampy is pictured here steering his party boat, *Ethel*, by York's Landing in Lowell's Cove.

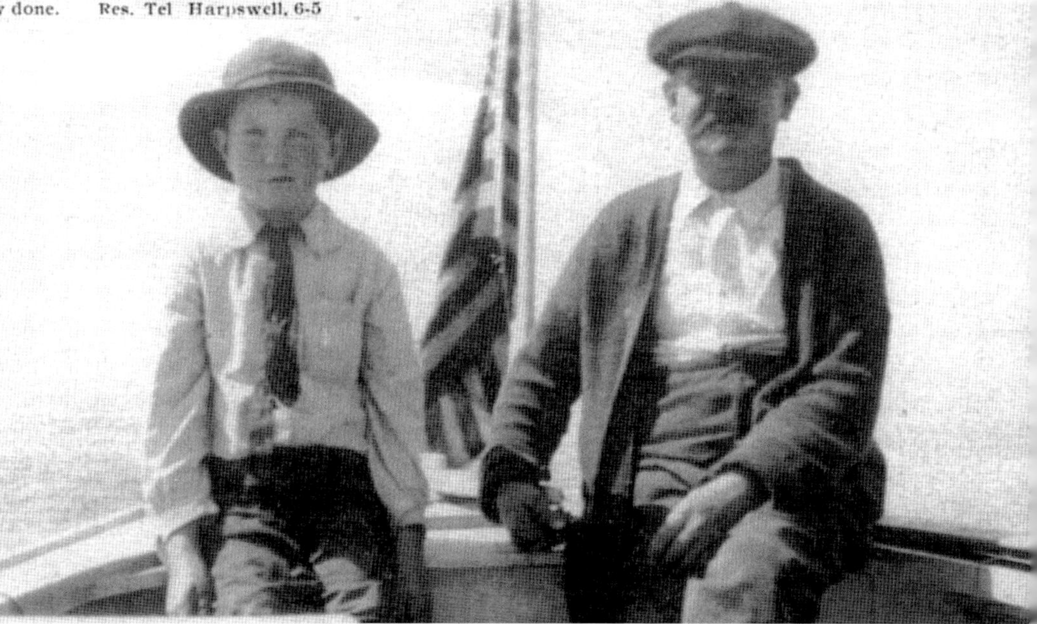

Above: Linwood Johnson and Grampy Orrin Johnson—about 1917.

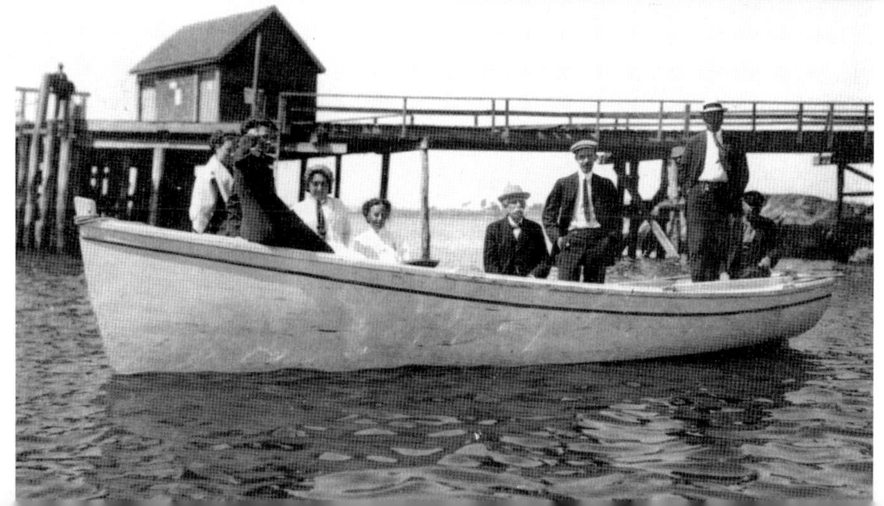

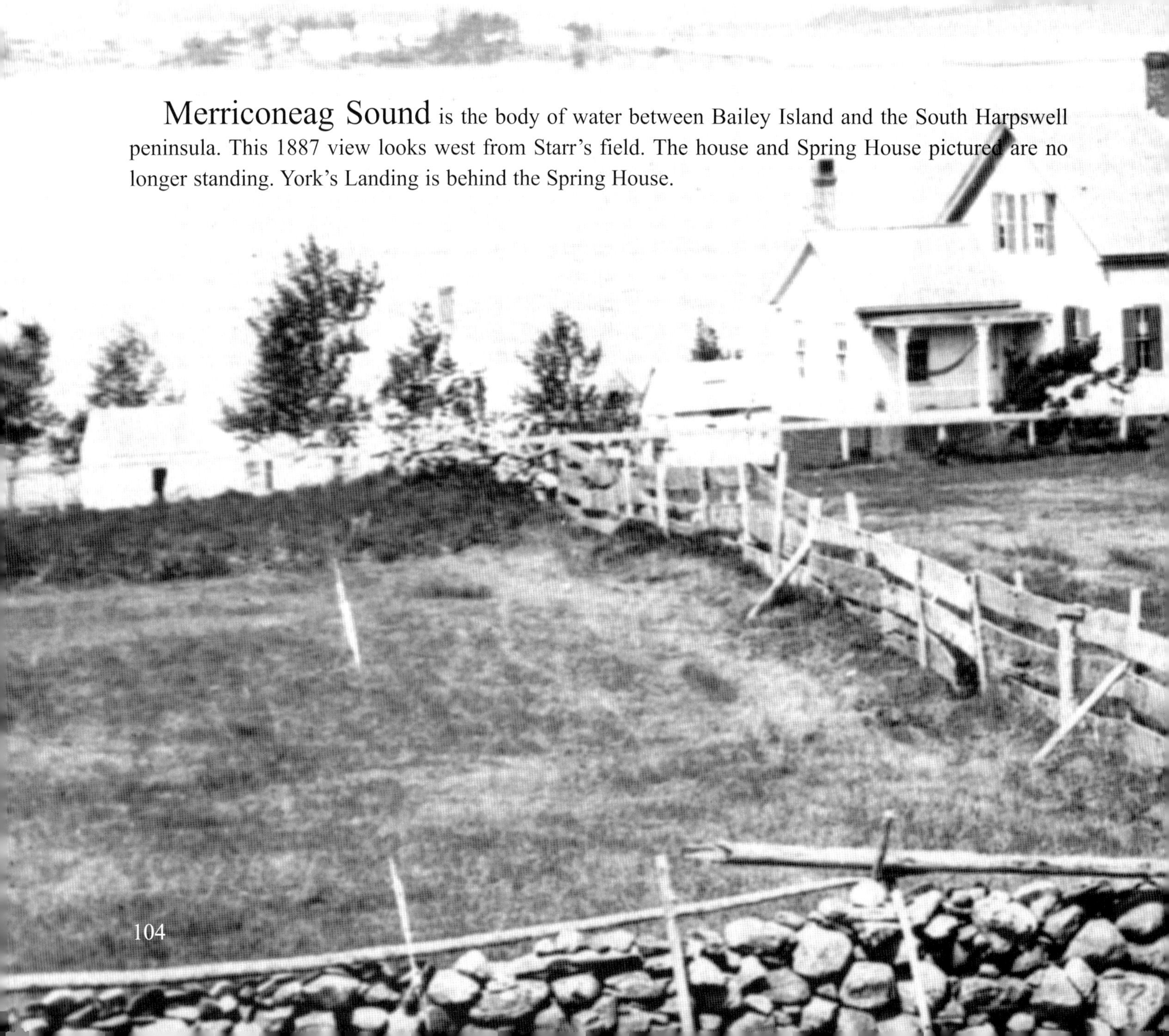

Merriconeag Sound is the body of water between Bailey Island and the South Harpswell peninsula. This 1887 view looks west from Starr's field. The house and Spring House pictured are no longer standing. York's Landing is behind the Spring House.

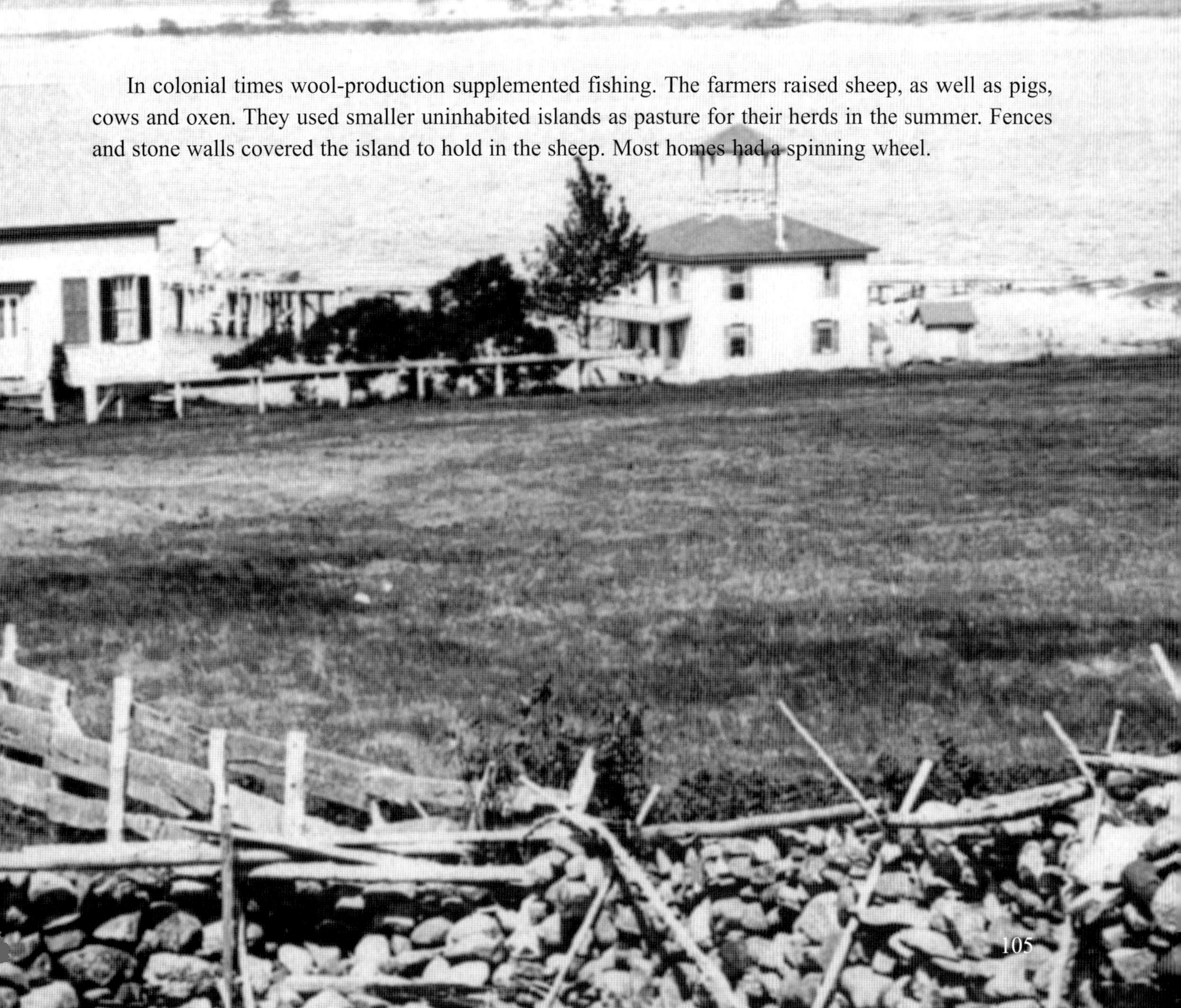

In colonial times wool-production supplemented fishing. The farmers raised sheep, as well as pigs, cows and oxen. They used smaller uninhabited islands as pasture for their herds in the summer. Fences and stone walls covered the island to hold in the sheep. Most homes had a spinning wheel.

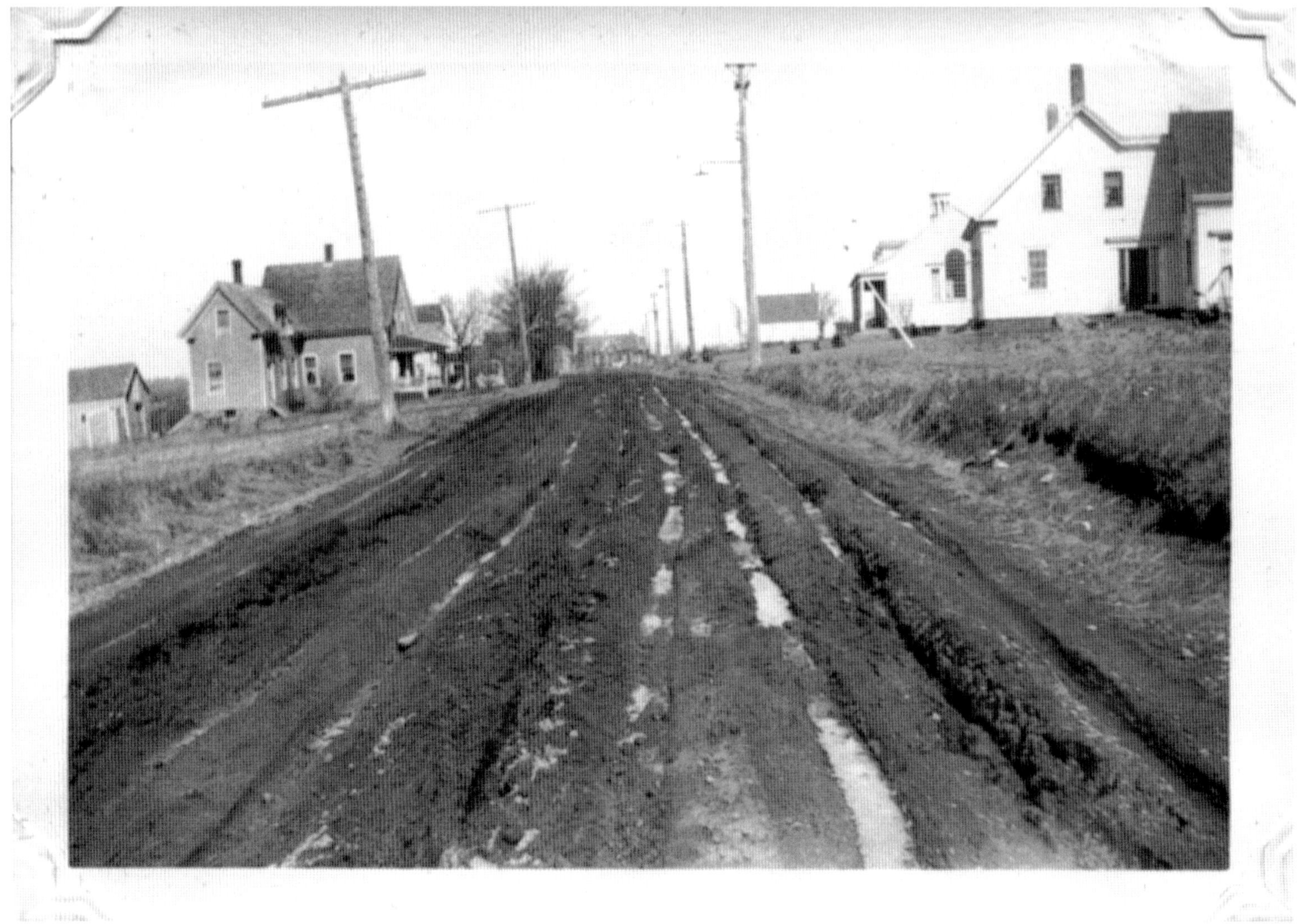

Charlie York recalls the road on Bailey Island: "Our ro'd wa'n't much, just a three-way track along the middle of the island, two for the wheels and one between, where the horse walked. Some places it went over bare ledges, and then through mudholes after a rain."

—*Charlie York: Maine Coast Fisherman*, by Harold Clifford, 1974

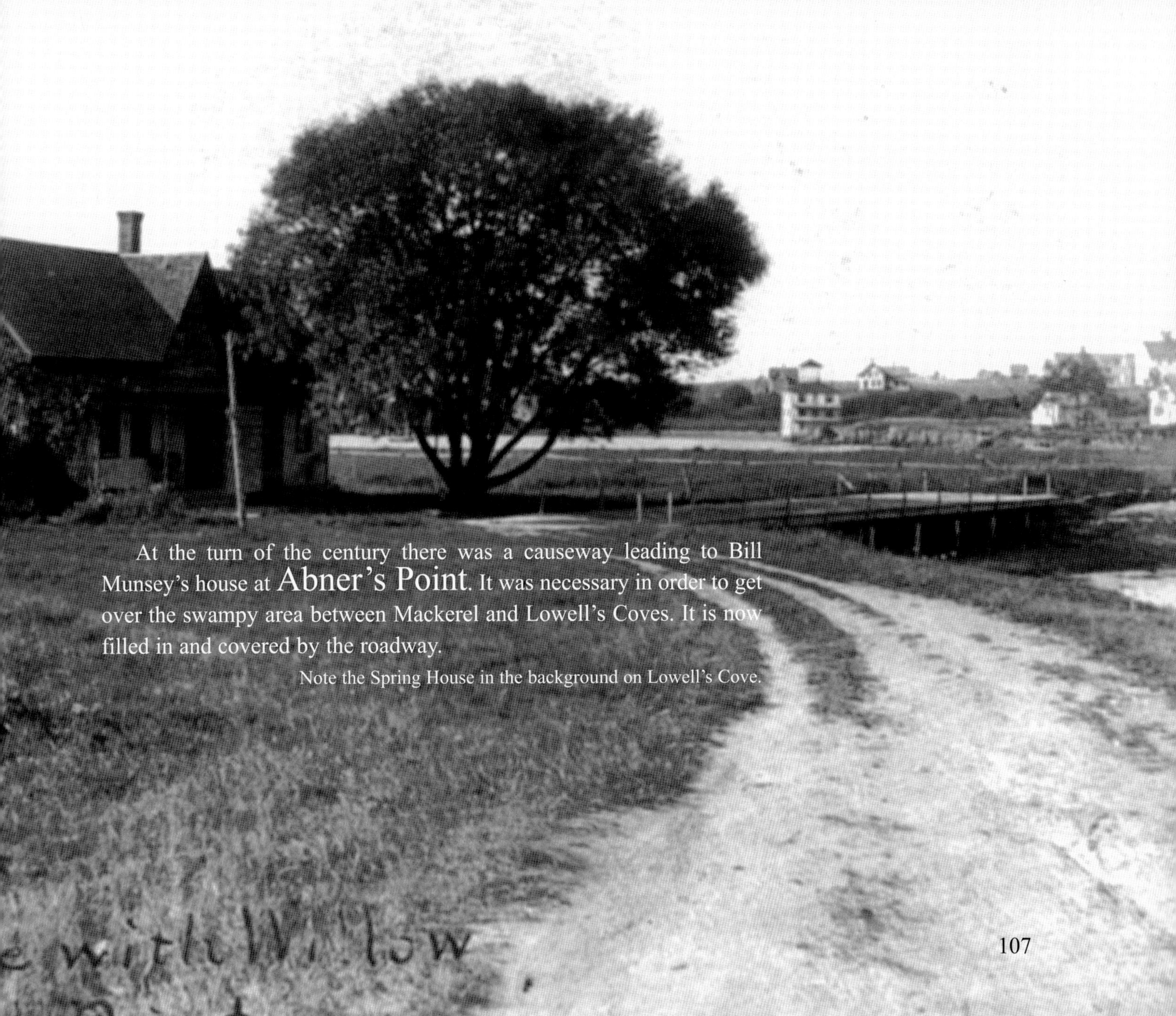

At the turn of the century there was a causeway leading to Bill Munsey's house at **Abner's Point**. It was necessary in order to get over the swampy area between Mackerel and Lowell's Coves. It is now filled in and covered by the roadway.

Note the Spring House in the background on Lowell's Cove.

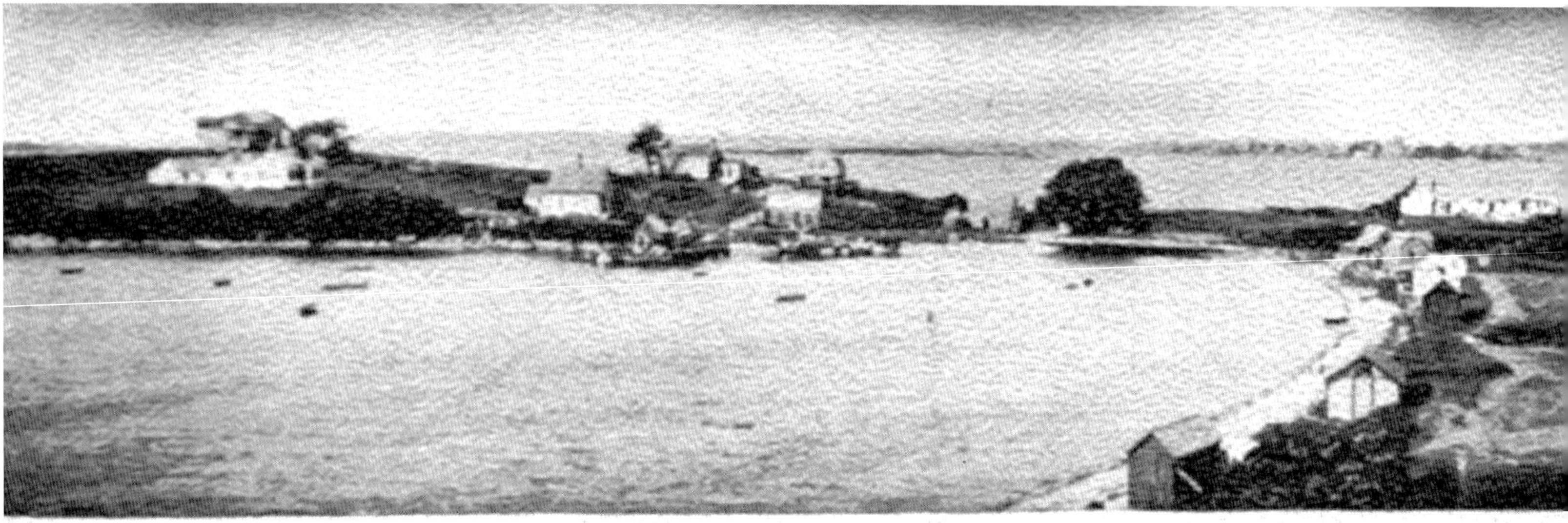

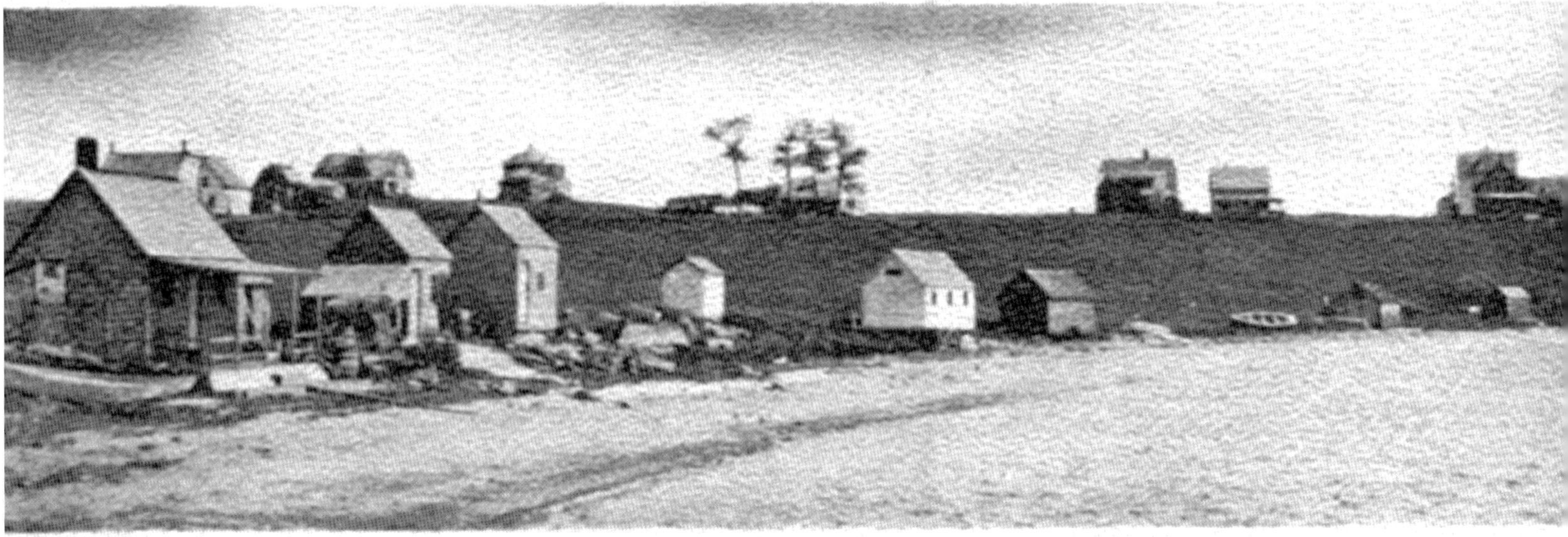

BAILEY'S ISLAND, ME. Two views of the Bathing Beach, Mackerel Cove.

Mackerel Cove and Steamer Landing

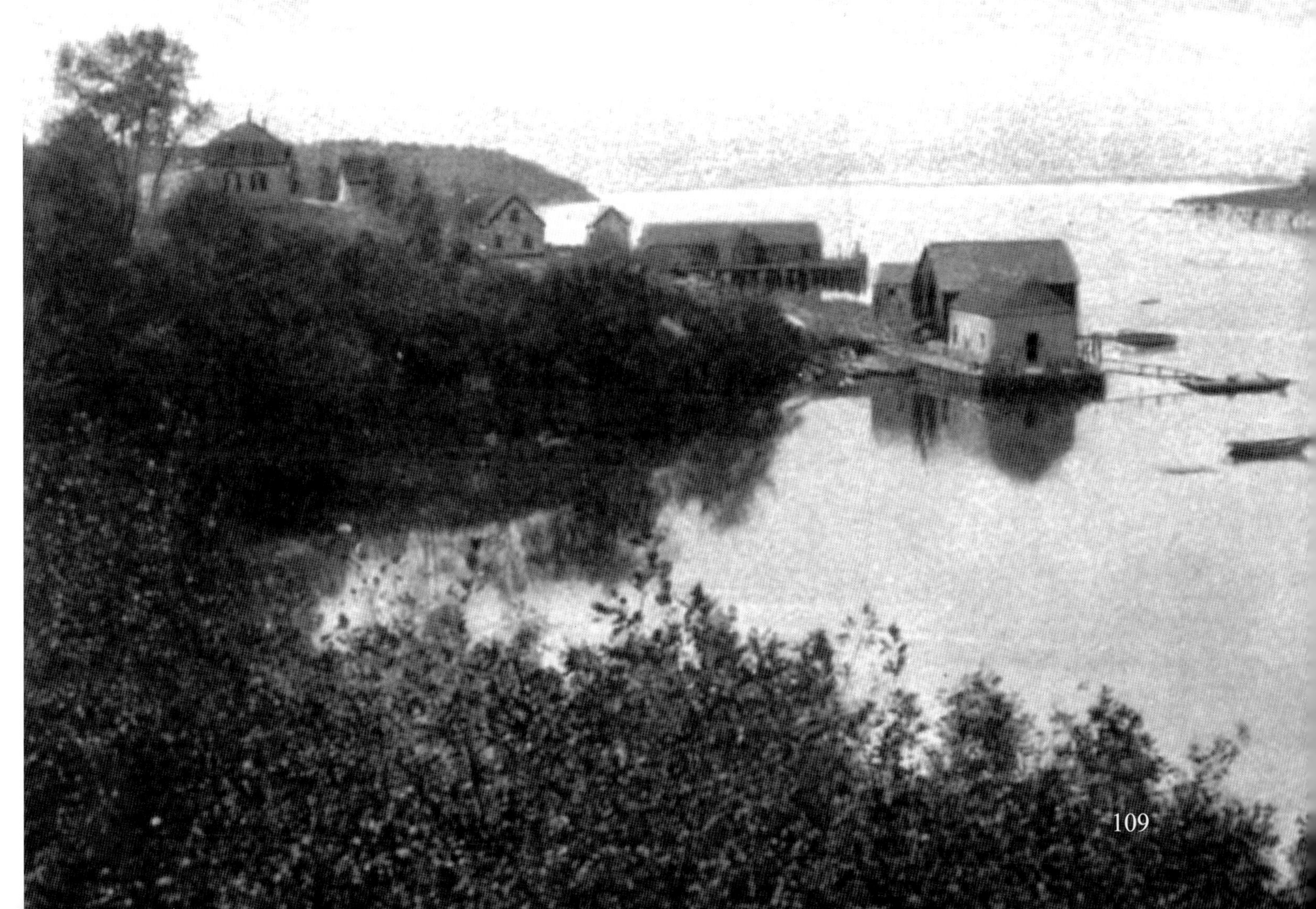

Steamboat Wharf and two-lane road near Ocean view Hotel—1907.

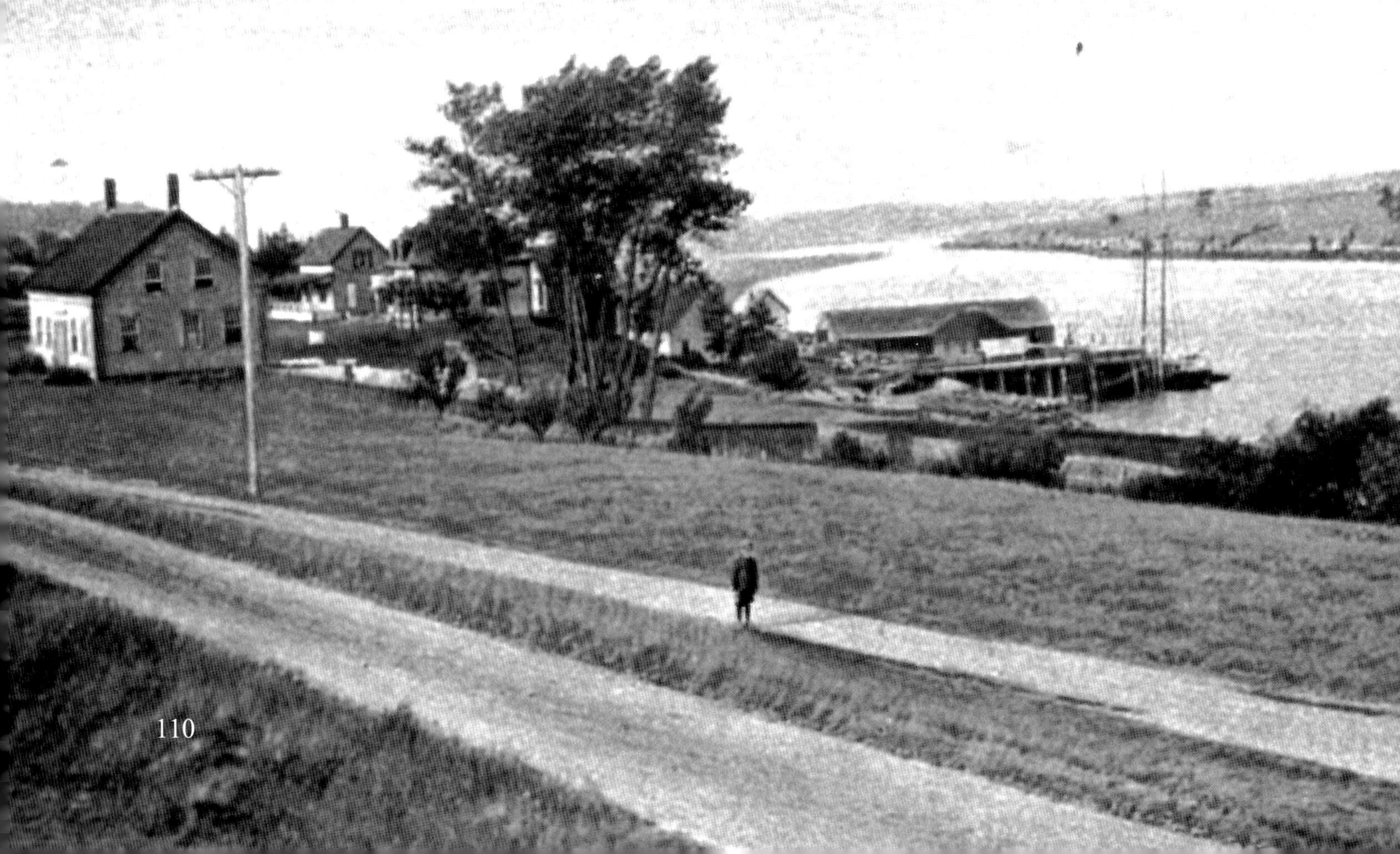

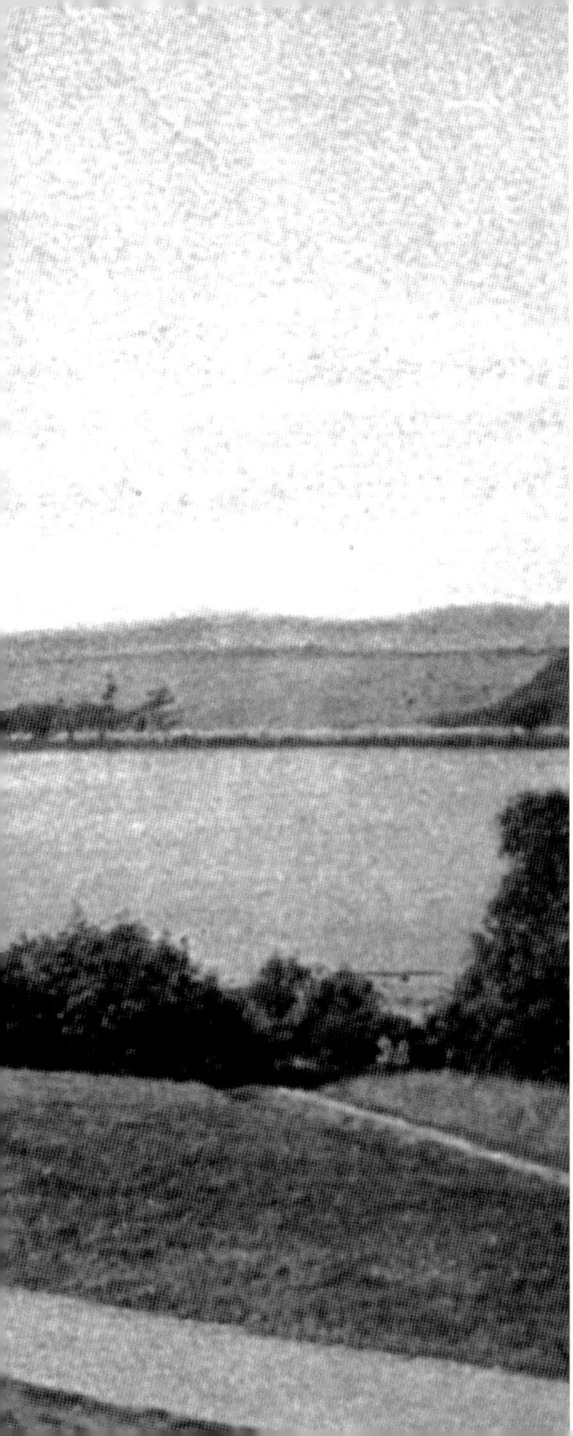

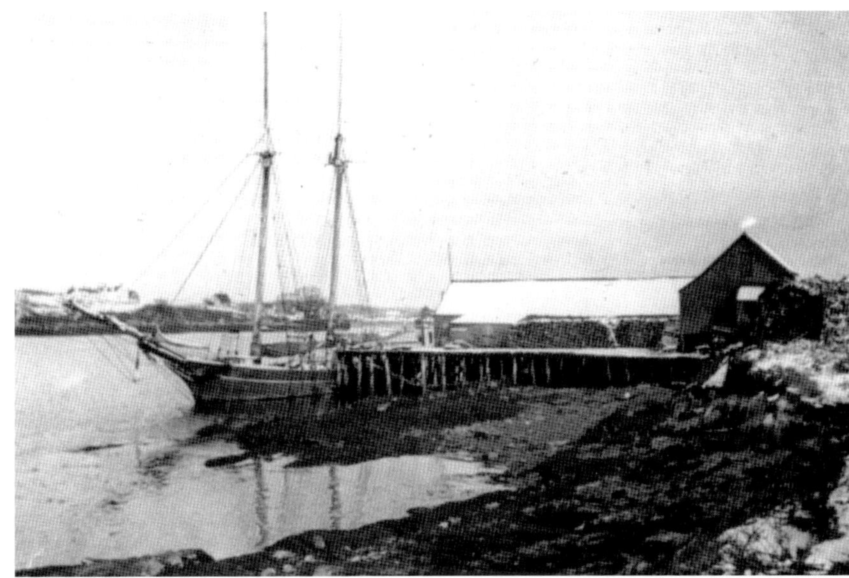

Schooners were a common sight in Mackerel Cove at the turn of the century. *Coaster Regina* stops at Steamboat Wharf in Mackerel Cove to deliver wood. About 1900.

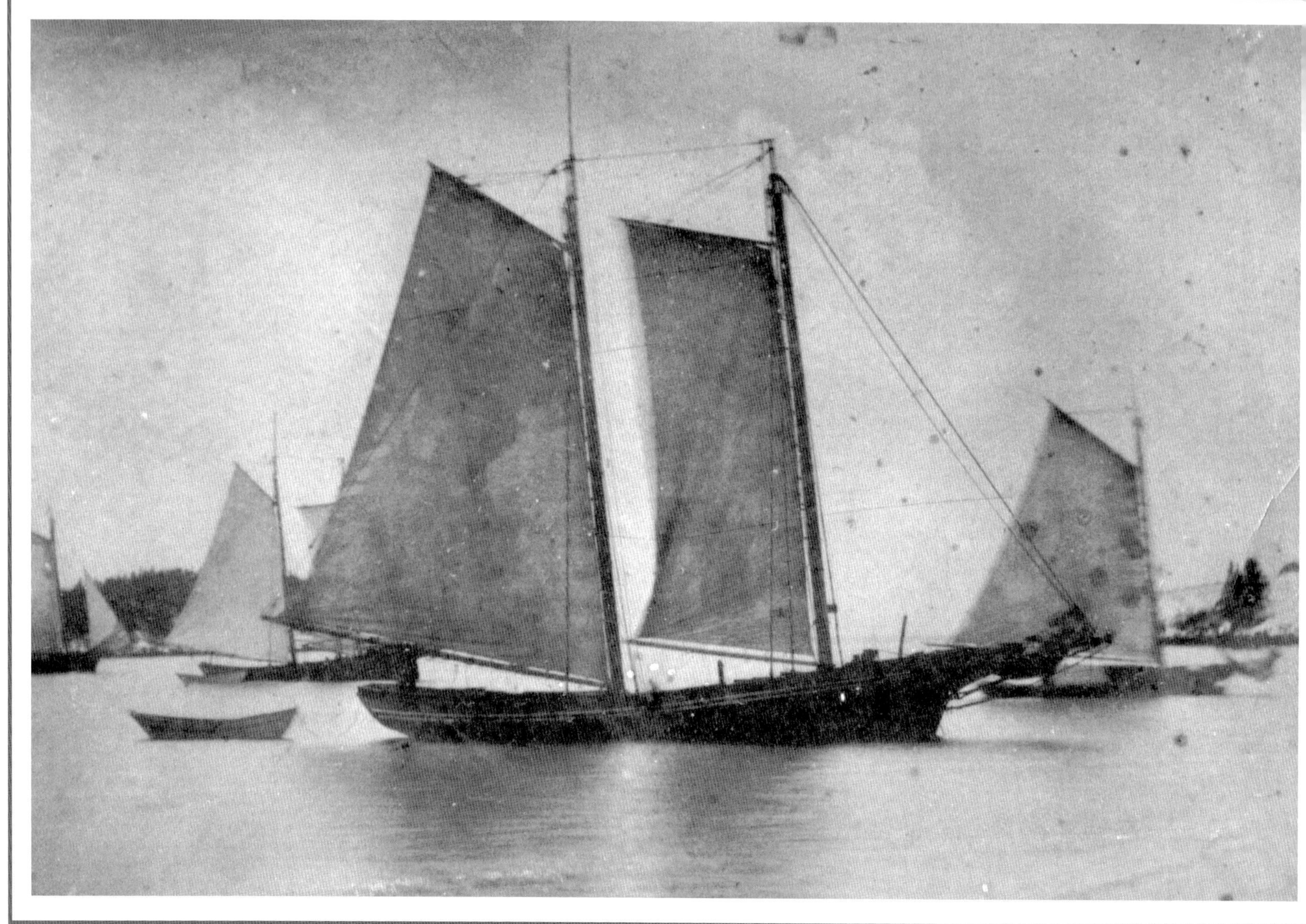

Great-grandfather James Lewis Orr was the captain of the schooner *Forest Maid*, shown here in the late 1800's.

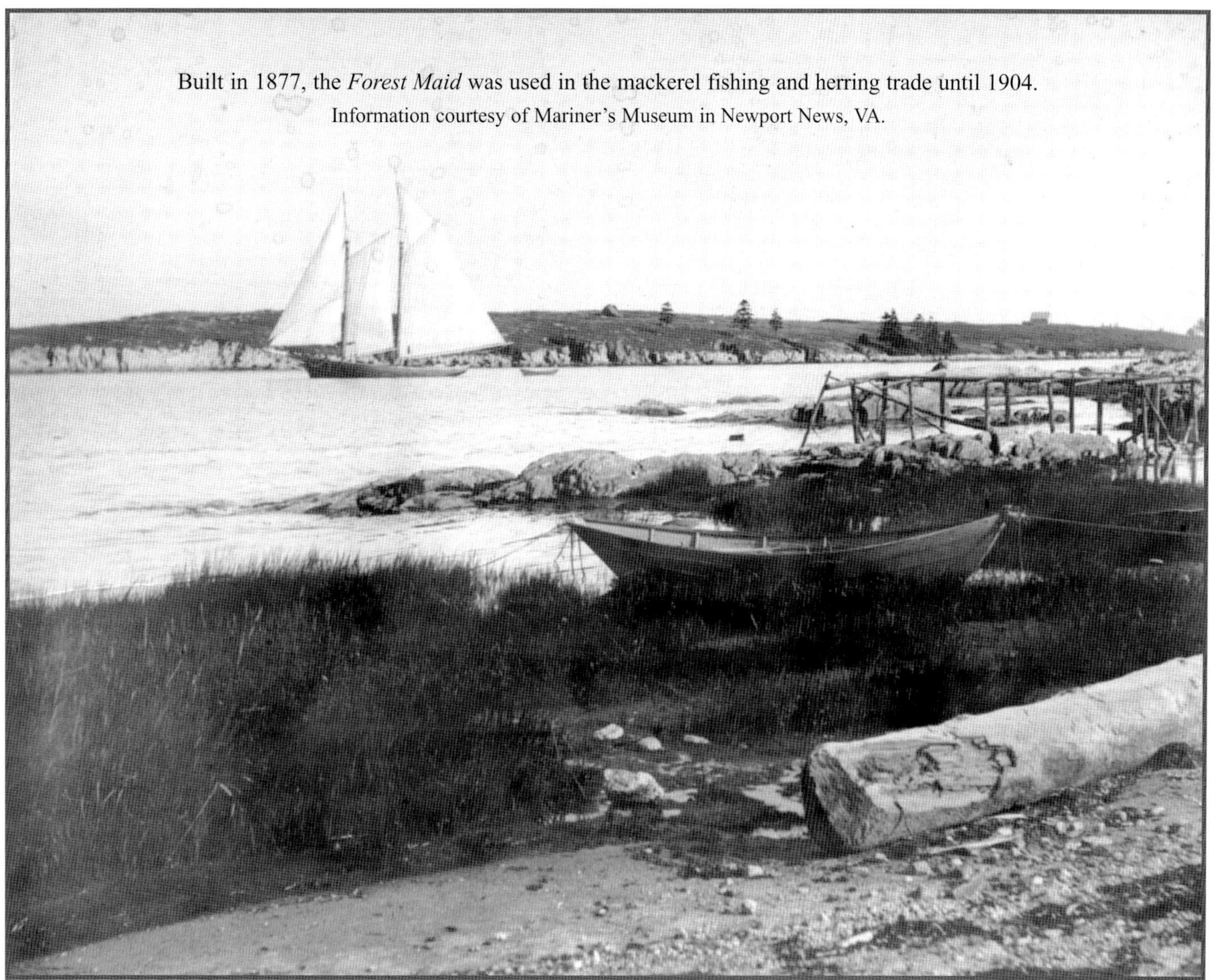

Built in 1877, the *Forest Maid* was used in the mackerel fishing and herring trade until 1904.
Information courtesy of Mariner's Museum in Newport News, VA.

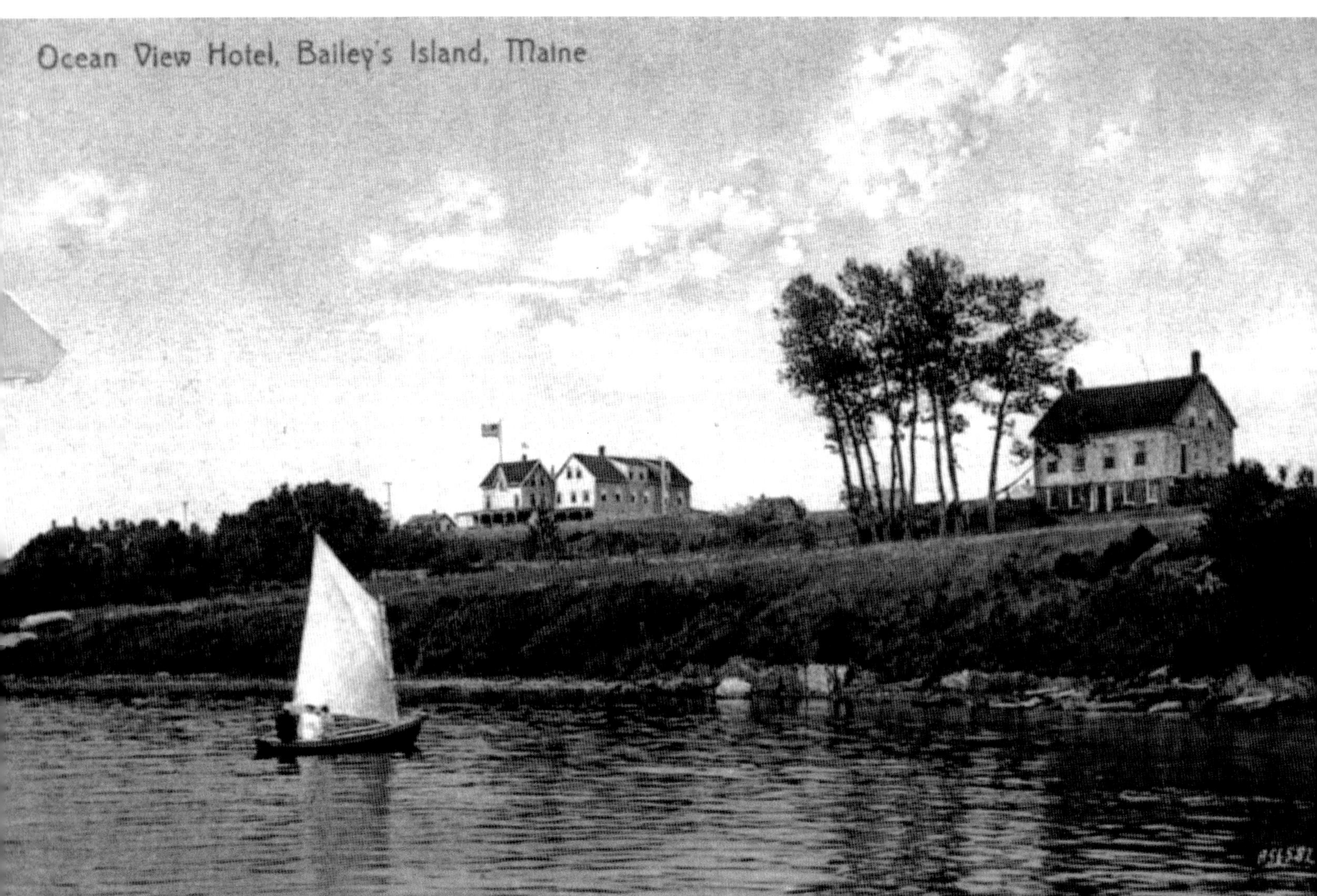
Ocean View Hotel, Bailey's Island, Maine

Steamboat Wharf at Mackerel Cove before 1910.

Most islanders and summer folks of the early to mid 1900's have wonderful memories of Steamboat Wharf and the *Aucocisco*. In 1978 hurricane-force winds ripped Steamboat Wharf off its pilings and it floated out into Mackerel Cove.

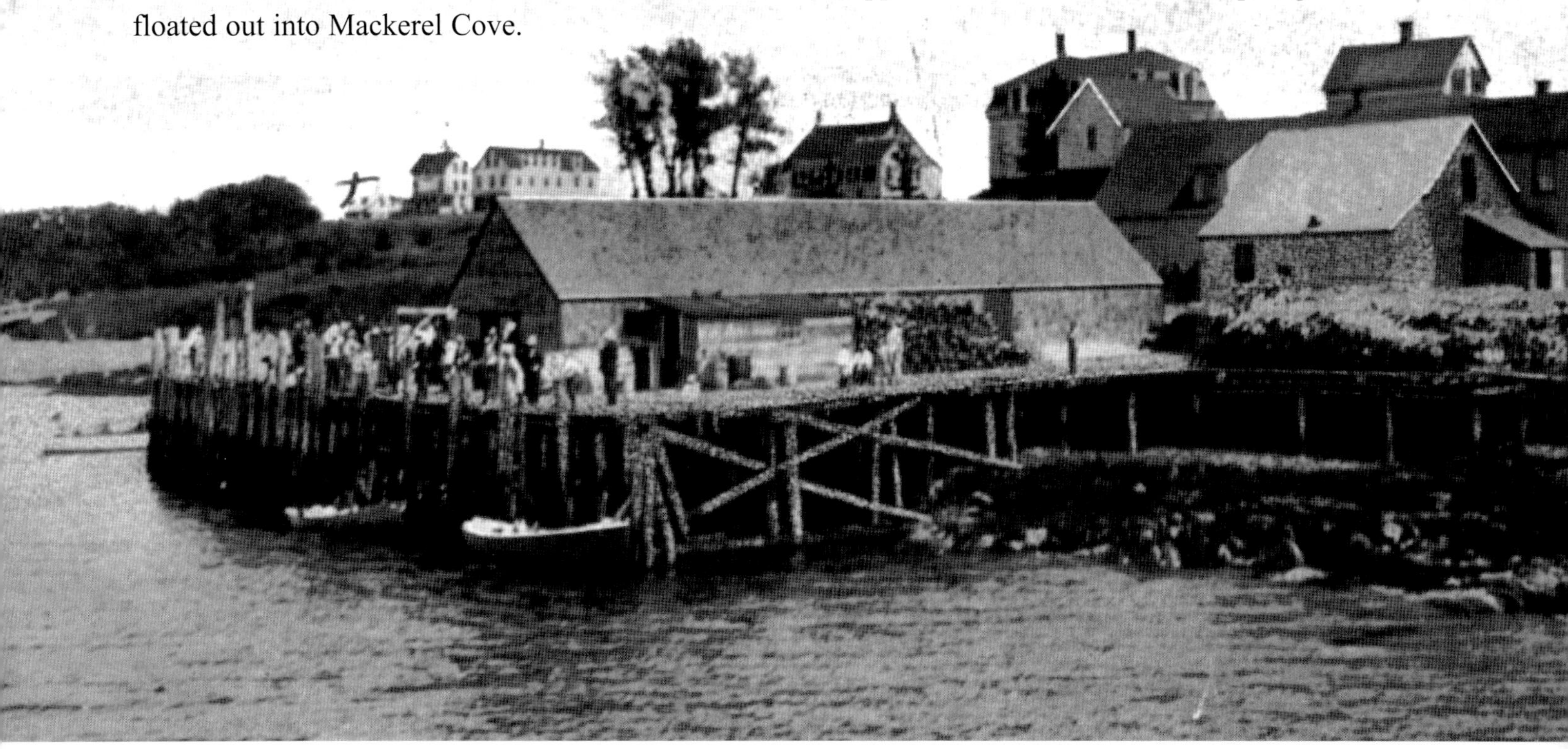

Marjorie Johnson lived most of her life on Bailey Island. She owned and managed Willow Cottage, a boarding house with cottages that overlooked Mackerel Cove. In 1975, a book of her poems, *Songs From an Island,* was published. One of my favorites is "When the Cove Silvers."

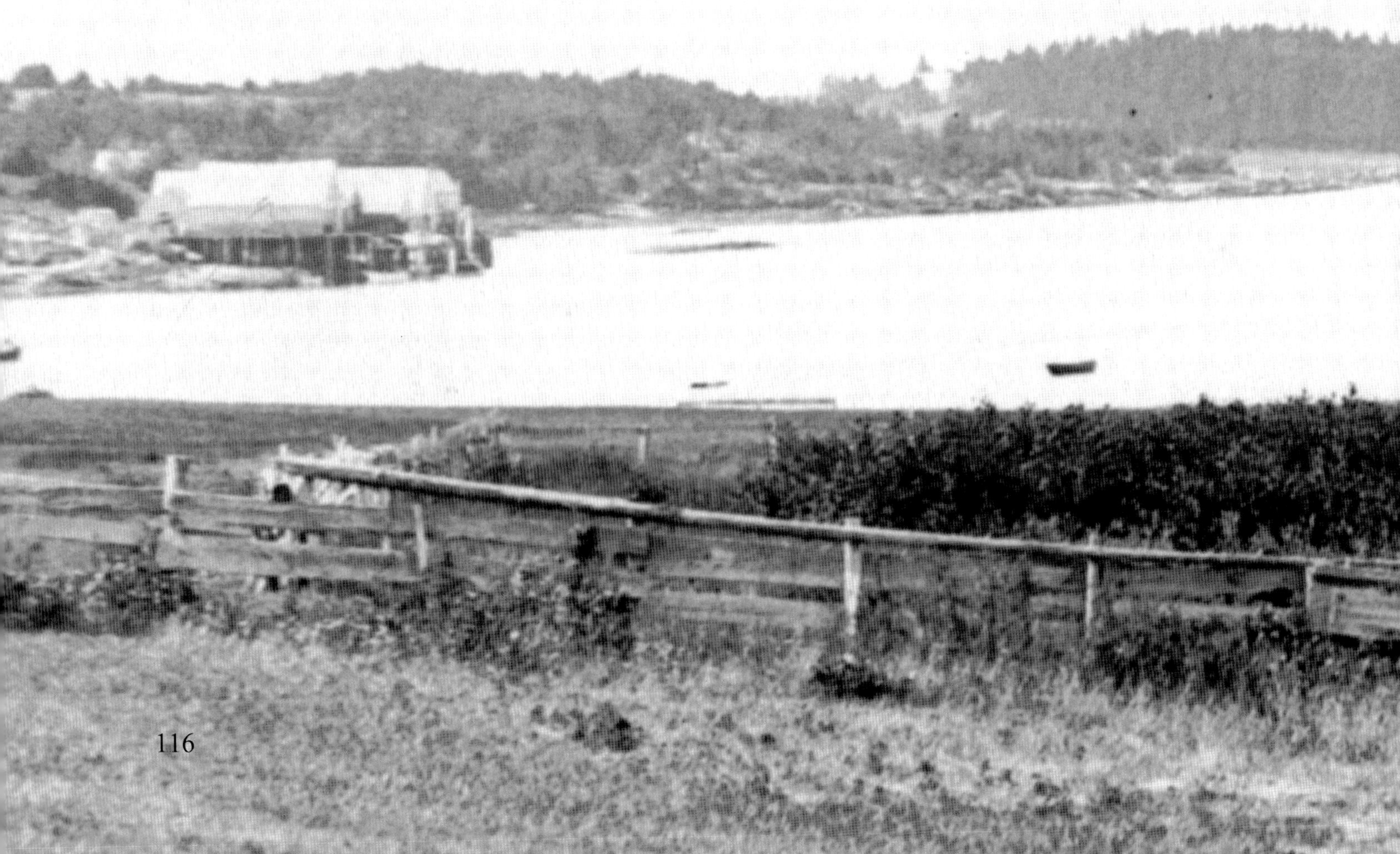

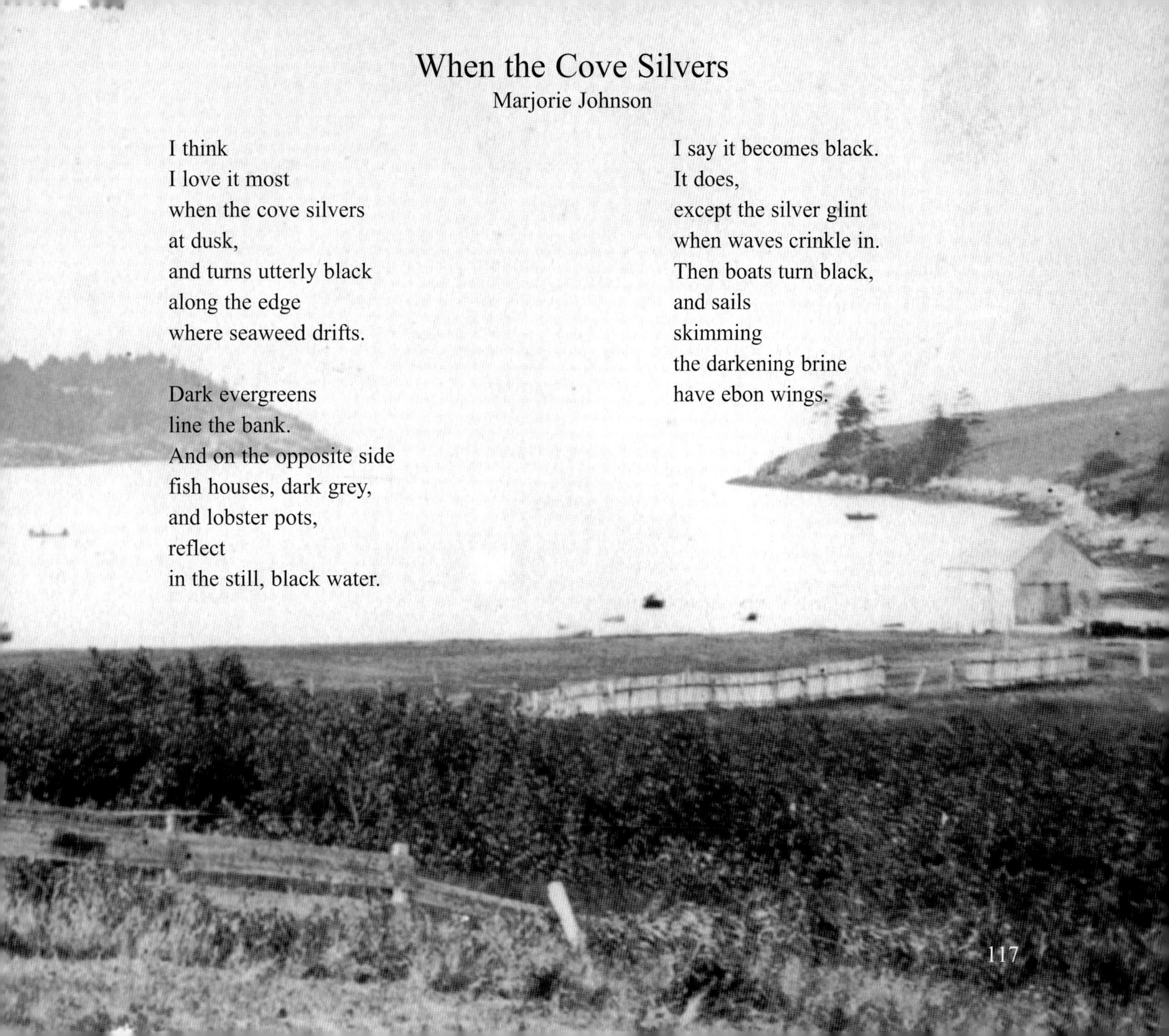

When the Cove Silvers

Marjorie Johnson

I think
I love it most
when the cove silvers
at dusk,
and turns utterly black
along the edge
where seaweed drifts.

Dark evergreens
line the bank.
And on the opposite side
fish houses, dark grey,
and lobster pots,
reflect
in the still, black water.

I say it becomes black.
It does,
except the silver glint
when waves crinkle in.
Then boats turn black,
and sails
skimming
the darkening brine
have ebon wings.

Mackerel Cove has long been the center of activity on Bailey Island and is still one of the most picturesque coves in Casco Bay. As kids in the 1950's we often hung around at Mackerel Cove, swimming, fishing for pollock, cunners and sculpins, and rowing any of the punts that might be tied up on the floats near Abner's Wharf.

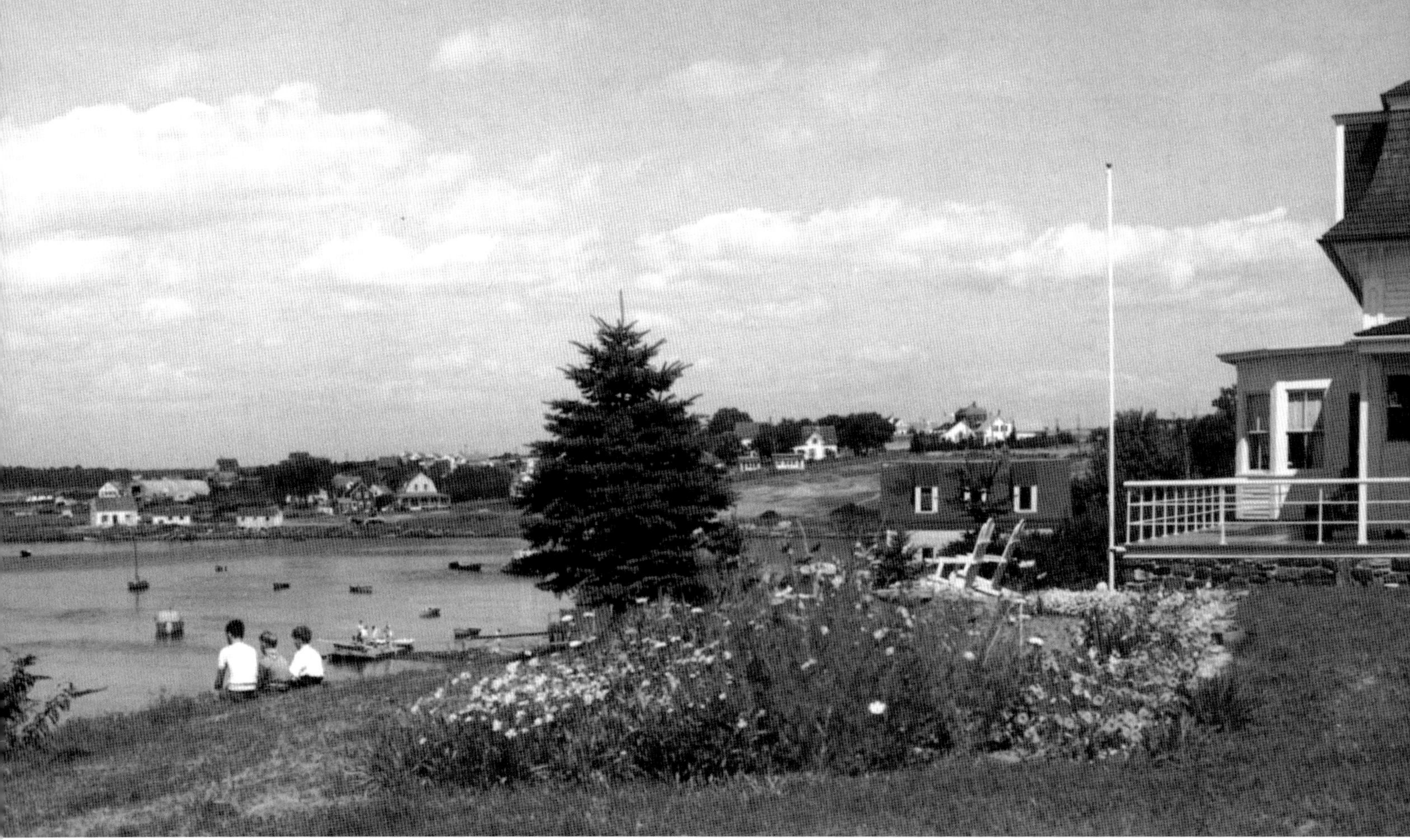

The Bathing Beach at Mackerel Cove, looking west, around 1891. On the beach—Sinnett Johnson's fish house. On the far right is Lowell's Cove and Lowell's Cove Point. Captain James Sinnett, nicknamed "Labrador Jim" because he fished off Labrador in the mid-1800's, owned a building on the point where he slack-salted fish and shucked clams. Slack-salting fish was a method used to preserve fish by soaking the fish in barrels of salt brine and then hanging them to dry.

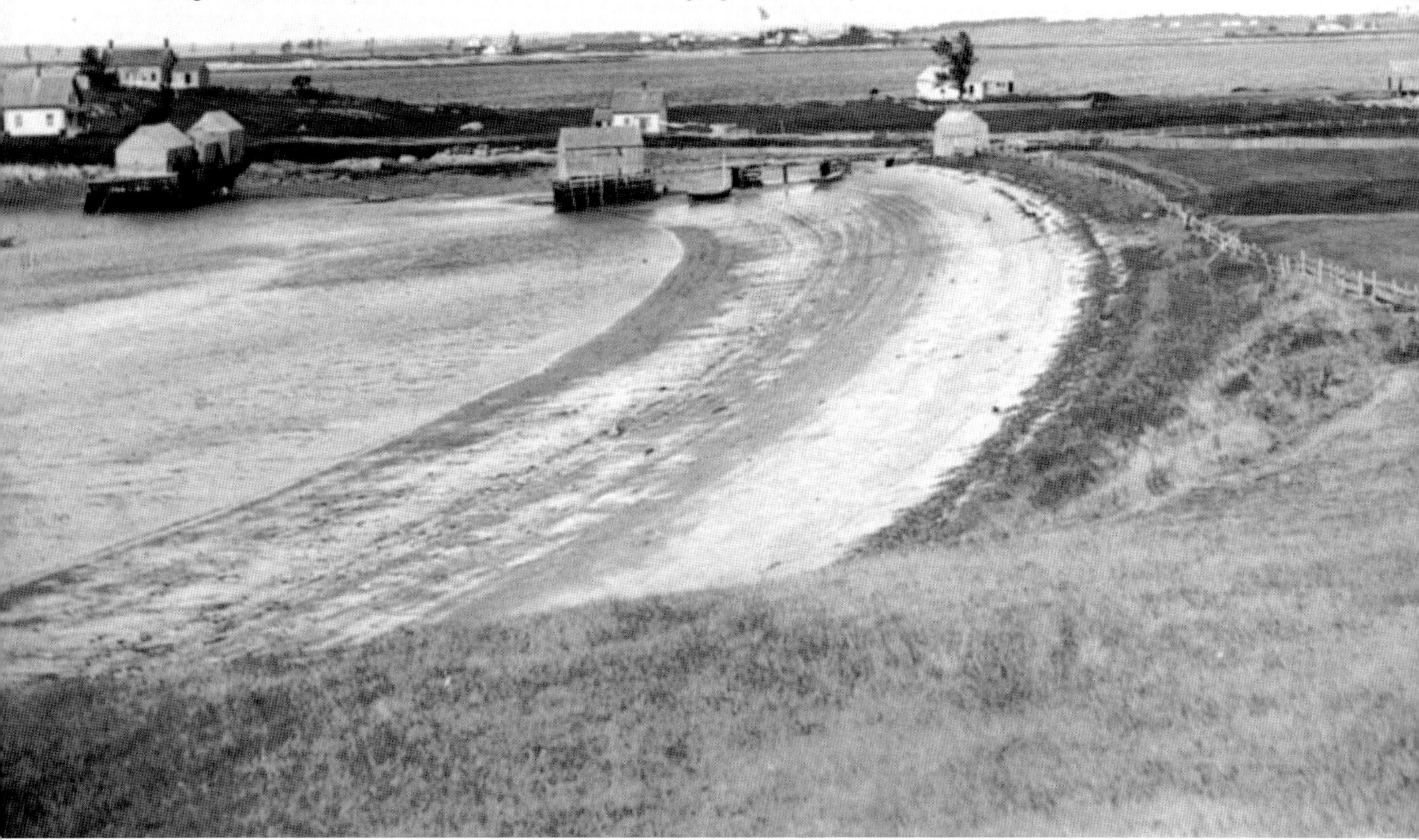

Great-grandfather Sinnett Johnson's fish house on Mackerel Cove Beach.

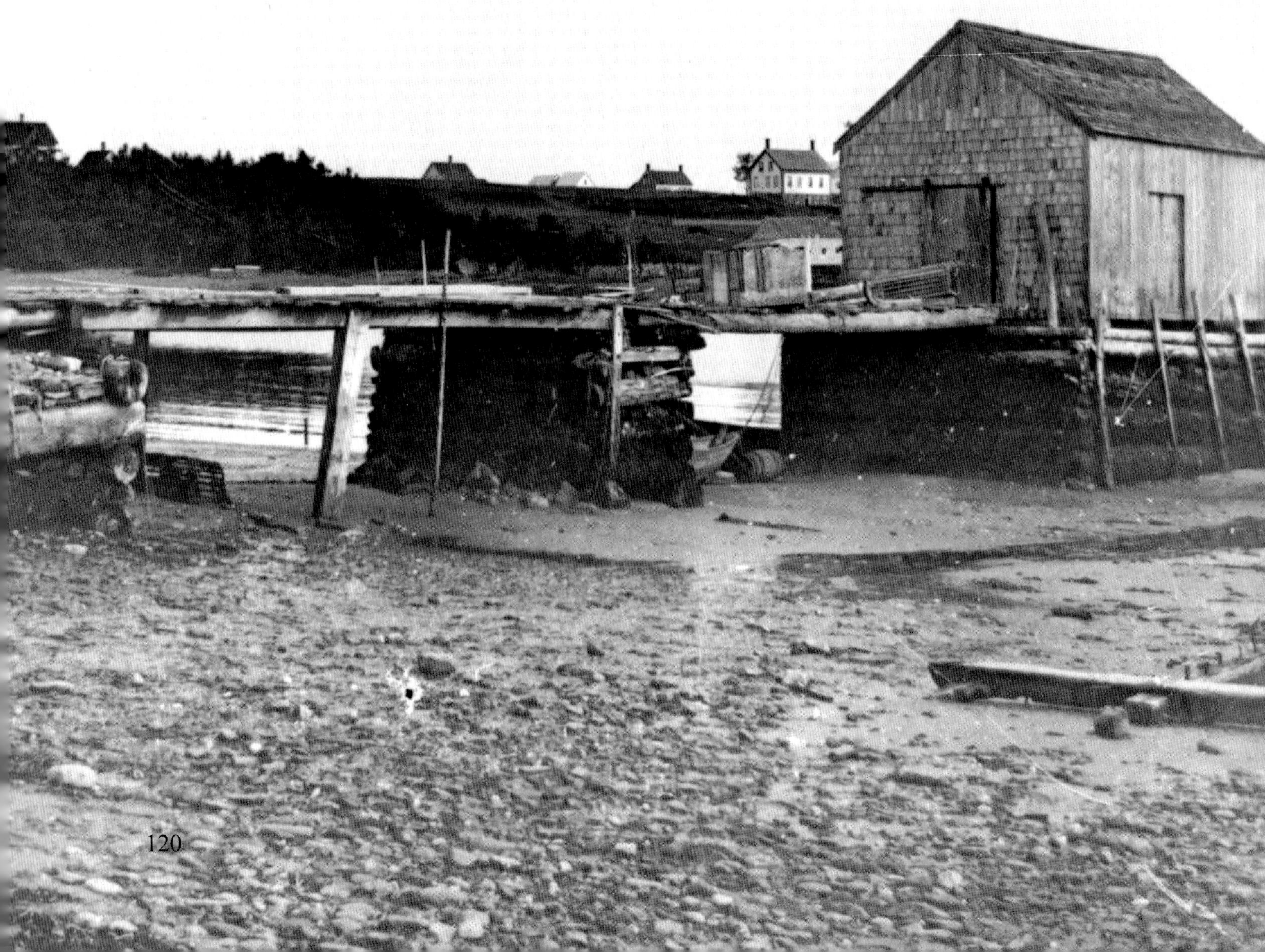

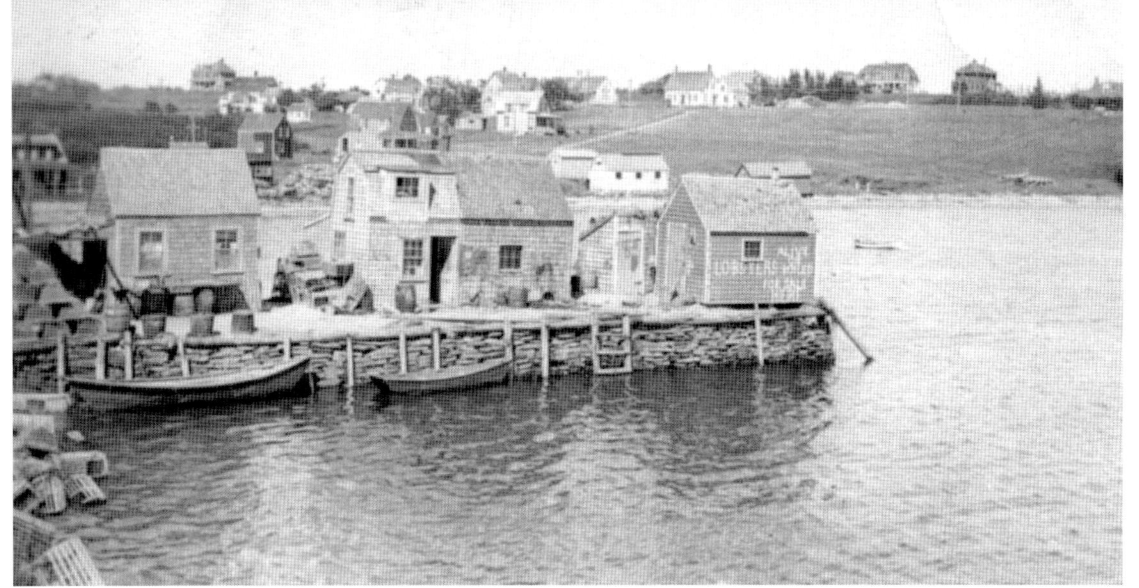

Fish houses of Mackerel Cove around 1891.

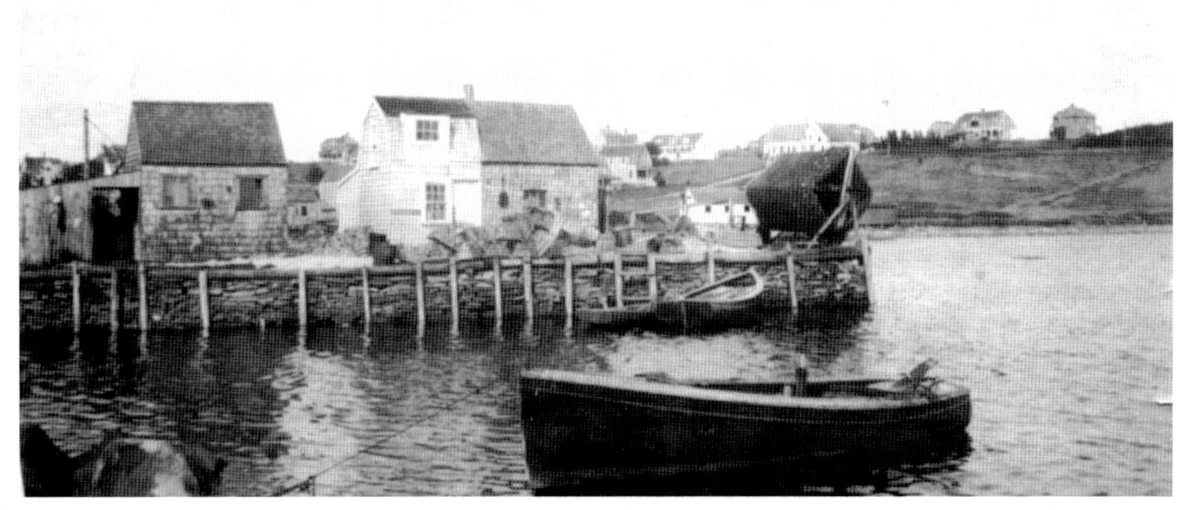

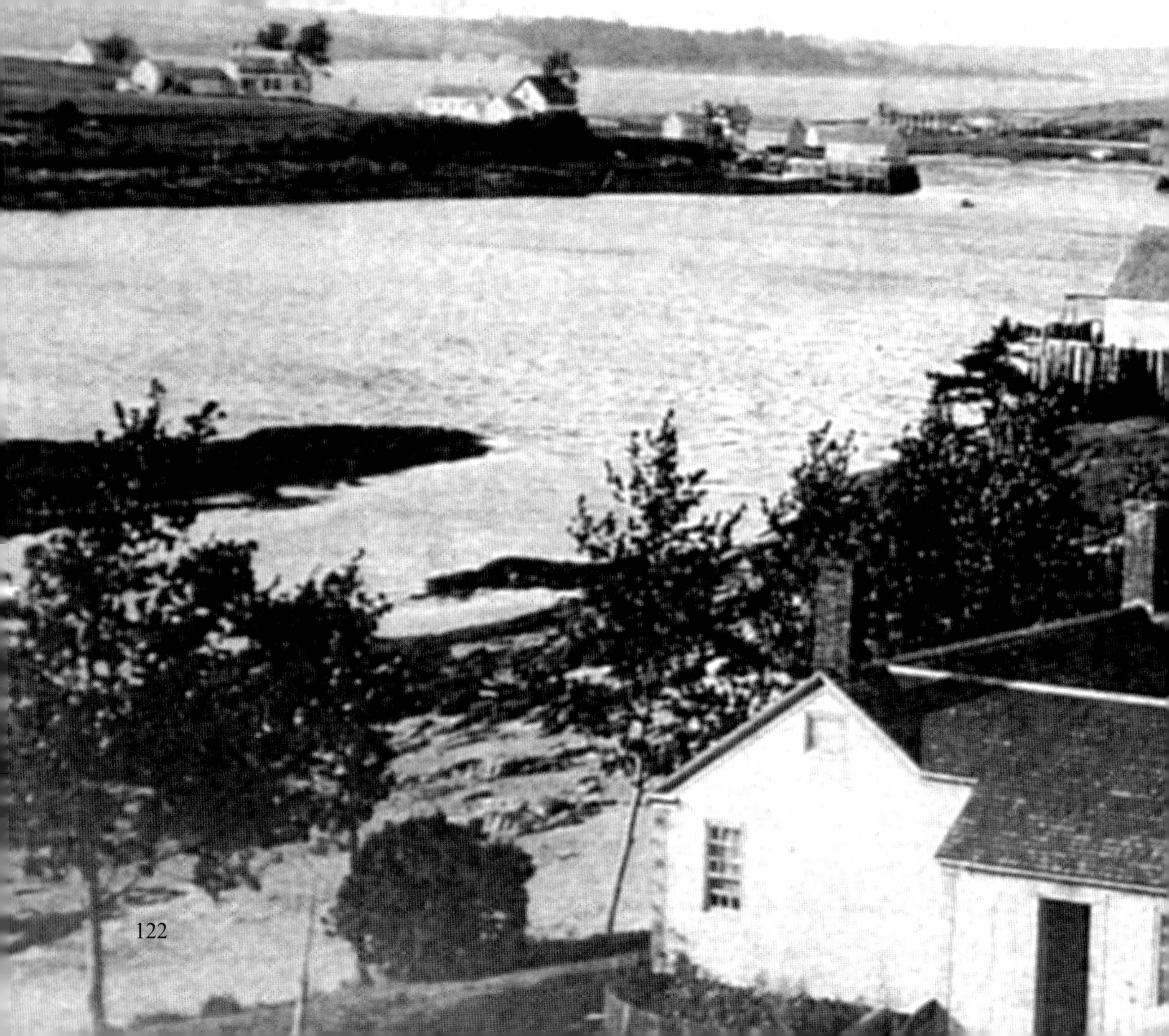

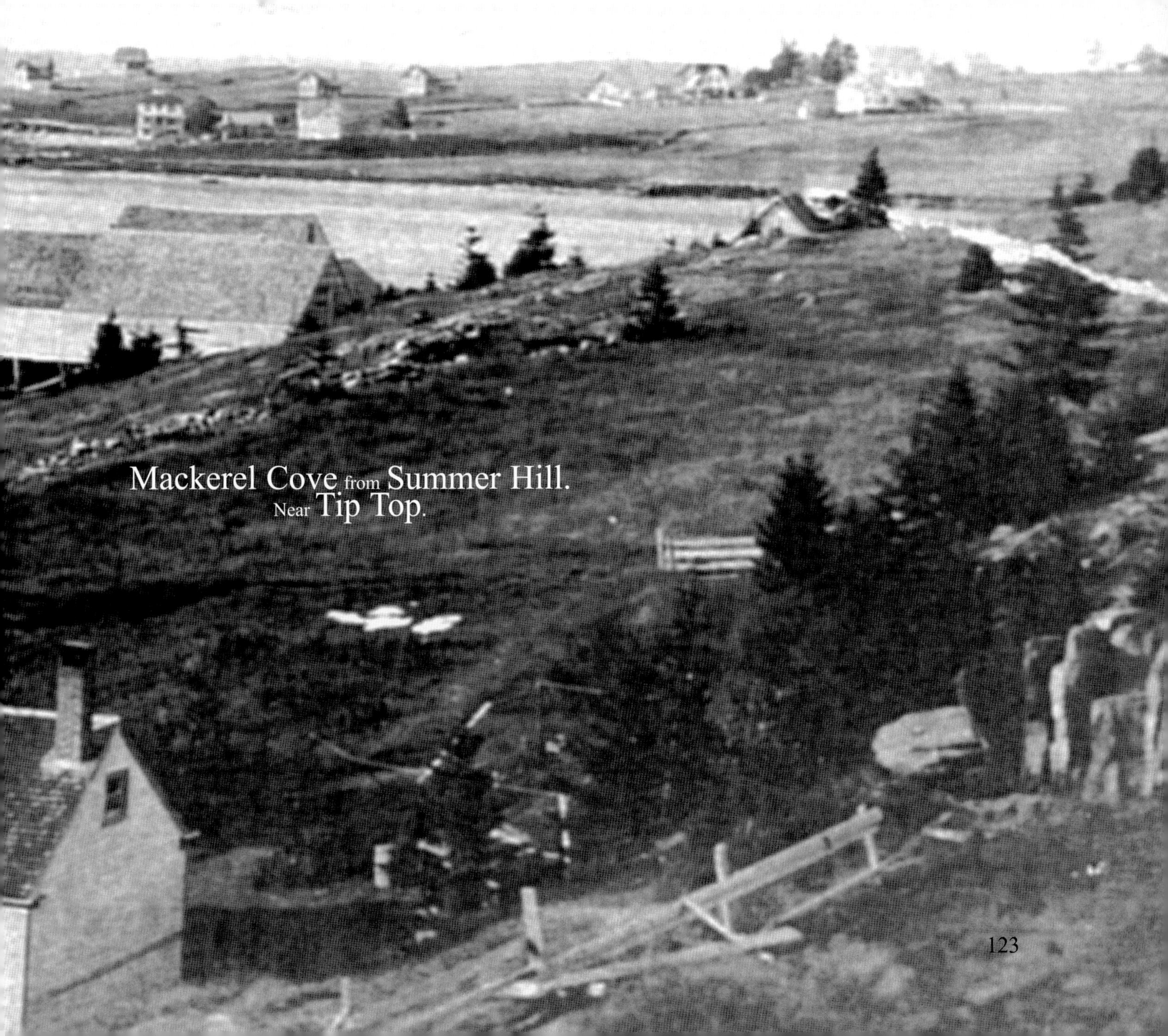

Mackerel Cove from Summer Hill.
Near Tip Top.

The *Merriconeag* arrives at York's Landing in Lowell's Cove

Steamboat service came to Bailey Island in 1888. The boat left Orr's Island at 7:00 in the morning and arrived at York's Landing, also called Old Wharf, at Lowell's Cove on Bailey Island twenty minutes later. From there it headed for Portland and returned to Orr's Island at the end of the day. The steamboat delivered freight, coal, lumber, dry goods and mail, as well as passengers traveling to and from Portland.

A number of different steamboats serviced the island. The *Aucocisco*, the *Sebascodegan*, the *Merriconeag*, the *Machigonne*, the *Emita* and the *Maquoit*, could be seen, at one time or another, until the mid-fifties.

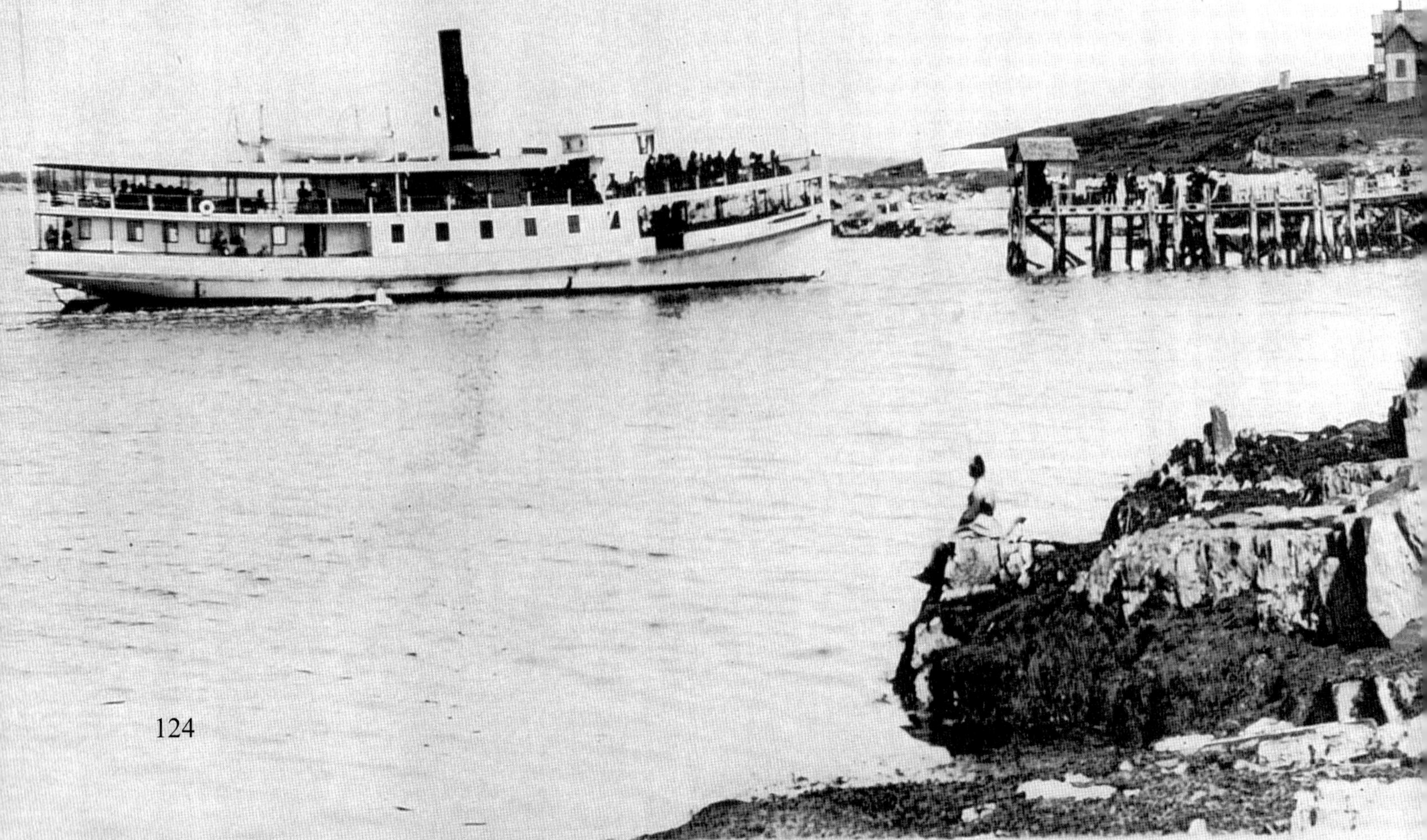

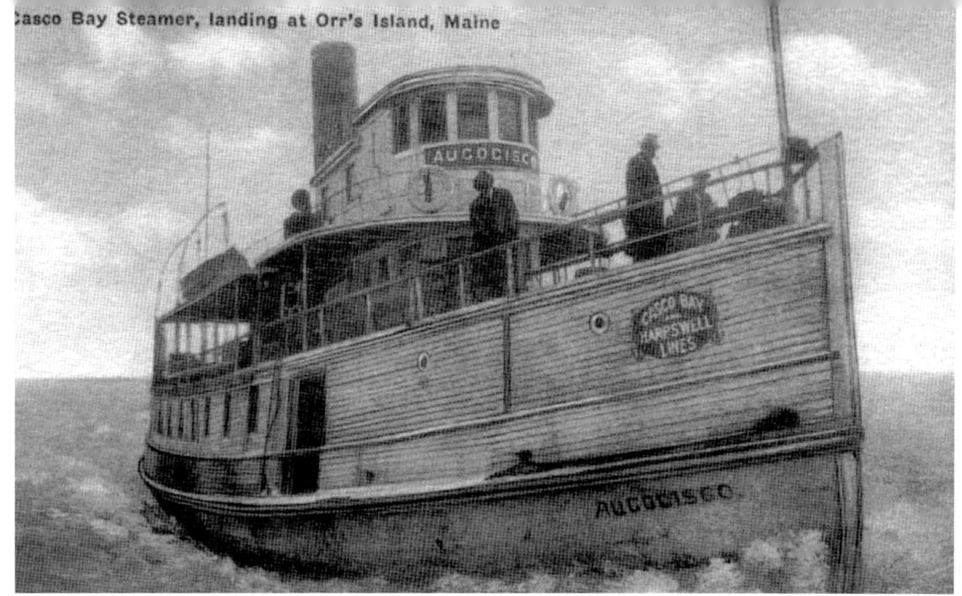

The *Aucocisco*, called *Auco* or *Queen of the Fleet*, was launched in 1897 in South Portland, Maine. It was the most popular of the steamboats that serviced Bailey Island from the late 1800's to the mid-1950's. Captain Charles Morrill from Orr's Island, who sailed the *Auco* for many years, was very popular among the islanders and tourists. During World War II it was used to carry soldiers from Portland to forts in the bay. In 1952, the *Auco* was retired.

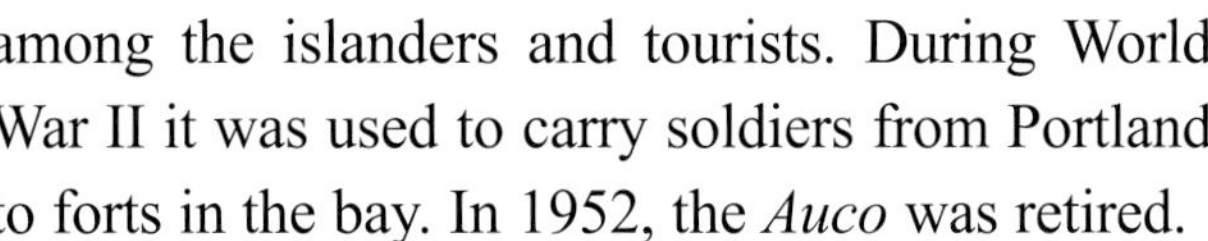

On hot days, the island children joined the Aucocisco crew diving off the pilings of the wharf into the cold ocean. (I suppose we were showing off for the tourists as much as anything.) If the tide was low, we went under the wharf to check for coins that might have fallen through the cracks. We then went to Sinnett's Store, right next door. It was also the Post Office. We joined all of the islanders to wait as the mail was sorted.

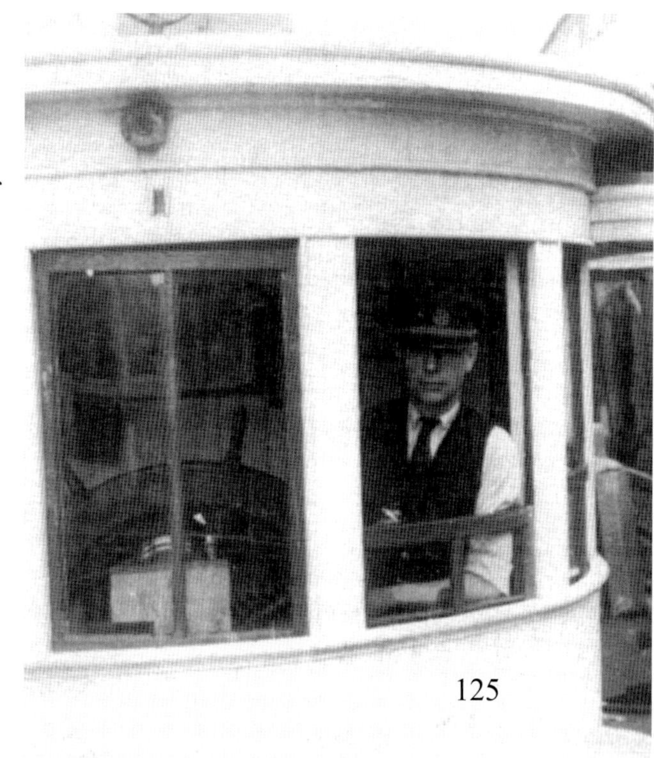

At right: Captain Carleton Morrill, son of Captain Charles B. Morrill, in the Pilot House of the *Gurnet*.

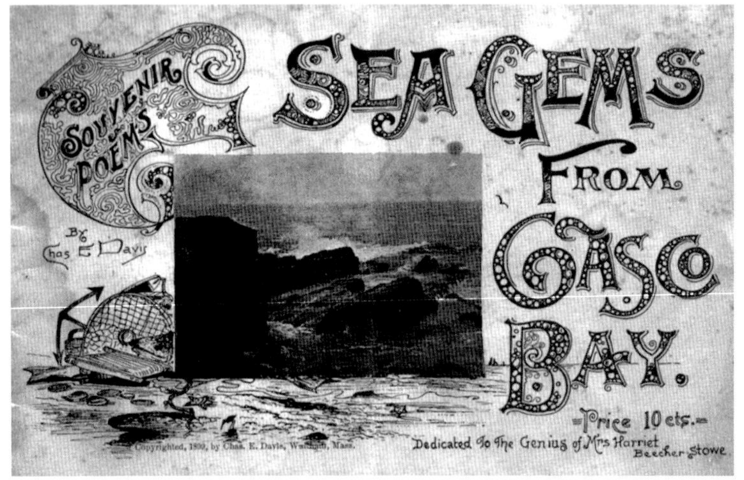

The following poem and picture were taken from *Sea Gems From Casco Bay*, a booklet of poems by Chas. E. Davis, printed in 1899. The cover, photo and poem are reproduced on these two facing pages.

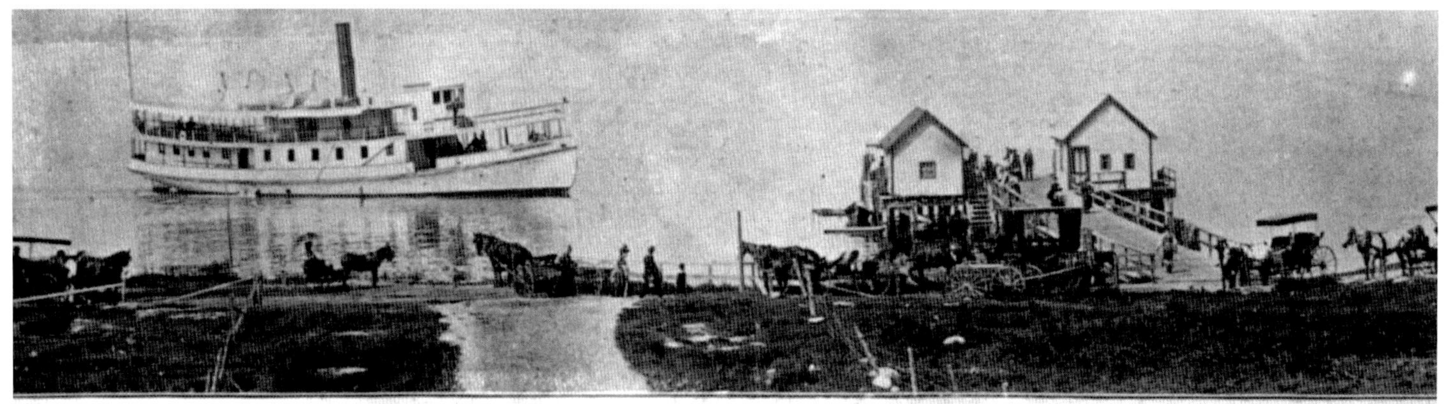

A Cruise Among the Isles.

(On Steamer Aucocisco.)

"Way down east" in Casco,
The bay of thousand isles,
Scenes of peace and beauty
Extend for many miles.

From Portland city eastward,
Toward the land of bright sunrise,
The sea-bird, Aucocisco,
Her journey daily flies.

Old Casco's emerald gems
Appear on every hand,
As onward flies our sea-bird
Toward Orr's, the promised land.

First the grim old forts we pass,
The lights and beacons, too,
While Cushings Peak's and Diamond
Quickly fade from view.

Onward speeds our sea-bird,
New scenes now heave in sight;
The two Chebeagues are fading,
With Hope upon our right.

But Bang's Stave and Clapboard
Are isles so very queer,
We passed them long ago;
Old Harpswell's drawing near.

"Haul in the gang-plank," the Cap'n shouts,
The steam is up and blowing;
We're off for Orr's and Bailey's,
A twelve-knot clip we're going.

Now the Geese and Goslings
Are clothed in emerald light;
"Old Whaleboat" in the distance,
A grand, majestic sight.

Eagle, Cliff and Jewell's
Vanguards of the ocean;
The wintry gales they break:
This is no idle notion.

In our hurry we most forgot
To merely make a mention
Of Haskell's Birch and Brown Cow
Thinking is such a tension.

Mackerel Cove, that gem serene,
Beautiful haven of rest;
Art can never hope to imitate,
Nature has outdone the best.

The "Pearl of Orr's Island";
A New England tale of long ago,
Written by that famous authoress,
Mrs. Harriet Beecher Stowe.

And thus, like the brook,
We might "run on forever,"
Casco's beauties to describe,
Exhausted they can be never.

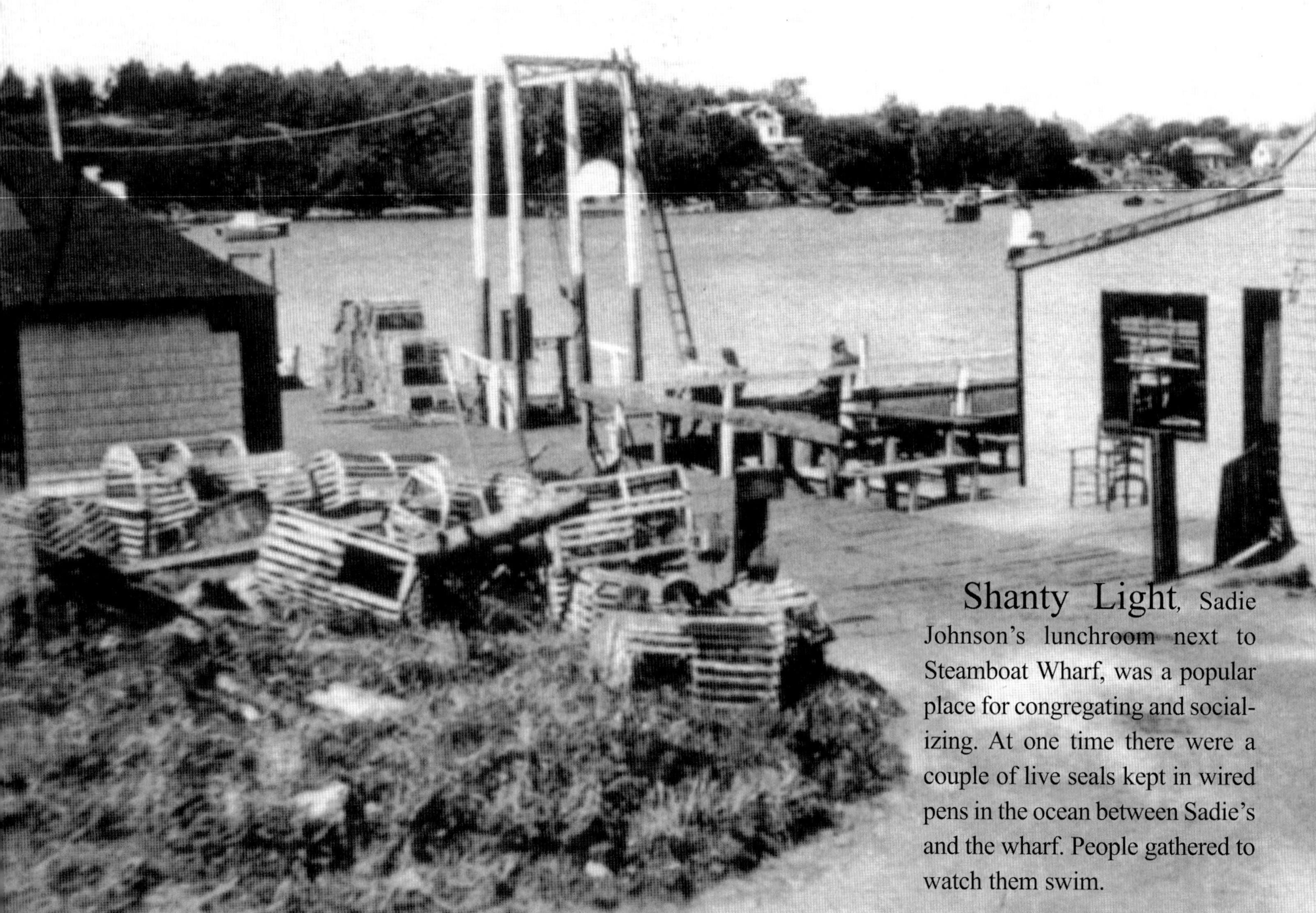

Shanty Light, Sadie Johnson's lunchroom next to Steamboat Wharf, was a popular place for congregating and socializing. At one time there were a couple of live seals kept in wired pens in the ocean between Sadie's and the wharf. People gathered to watch them swim.

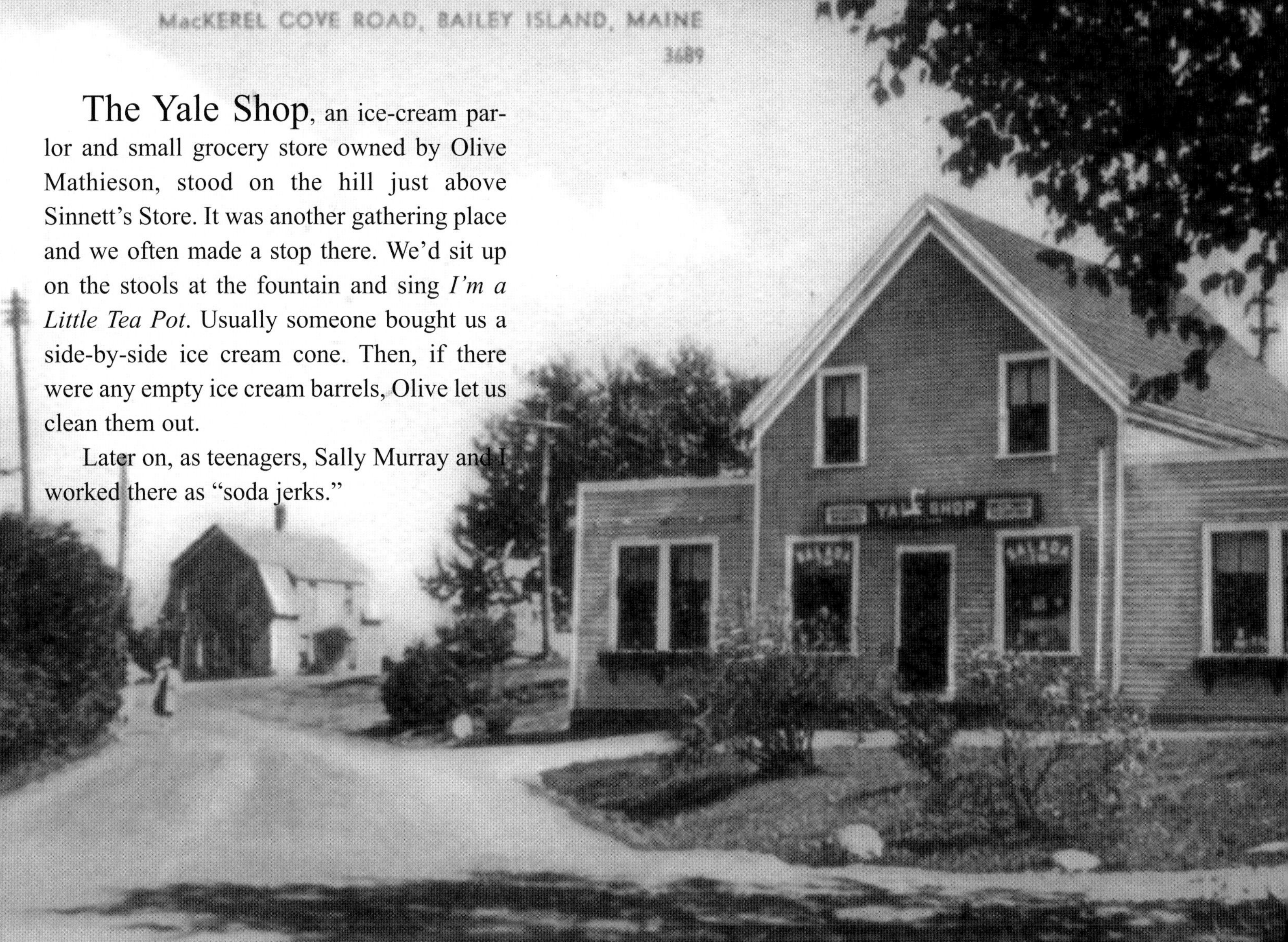

The Yale Shop, an ice-cream parlor and small grocery store owned by Olive Mathieson, stood on the hill just above Sinnett's Store. It was another gathering place and we often made a stop there. We'd sit up on the stools at the fountain and sing *I'm a Little Tea Pot*. Usually someone bought us a side-by-side ice cream cone. Then, if there were any empty ice cream barrels, Olive let us clean them out.

Later on, as teenagers, Sally Murray and I worked there as "soda jerks."

THE JOHNSON, **BAILEY ISLAND, MAINE**

Enlarged and Improved — **H. F. Johnson, Prop.** — Open June 15 to Sept. 20

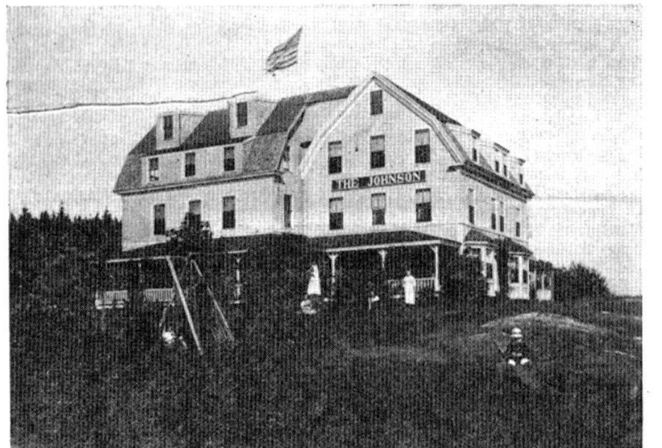

This is one of the houses which has made Casco Bay famous. The situation is picturesque, on a slight ridge between Mackerel Cove and Little Harbor. There's always a cool breeze, and the nearness of spruce and fir trees gives the air that tone which is so often recommended by physicians. Thirty sleeping rooms. Every convenience, open plumbing, etc. Table is supplied with every product of the bountiful sea and the house gardens. Bathing, Fishing, Motor and Sailboat Parties are always popular amusements. Accommodates with cottages 50 guests. Rates on application. N. E. Telephone.

H. F. JOHNSON, Boat-Builder... Casco Bay Hamptons and Launches of all kinds designed and built to order.

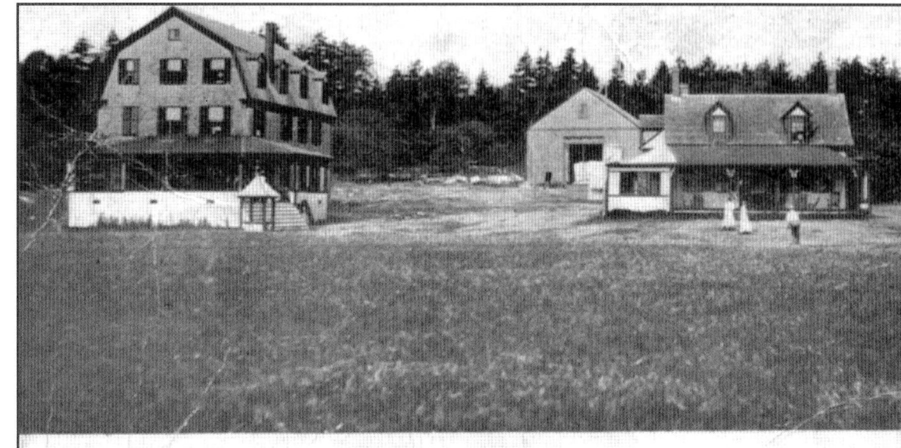

BAILEY ISLAND, ME. The Homestead.

Boarding Houses and Cottages

THE WOODBINE AND COTTAGES

BAILEY'S ISLAND.

Mrs. Humphrey Sinnett, Prop.

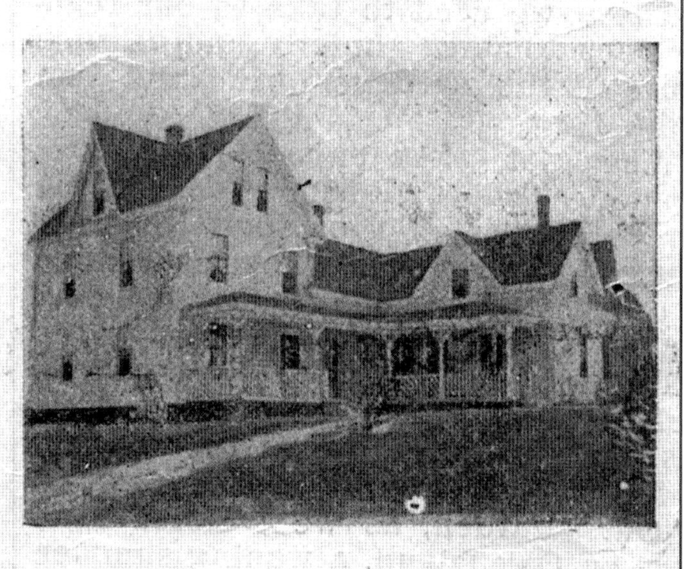

Our house is equal to any in the bay. Only a few minutes' walk from both wharves. Large rooms from which a fine view of the Atlantic can be had. All kinds of sports indulged in by our guests. Golf, Tennis court only a short distance from the house, Bathing, Boating and Fishing. No better table on the Bay. Open June 1 to Oct. 1. **Accommodates 60. Rates $8.00 to $12.00 per week.**

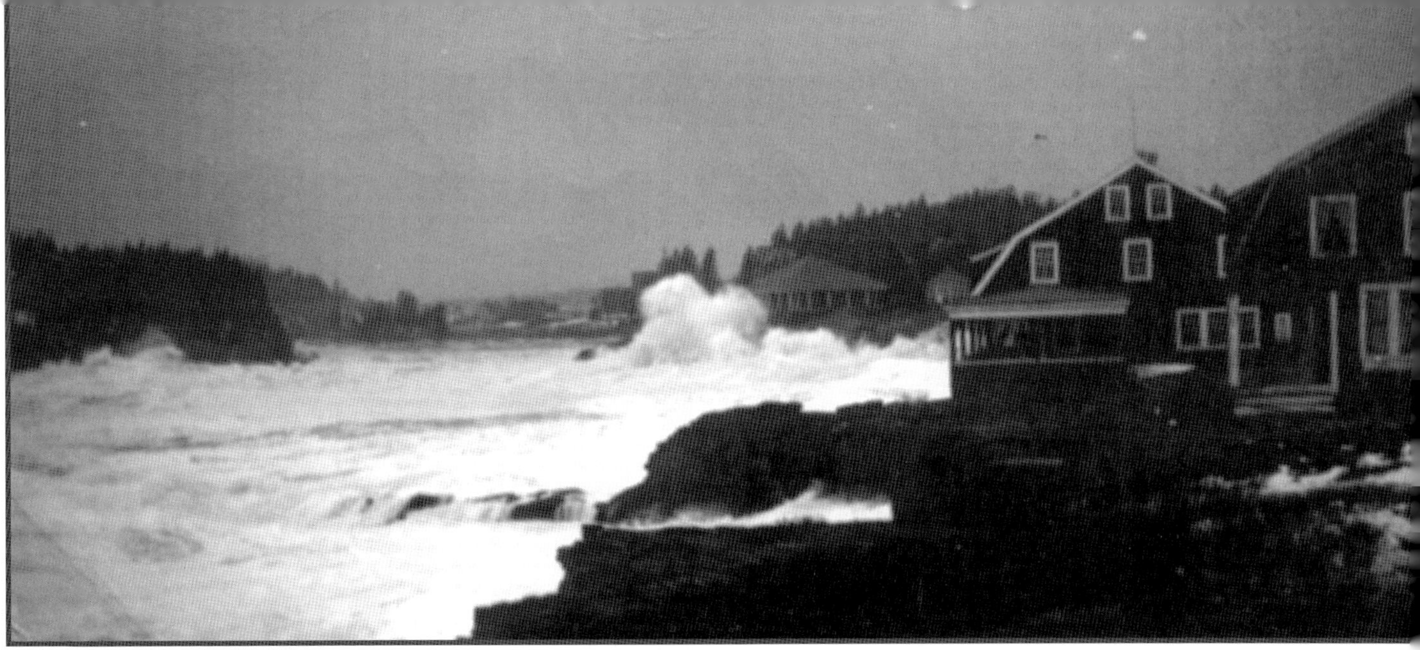

Once steamboat service from Portland came to Bailey Island in 1888, cottages and boarding houses sprung up. Some of the early boarding houses are now private homes. These include the Robinhood Inn near Cedar Beach on the northeast side of Bailey Island, the Johnson House on the east side of the road near the south end of the island, the Woodbine on the east side of the road overlooking Mackerel Cove, and the Homestead at the south end of Bailey Island. The Driftwood Inn, shown above, still operates as a boarding house with cottages. It overlooks Little Harbor on the east side of the island.

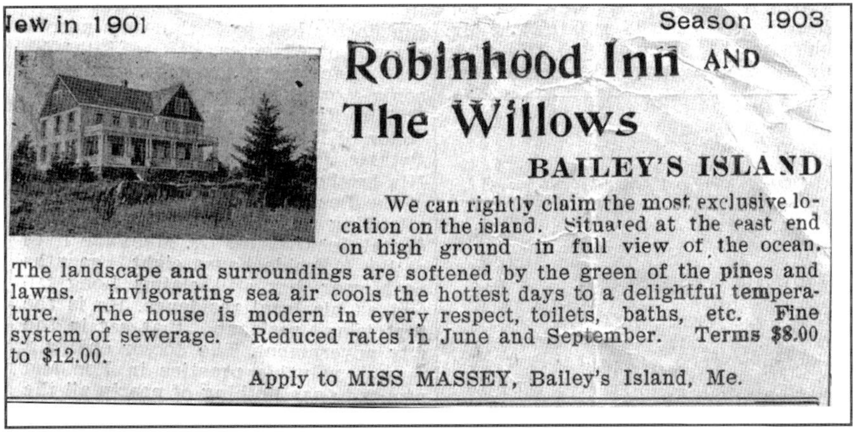

New in 1901 Season 1903

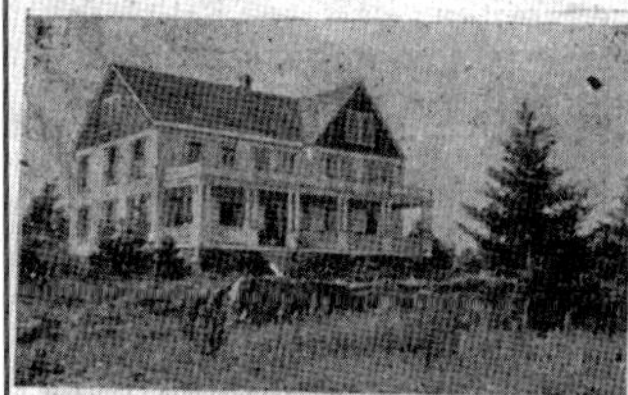

Robinhood Inn AND **The Willows**

BAILEY'S ISLAND

We can rightly claim the most exclusive location on the island. Situated at the east end on high ground in full view of the ocean. The landscape and surroundings are softened by the green of the pines and lawns. Invigorating sea air cools the hottest days to a delightful temperature. The house is modern in every respect, toilets, baths, etc. Fine system of sewerage. Reduced rates in June and September. Terms $8.00 to $12.00.

Apply to MISS MASSEY, Bailey's Island, Me.

Walter Crafts from Auburn, Maine, built the Ocean View Hotel, once located on the east side of the highway overlooking Mackerel Cove. On a visit to Casco Bay he was struck by the beautiful view of Mackerel Cove. There were only five summer cottages on the island at the time. There was no post office and no wharf. Mr. Crafts started out by having a cottage built above the cove in 1887. Because the tourist industry was expanding rapidly and the need for overnight rooms was great, he decided to add fifteen sleeping rooms and a dining room the following year. He continued to add on each year until the cottage became a substantial hotel able to accommodate 100 guests.

The Ocean View was torn down in the early 1960's.

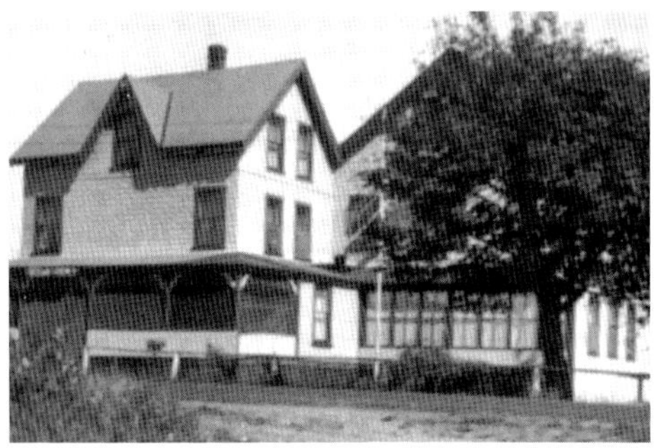

OCEAN VIEW HOUSE

WALTER D. CRAFTS, PROP.

BAILEY'S ISLAND, MAINE.

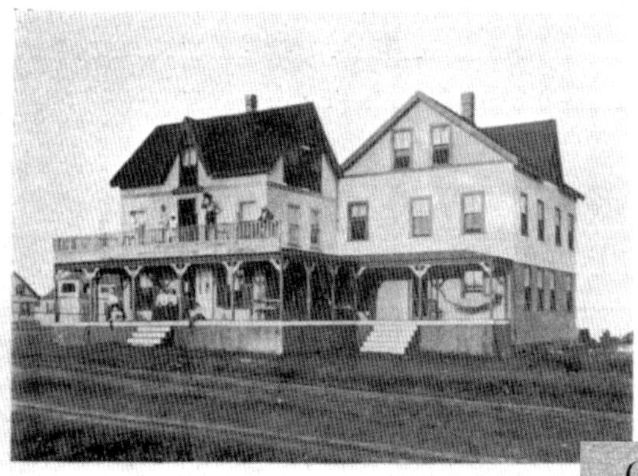

OCEAN VIEW HOUSE.

NEW and NEWLY FURNISHED. COOL, AIR

The Ocean View, as its name indicates, commands a wide and sw
of the ocean and the shores of Bailey's Island from each room i
We have no uncomfortable nights, and blankets are needed nearly
The house is within two minutes walk of the steamboat wharf an
and centrally located as regards the places of natural beauty on
Fine boating, fishing and bathing facilities. Fine sand beach at
the famous Mackerel Cove near the house. The water this seas
living spring in the granite rock near the honse, and is as clear
The proprietor requests that booking for rooms be made as far i
possible.

Rates { $1.75 per day,
$8.00 per week and upwards.
Table Board, $6.00.

MAIL COLLECTED AT THE HOUSE TWICE A DA

OCEAN VIEW HOUSE,

BAILEY'S ISLAND, ME.

WALTER D. CRAFTS, PROPRIETOR.

DINNER MENU.

SOUP.

Clam stew. Barley soup.

FISH.

~~Baked mackerel~~ Boiled haddock egg sauce.

BOILED.

Boiled fowl with pork.

ROASTS.

Roast lamb. Rib. of beef

ENTREES.

Lobster salad

VEGETABLES.

Mashed and plain boiled potatoes Onions Shell beans.

RELISHES.

PASTRY AND DESSERT.

Mince and apple pie. Custard pudding Vanilla ice-cream

TEA. COFFEE. ~~COCOA~~

DINNER SERVED FROM 12.30 TO 1.30.

In the late 1800's many literary people from out-of-state found that Bailey Island was, and is, an ideal place to spend summers. The beauty of the sea, the rolling surf, and the pounding waves on the rocky shores attracted many.

Friends and relatives of the Reverend Adams' family built the Mission Cottages on the narrow ridge of Sea Bank overlooking Pebbly Beach in the late 1800's. The Sea Shell was the first built in 1883, the Barnacle in 1885, the Nautilus in 1887, and the Tides in 1888.

Erastus Starr of Massachusetts was a lover of nature, and when he visited Bailey Island he was easily convinced to locate there for the summer. In 1901 he built his attractive cottage high on the hill above the Bailey Island Union Church, keeping the field below open to save the view. His family still owns the cottage and continues to come to the island every summer.

Parker Luckey's summer home overlooking Mackerel Cove, around 1950.

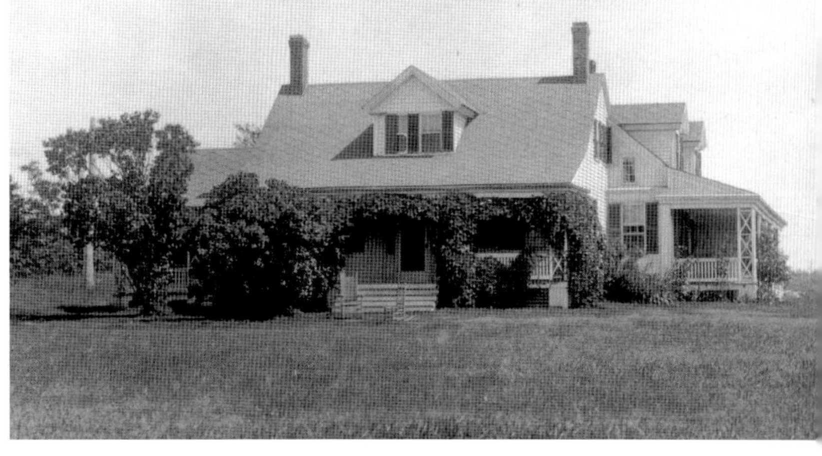

Starr Cottage

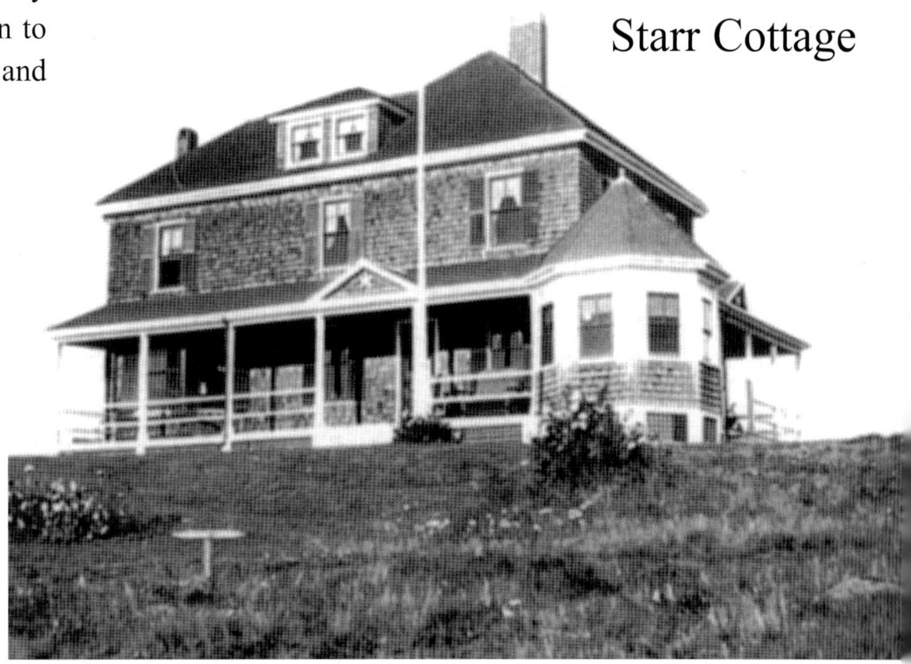

The Mooring on Jockey Hill.

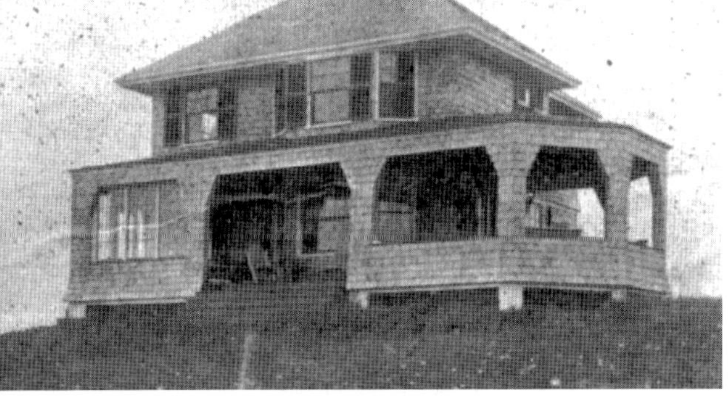

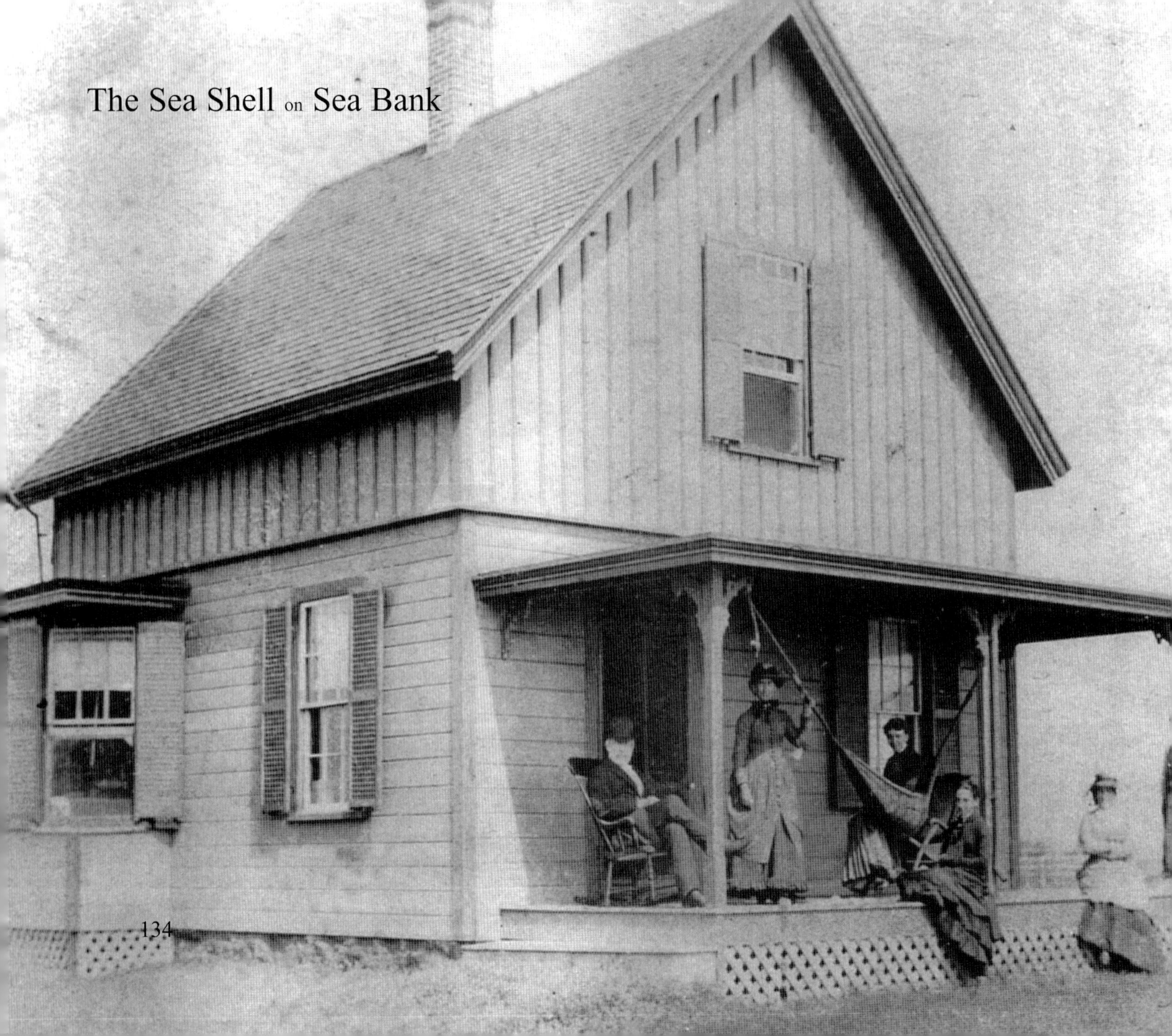

The Sea Shell on Sea Bank

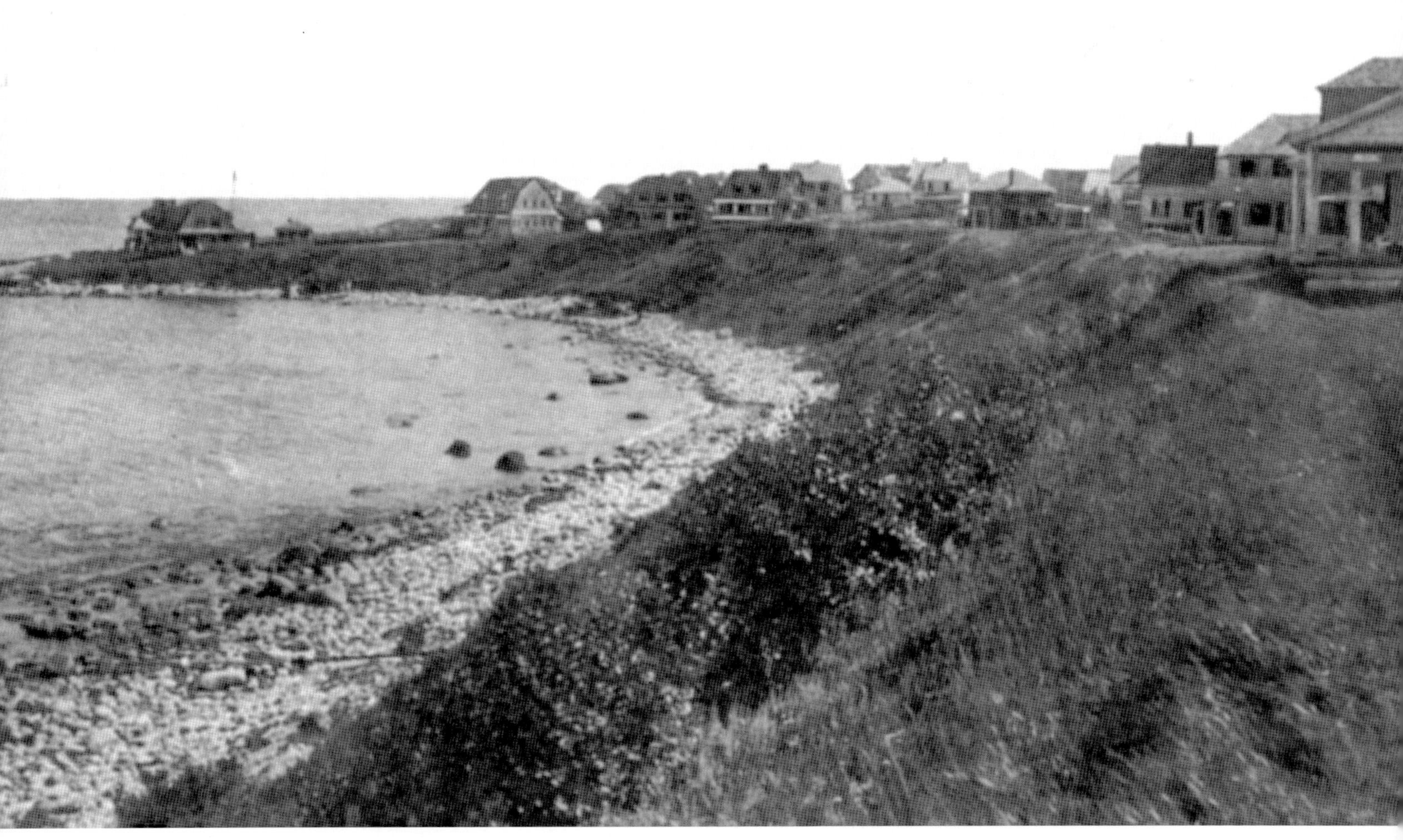

In the middle of the island, on the east side, many cottages face the ocean. This postcard shows the shoreline south from behind the Library Hall.

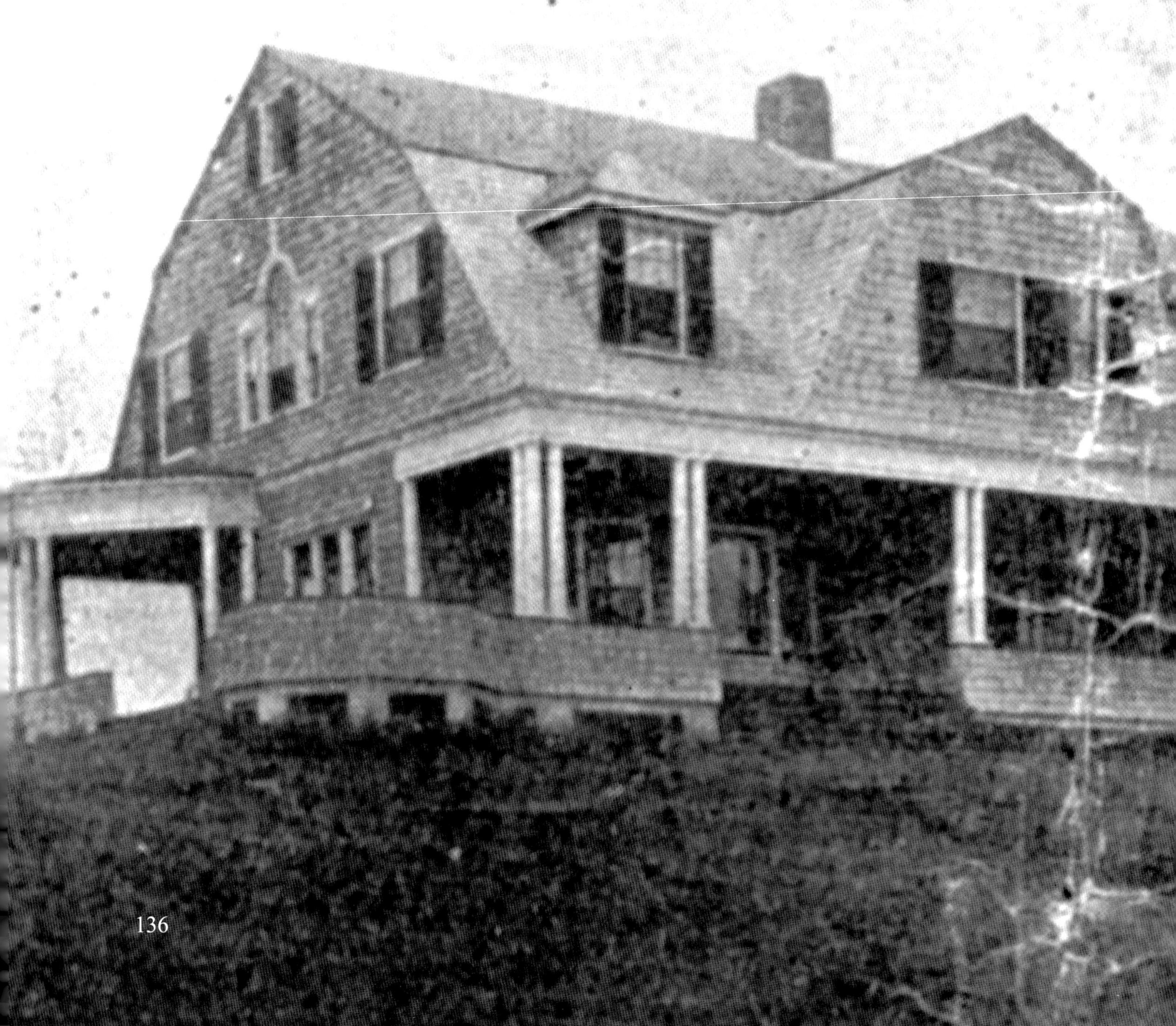

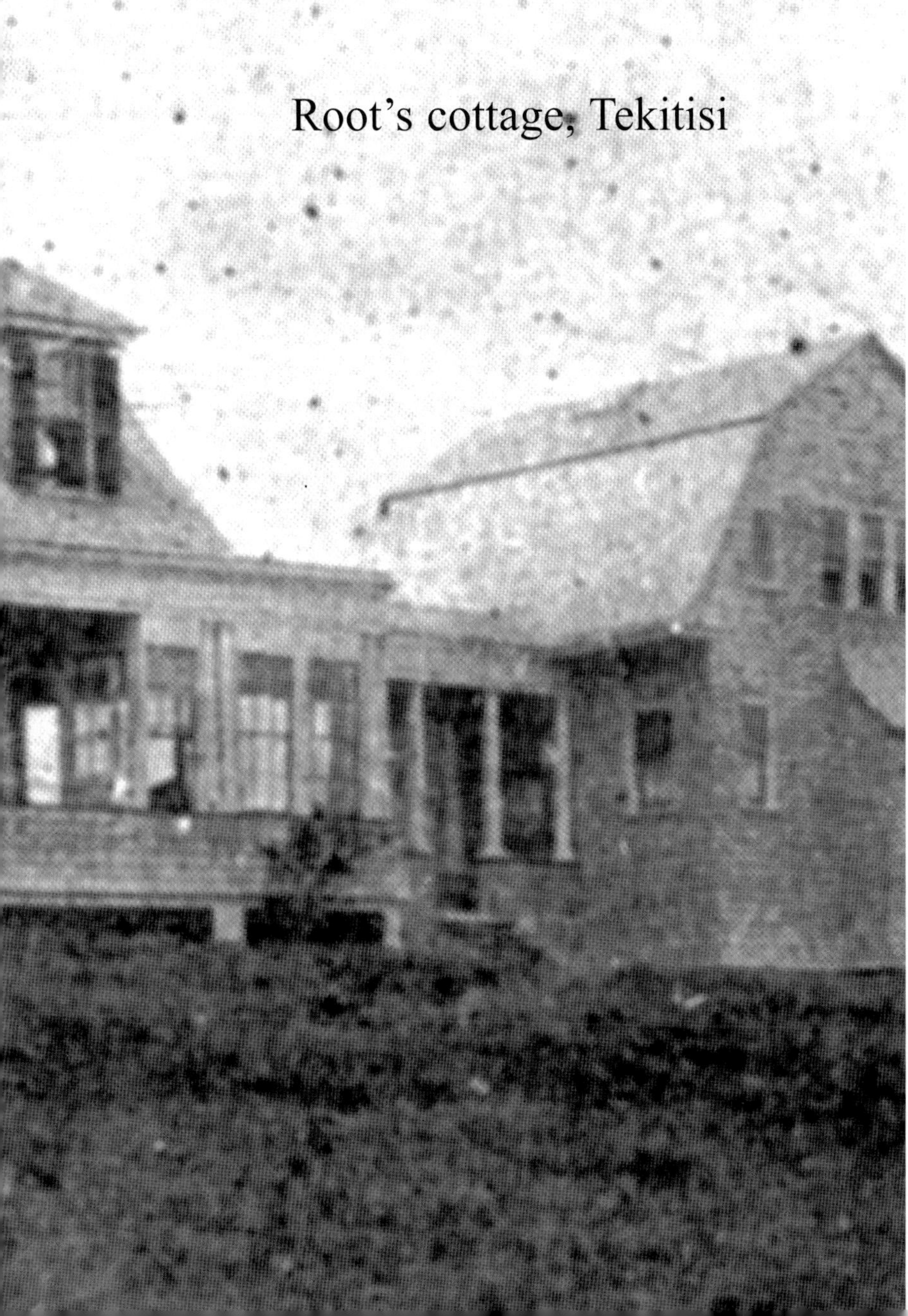

Root's cottage, Tekitisi

By 1903 there were over 60 summer cottages on Bailey Island. Many of the cottages built at the turn of the century are still standing. Today on Jockey Hill you can see the Root cottage, "Tekitisi" built in 1895 by Charles F. Root of New York. He was president of the Root Newspaper Association. His father, George F. Root, died on Bailey Island at the cottage. He was the composer of many Civil War songs, including, *The Battle Cry of Freedom*, ("Yes, we'll rally round the flag, boys...."), *Tramp, Tramp, Tramp* and *Tenting on the Old Camp Ground*. Charles' sister, Clara Louise Burnham, built a cottage next door. Besides her musical ability, she wrote many novels. Bailey Island is the setting for *Dr. Latimer*, published in 1893.

Jockey Hill

In the middle of Bailey island, behind the Library Hall, is a hill overlooking the ocean on both sides. This hill, which now has three lovely summer cottages, is called Jockey Hill. Here is a hand-written account from the memoirs of my father, Linwood O. Johnson:

> The story of the origin of the name has been handed down from one generation to another and is as follows: "Deacon Timothy Bailey's wife had a brother, Benjamin Curtis, otherwise known as "Jockey Ben." This being before the days of prohibition, Jockey Ben was in the habit of imbibing rather freely and at these times would seize his old flint and fire, the Indian alarm. The good Deacon (his brother-in-law) would remonstrate and even pray with him, but it was all of no use, and at last the Deacon told Ben he must go away. So he came down the island and selected the spot which was always afterwards known as Jockey's Hill and built for himself some sort of a shelter where he lived for many years.

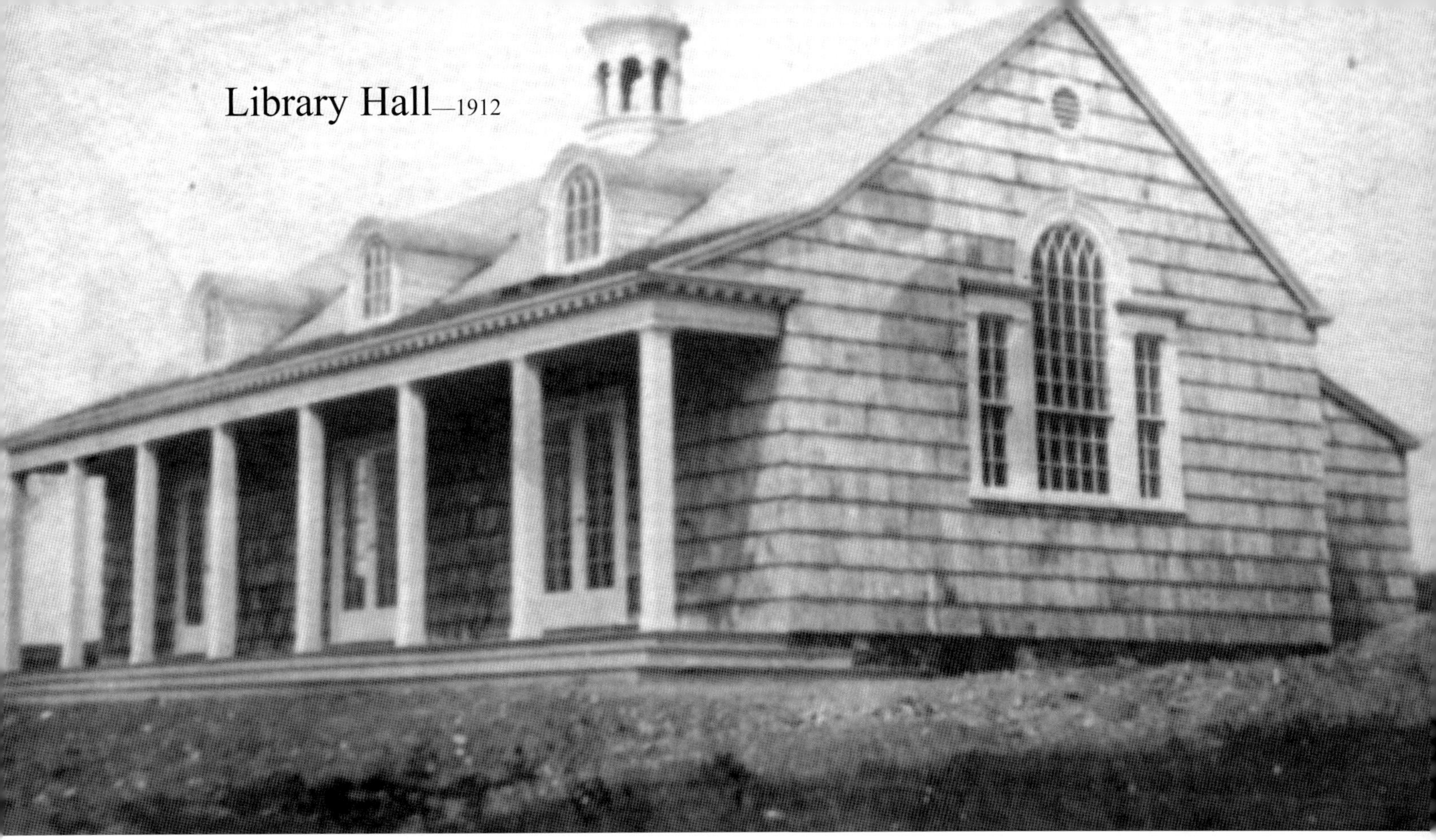

Library Hall—1912

The renowned architects Horace Mann and Perry MacNeille of New York, who were partners in the same firm, designed Library Hall in 1909. They had family connections on Bailey Island and later became brothers-in-law. Before designing Library Hall as a miniature Mount Vernon, they designed the MacNeille cottage on the hill above the Library Hall. They spent summers there for seventeen years.

The Library Hall was a significant building in design and used as a model for later community centers by Mann and MacNeille. Constructed in 1910, the Library Hall was dedicated in 1912 to be used as a library and to serve as a place for social functions.

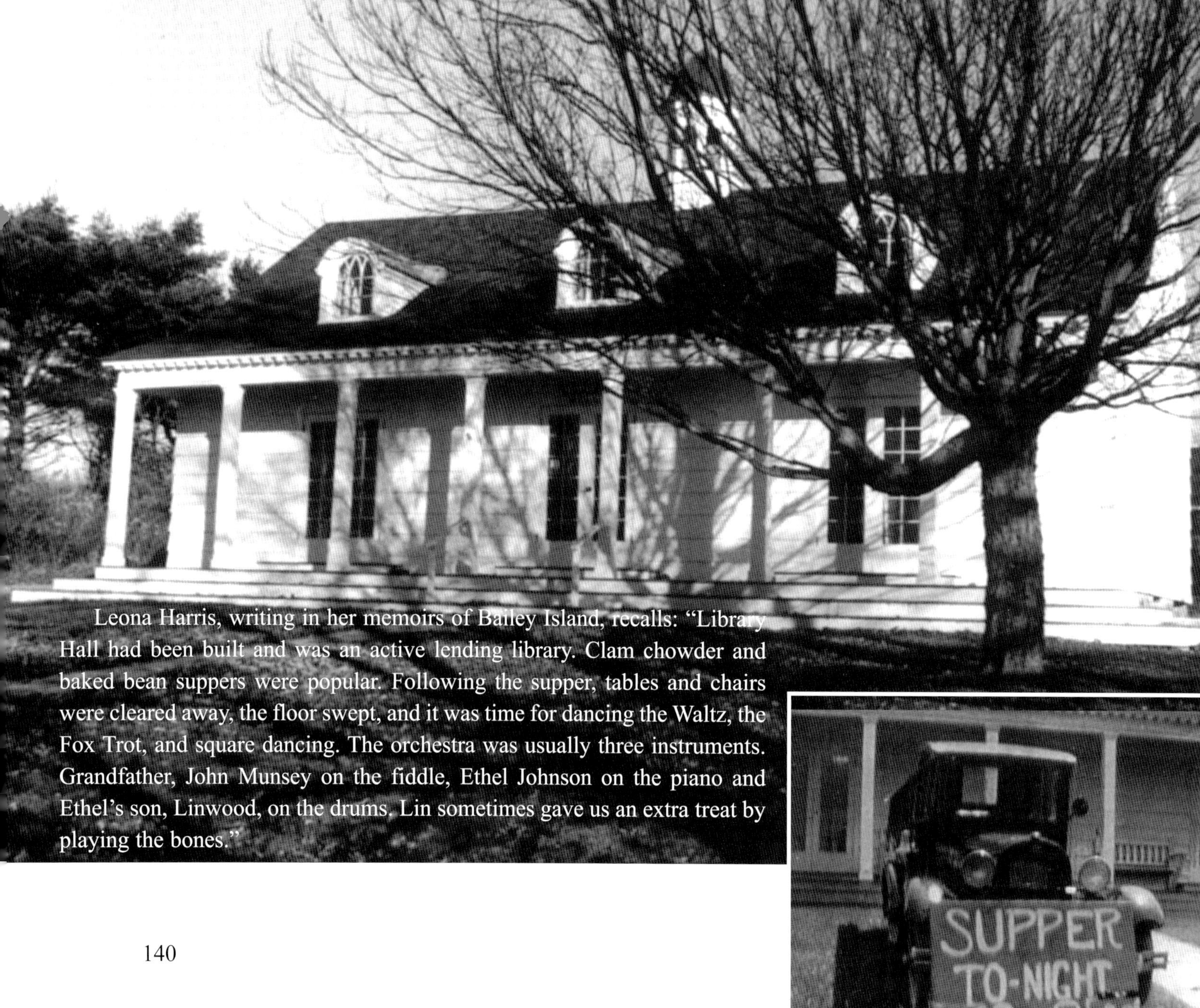

Leona Harris, writing in her memoirs of Bailey Island, recalls: "Library Hall had been built and was an active lending library. Clam chowder and baked bean suppers were popular. Following the supper, tables and chairs were cleared away, the floor swept, and it was time for dancing the Waltz, the Fox Trot, and square dancing. The orchestra was usually three instruments. Grandfather, John Munsey on the fiddle, Ethel Johnson on the piano and Ethel's son, Linwood, on the drums. Lin sometimes gave us an extra treat by playing the bones."

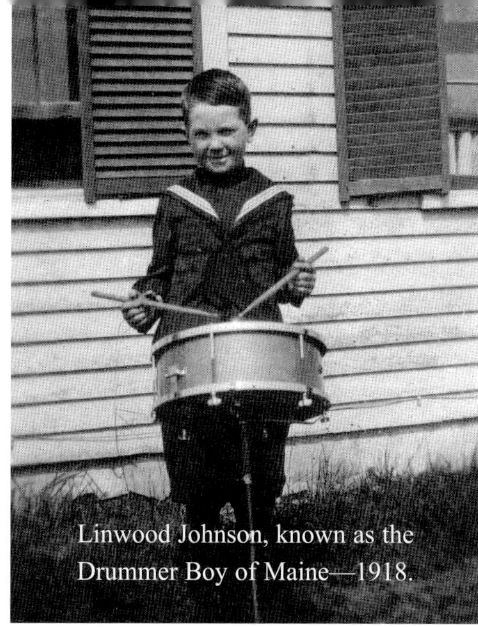
Linwood Johnson, known as the Drummer Boy of Maine—1918.

In 1975 my father, Linwood Johnson, spoke about the Library Hall and entertainment on Bailey Island in an interview with David A. Taylor, now a folklife specialist at the American Folklife Center, Library of Congress in Washington, D.C.

Linwood: Back in the days before the bridge, you know, these traveling shows would come around. They had a minstrel show up here at the hall and there was a bunch of us kids that—of course, every kid that could git the money was there. Well, after the show we all went home and started makin' some bones out of trap lathes—hardwood lathes, saw 'em up, whittle 'em out. Grandmother, she was interested in music.

I played the drums anyway, so she—she turned around and sent outright to Sears and Roebuck and got me some bones. That's the first ones I had.

David: Where did the minstrel show come from?

Linwood: Probably a traveling show. They traveled all over the place.

David: Come by boat?

Linwood: Oh, yeah. Had to. Either that or swim.

David: But it didn't go up and down the coast on the boat? It just came over here to the island?

Linwood: I wouldn't be surprised if it traveled the whole coast of Maine before it was over with. My mother, you know, played for dances since she was 16 years old. From then on that's just about all she did. She played all over the bay here from Small Point to Portland. Them days there was fiddles around, too. John Munsey, from over across the cove, he's been dead for years. He used to play with her. He was a good fiddler but gosh darn, you know he wasn't about to play with anybody but her. Just a notion he got in his head. And she could play, though. Jigs and reels mostly.

"Bones," a rhythm instrument, four to a set, two for each hand, were played like "spoons." These ebony bones were Dad's.

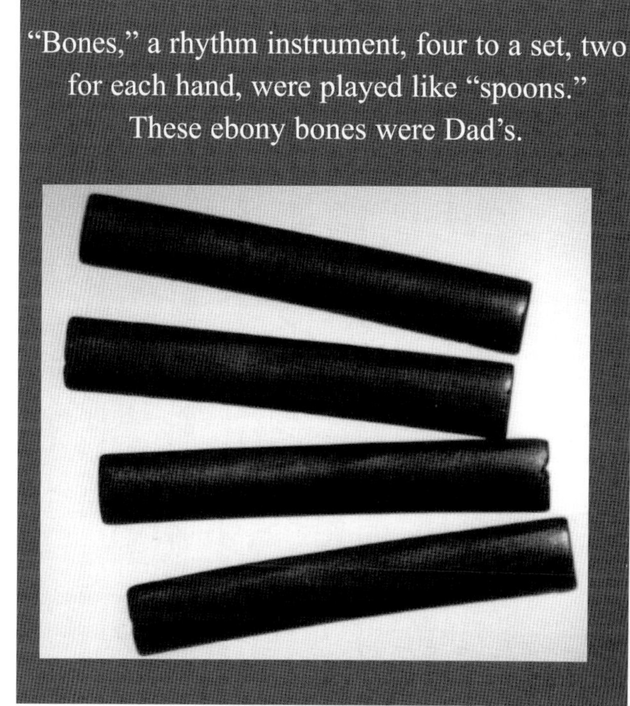

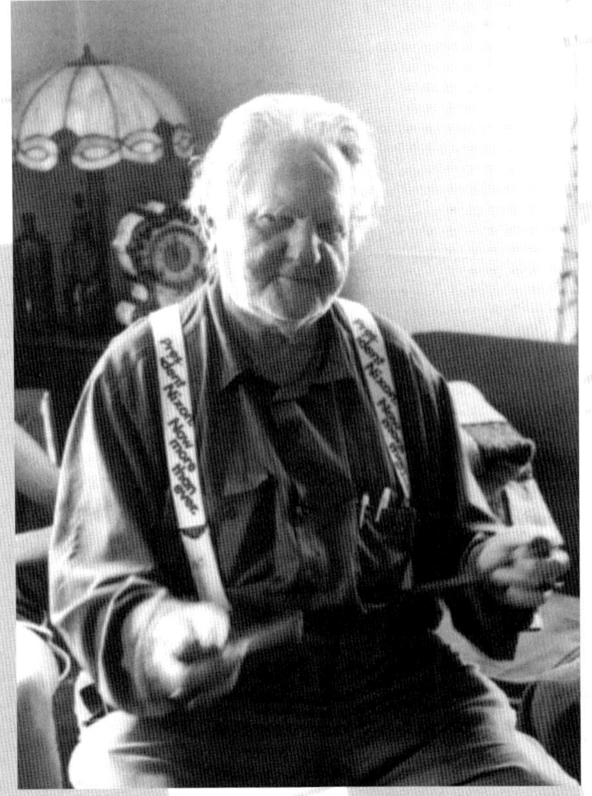

David: Did you ever play in any of those dances?

Linwood: I played the drum with Munsey over here and my mother and then World War I. I was a kid then. We used to play up here at the Library. Used to go to dances all the time up there.

David: Are the jigs and reels the tunes you like best to play the bones with? You like playing fairly rapidly, not slow?

Linwood: It's the beat of the darn thing. I don't know what you call it. I don't know nothin' about music. When I played that night here up to the Hall. We practiced quite a bit here. That time I was playing quite a bit, too. That place was plum full, gosh darn, lots of summer people. I worked for 'em, painting. I don't think one of them knew that I played the bones. Anyway, we come out on the stage, Prosper Richards I told you about, we sat down. and I had a suitcase and a raccoon coat, right in the middle of the summer. By Gosh, I took off that coat, Gin, my wife, folded it up just as careful, afraid I'd get some dirt on it—old moth eaten thing, laid it down in the chair and I opened up the suitcase and I had 2 pairs of bones in the suitcase. That's all I had. Well, they was still wondering what in the Devil they was gonna hear. Gosh, we got started on that Hornpipe. I'm telling you, Mister, it brought the house down. I don't give a darn, it did. They roared, they howled, and they screeched. I don't remember if there was an encore or not. I doubt there was.

Note: Linwood's suspenders say: "Nixon Now More Than Ever." This picture was taken in 1983.

Linwood Tells David Taylor Another One

“They used to gather around the houses, you know, and have sings, play the piano and have a great time. They’d have anywhere from 25-30 people a night, right here in this house. In the winter months the piano would be out in that dining room. And just as soon as it come summuh they brought it in here, and it set right there where that plant stand is. In the winter months they didn’t try to heat this room. They closed it up. I’d see ’em come up here and they’d haul kids on sleighs. They used to do it everywhere in the old days up and down the coast. They’d bring the kids up in the sled and put the kids to sleep. Laud, they’d sit there and sing ’til way onto almost 10 or 11 o’clock at night.

“Another thing, old Wood Bibber down the road here. He had a phonograph, one of them ones with the southern records and he’d wheel it up on his old wheelbarrow and he’d, uh, play it and I had to sit right quiet. Oh, I hated to see him come because when he’d come I had to keep quiet. I couldn’t say one word, nobody else, because he was playing that for our benefit and we want sposed to talk. He’d grind that thing and he’d play that, he’d play that darned thing and when he got all through, he’d say, “Well now, I’m going to leave that machine right here and you can play it all you want to.” And he’d take the crank home with him.

“He loved music. He was awful close but he loved music. He come up one night, wanted to hear the radio. I had a radio in 1922. That’s along time ago. That’s the early days of radio. My grandmother had a nephew worked for Westinghouse. He sent me this radio. It was just a panel, a mess of wires and three sets of batteries; a stored battery, which was an A battery. Then it had a B battery and a C battery. Anyway I had headphones; I had three pairs of headphones hooked up together. It was a winter night. Cold! And he walked pretty near a mile, come in, and I got them headphones out in that room out there. I got the headphones on his head and I turned them darn things on. They was just as clear, them old batteries, clear. By Gorry, they played *The Mocking Bird* from a New York station. He set there and he never said a word. When they finished the piece, he took off the headphones, he layed them down just as careful afraid he’d break them. He got up. He never said ‘Good Night.’ He never said, ‘Thank You.’ Never said a word. He went out through the kitchen. My mother, my father and grandmother was out there. He went right out by them and never spoke. He was bewildered, the old fella. He got out in the back yard, by the back door and he looked right up into the heavens hazin’ over with snow, coming on No’theast, looked up into the heavens and he said, ‘Godfrey Mighty, Godfrey Mighty,’ he said, ‘coming up here in a head of wind.’ He couldn’t imagine how that music from New York got up here with a wind No’theast. Poor old fella.”

~Order of Dances~

March & Circle

Quadrille
Waltz
Lady of the Lake
Two Step
Hulls Victory
Waltz
Quadrille

Intermiss
(20 Minut

Waltz & Schottische
Portland Fancy
Lancers Quadrille
Waltz
Boston Fancy
Lady of the Lake,—Good Night.

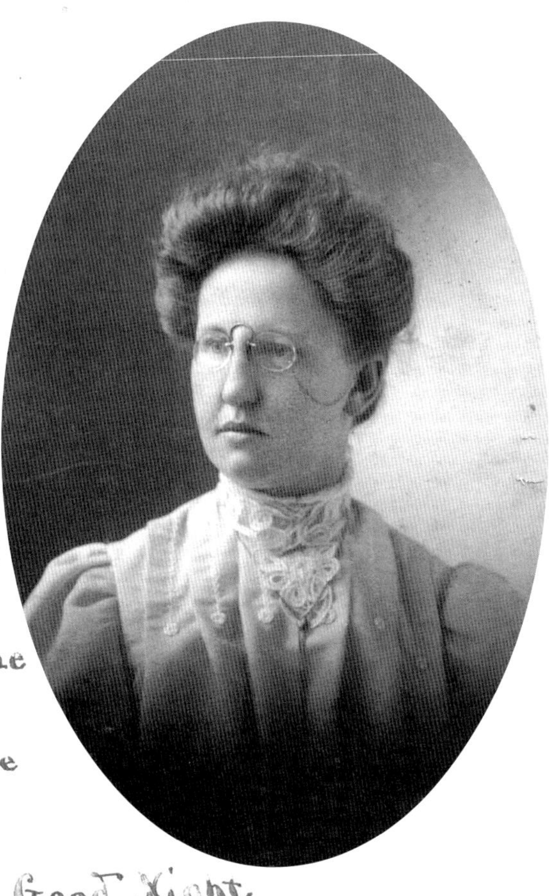

Grandmother Ethel Johnson's dance schedule next to a photo of her—early 1900's.

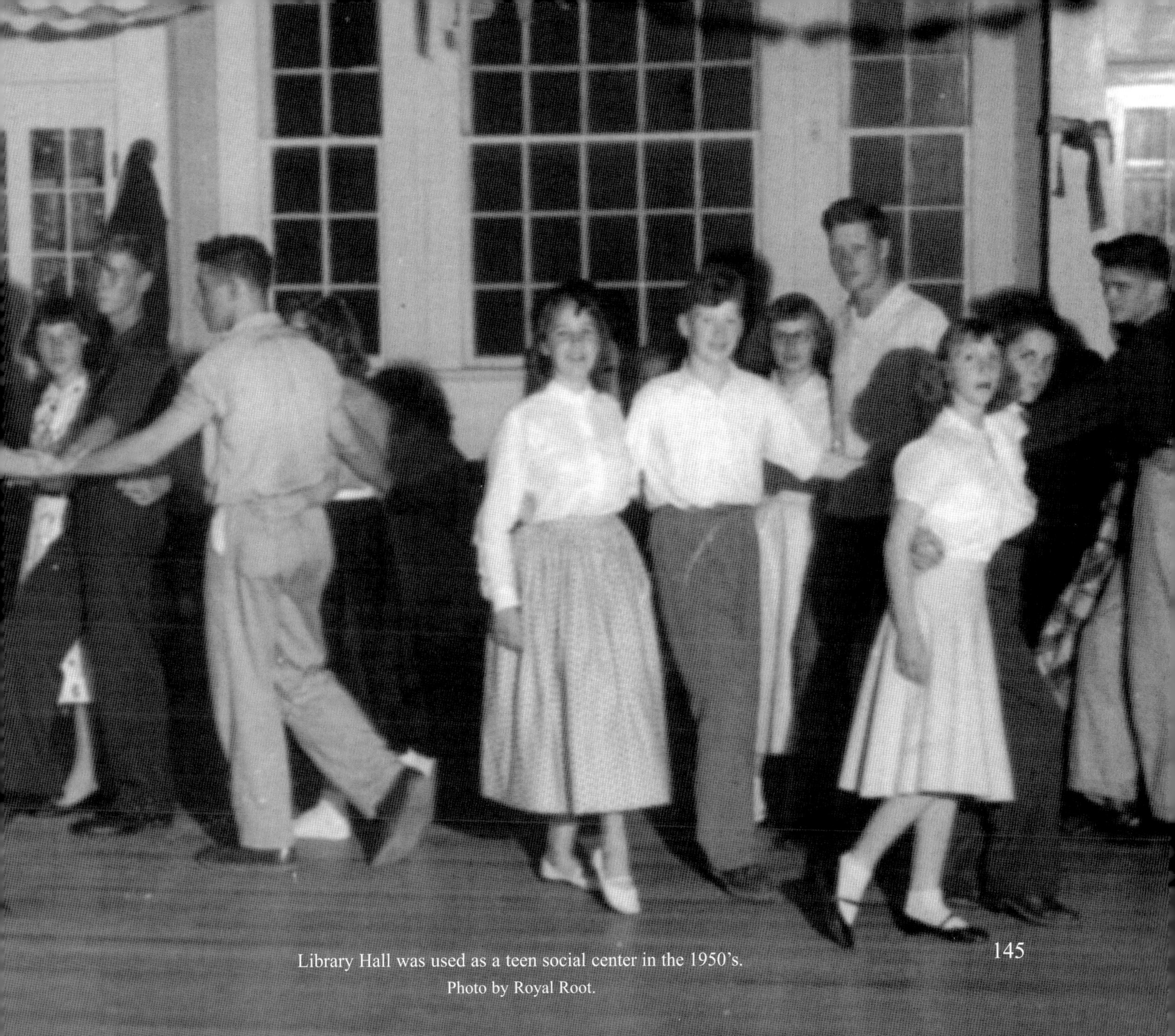

Library Hall was used as a teen social center in the 1950's.
Photo by Royal Root.

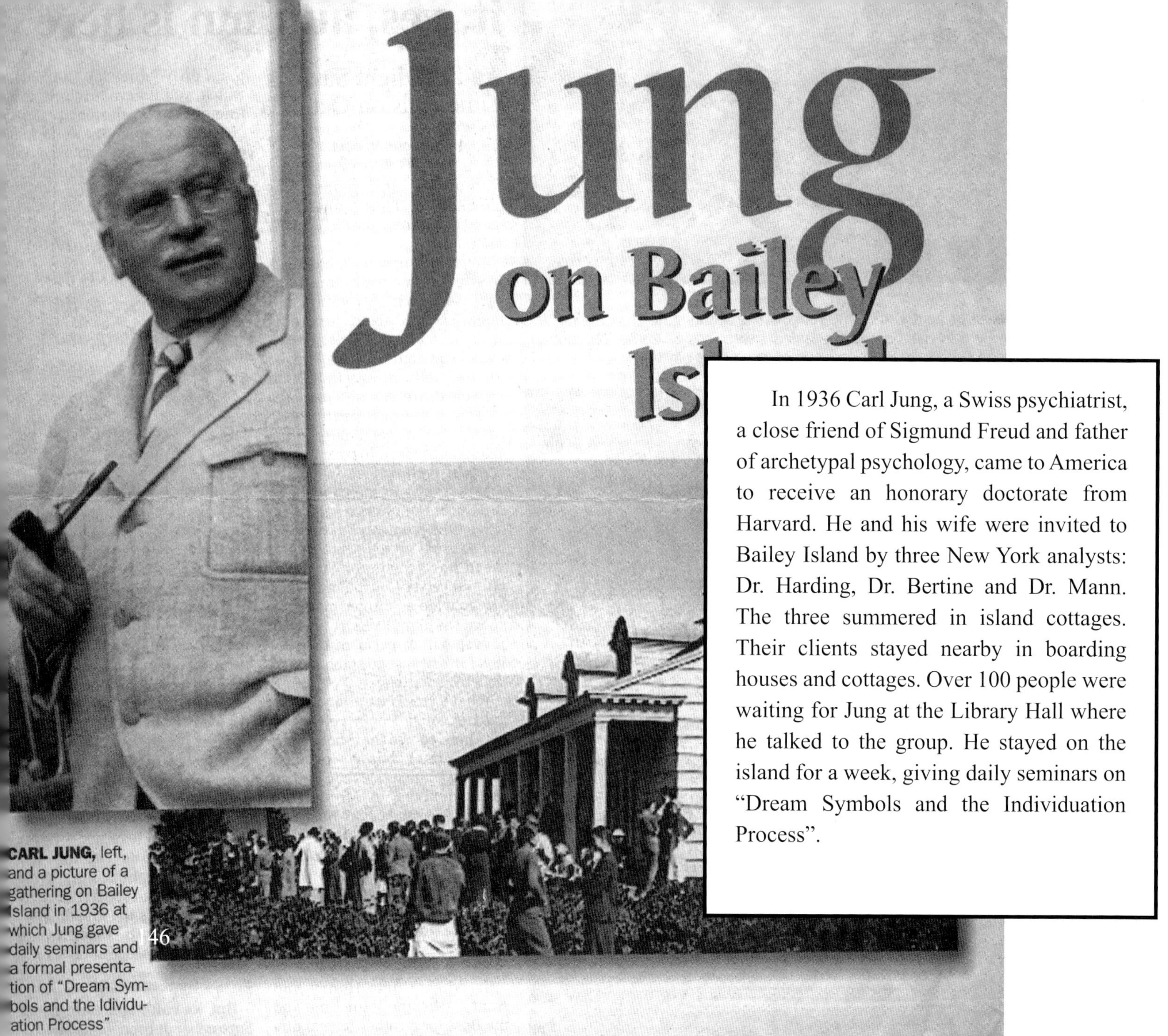

In 1936 Carl Jung, a Swiss psychiatrist, a close friend of Sigmund Freud and father of archetypal psychology, came to America to receive an honorary doctorate from Harvard. He and his wife were invited to Bailey Island by three New York analysts: Dr. Harding, Dr. Bertine and Dr. Mann. The three summered in island cottages. Their clients stayed nearby in boarding houses and cottages. Over 100 people were waiting for Jung at the Library Hall where he talked to the group. He stayed on the island for a week, giving daily seminars on "Dream Symbols and the Individuation Process".

CARL JUNG, left, and a picture of a gathering on Bailey Island in 1936 at which Jung gave daily seminars and a formal presentation of "Dream Symbols and the Idividuation Process"

The Fisherman Comes In

from *Songs From an Island*

Marjorie Johnson

The wind has blown
soft fragrance
of the fields,
and scent
of apple blossoms
after rain,
across the cove
to where
he moors his boat,
and rows ashore
with quick,
short strokes again.

With mighty shove
he sends it
through the sand,
slacks the hot oarlocks,
fits the oars
in place,
grasps the great fish
in gnarled
and horny hands.
And knows
there will be wonder
on her face.

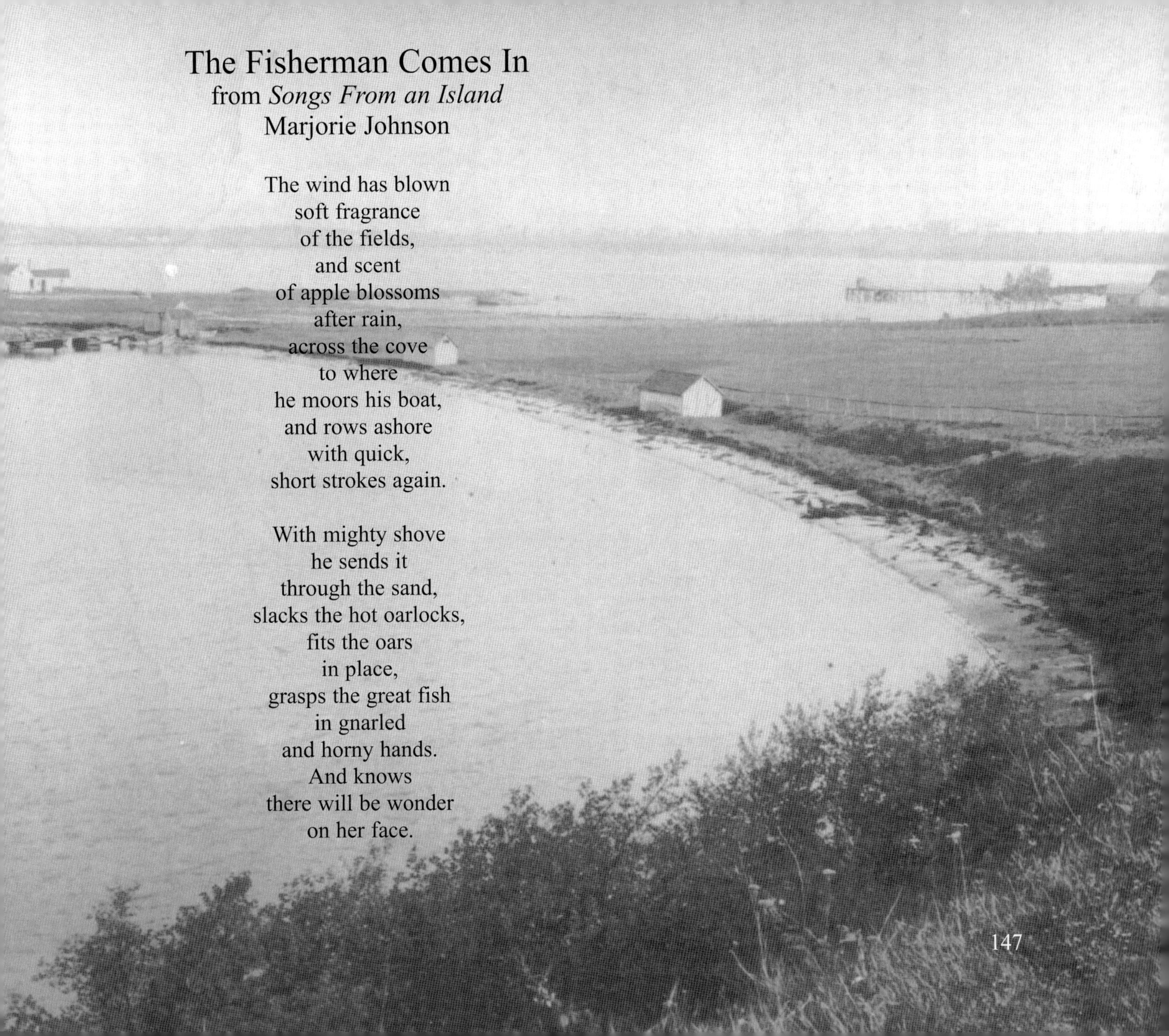

Lowell's Cove—1934. In any given year, islanders faced many storms. But in the winter of 1933-34 storms and severe temperatures froze solid the coves of Casco Bay. The ice breaker *Ossippee* was brought in to clear the way in Mackerel Cove. To get the mail from the steamboat, someone had to venture out on the ice to the head of Mackerel Cove, because that was as far as the steamer could come in. In 1917 local people were known to walk across the bay to Portland. Of course they probably walked in and around the bays, close to the shore, not in a direct line to Portland.

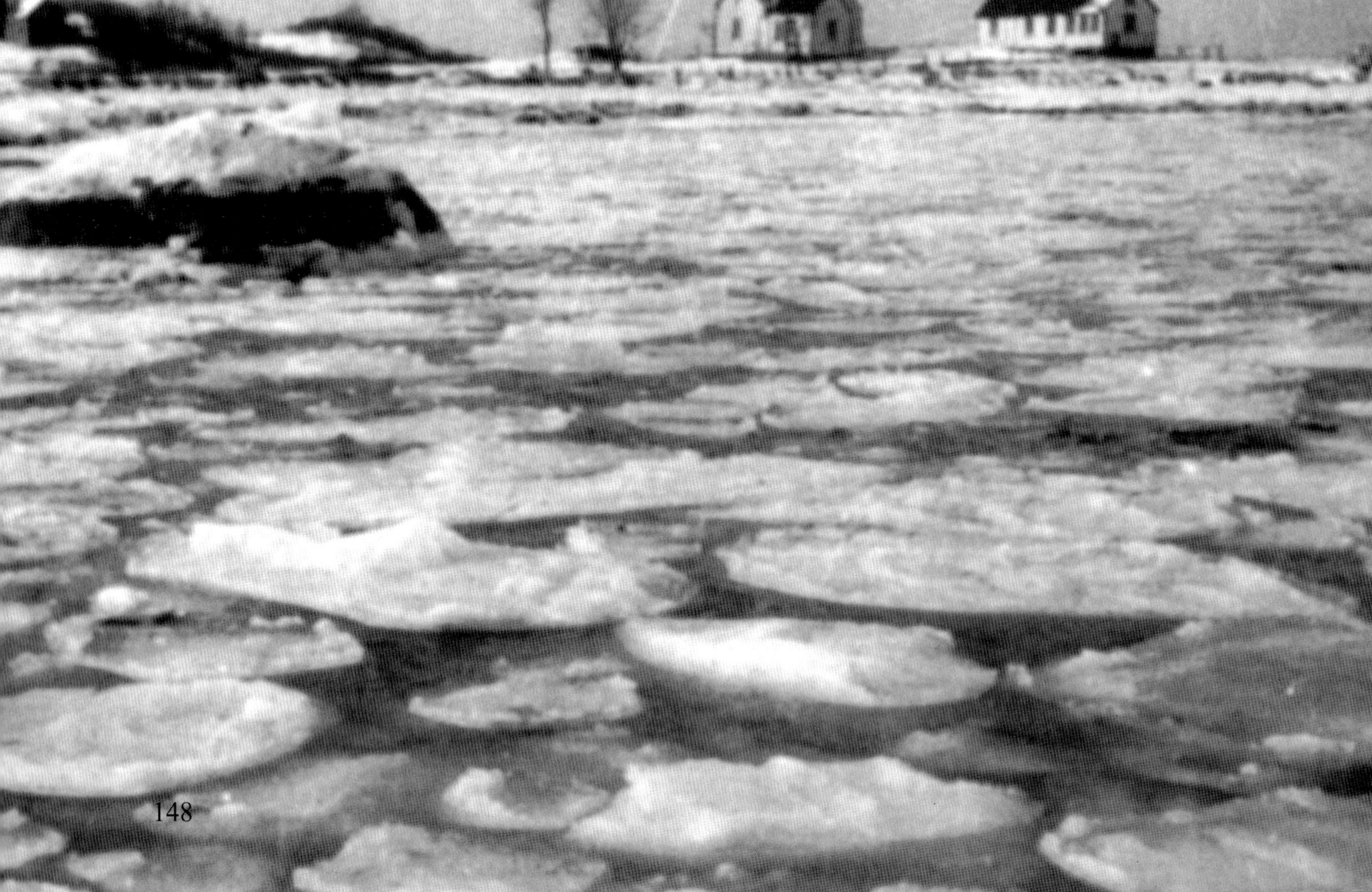

Ice Cakes in Lowell's Cove, 1950's. I remember many winters when there were "ice cakes" around the shoreline. It was great fun sledding down the hill from the main road to the cove, but we had to be careful not to slide over the bank and onto the beach because we couldn't tell for sure where the shore ended and the water began.

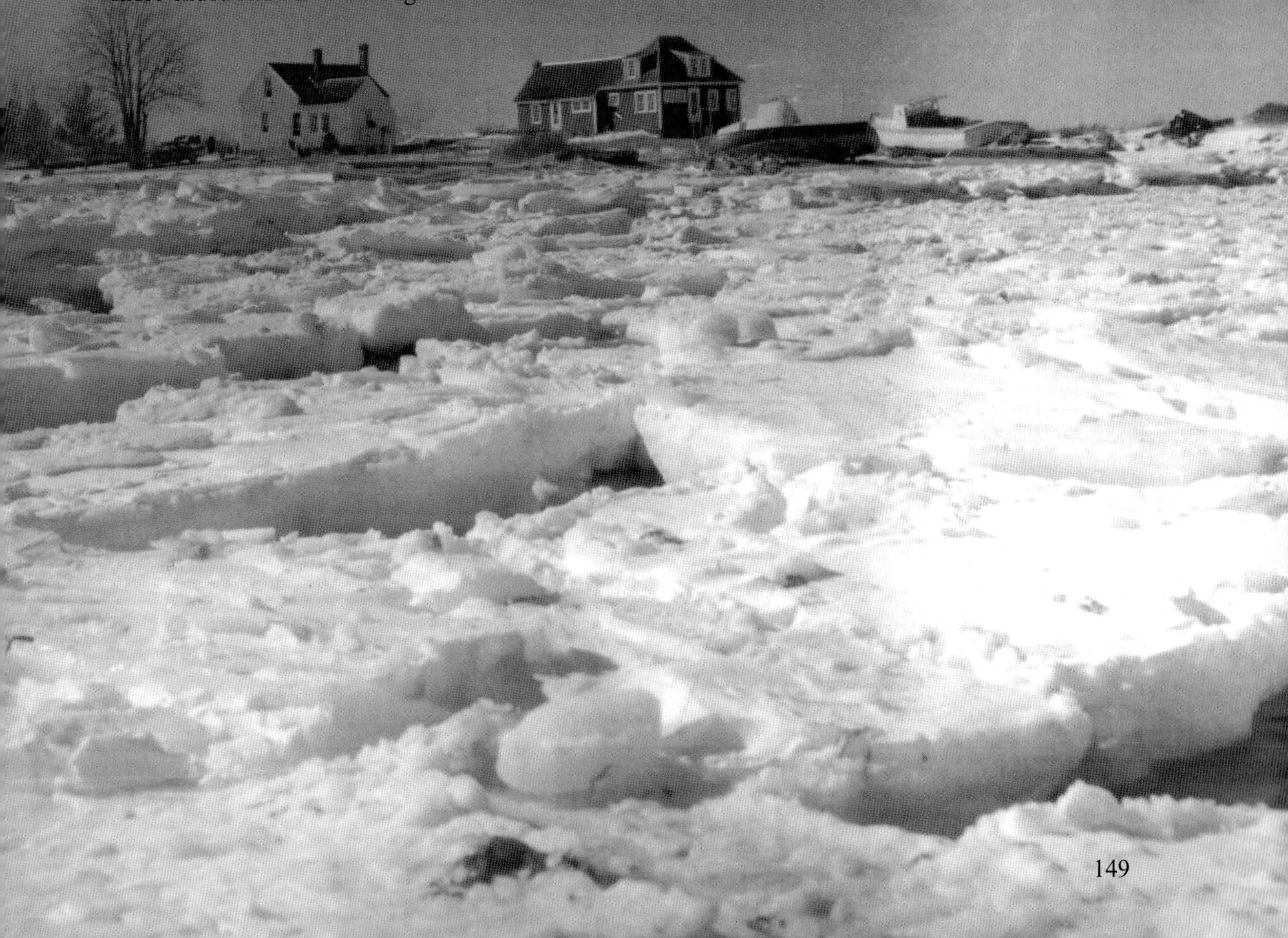

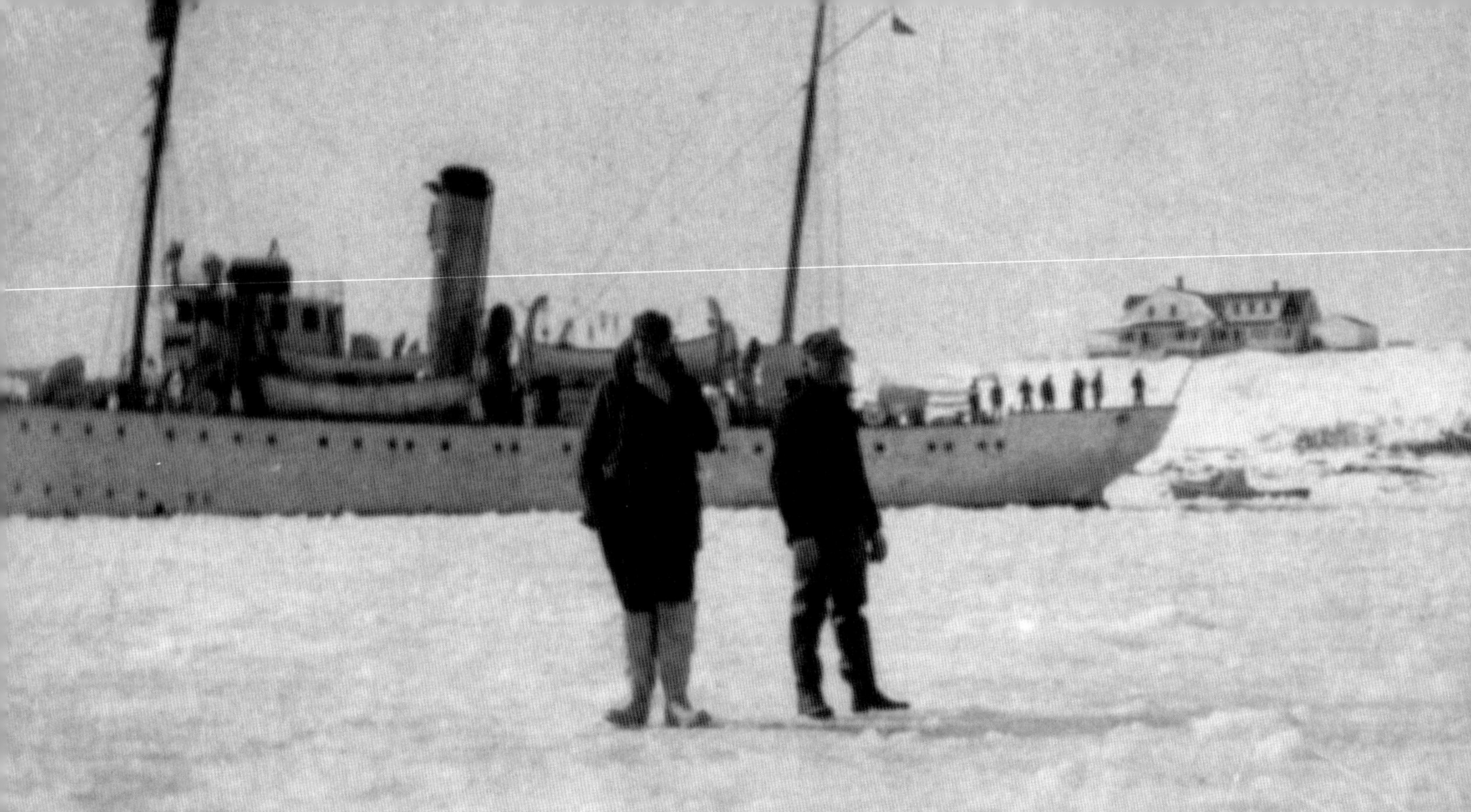

At left: Coast Guard cutter *Ossippee* moored in Mackerel Cove next to the trawler *Fannie Belle*.
Phil Johnson and Muffin Sinnett in foreground—1934.

At right inset is another view of the *Ossippee*.

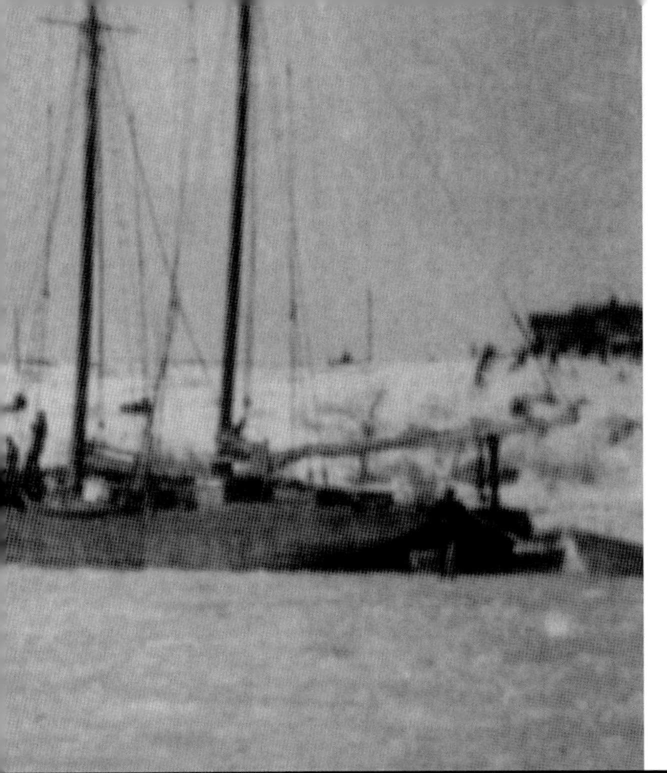

Bill Johnson, resident fisherman of Bailey Island, mentioned the ice storms in an interview for the *Brunswick Times Record* in 1979: "And one winter we got iced in. That were 1917, and the Portland packet-boats couldn't get here. You could walk to Portland that winter, and they went from Seguin to Portland by car acrost the ice! In 1934 the harbor again froze up, but by then they had a Coast Guard cutter to break it up."

Below is Grampy's car during a winter storm.

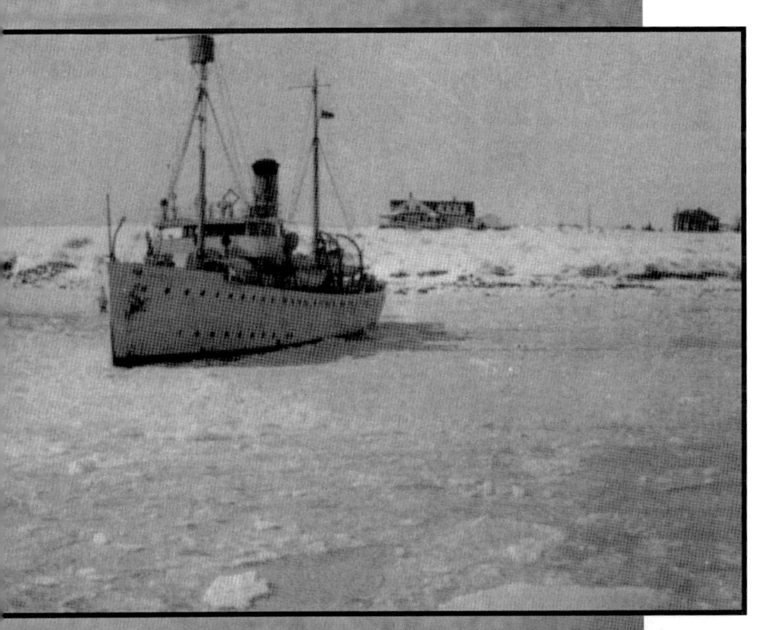

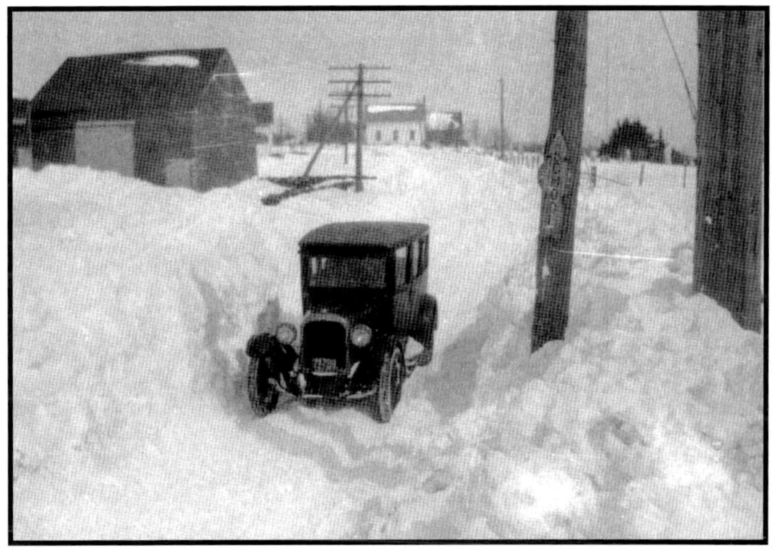

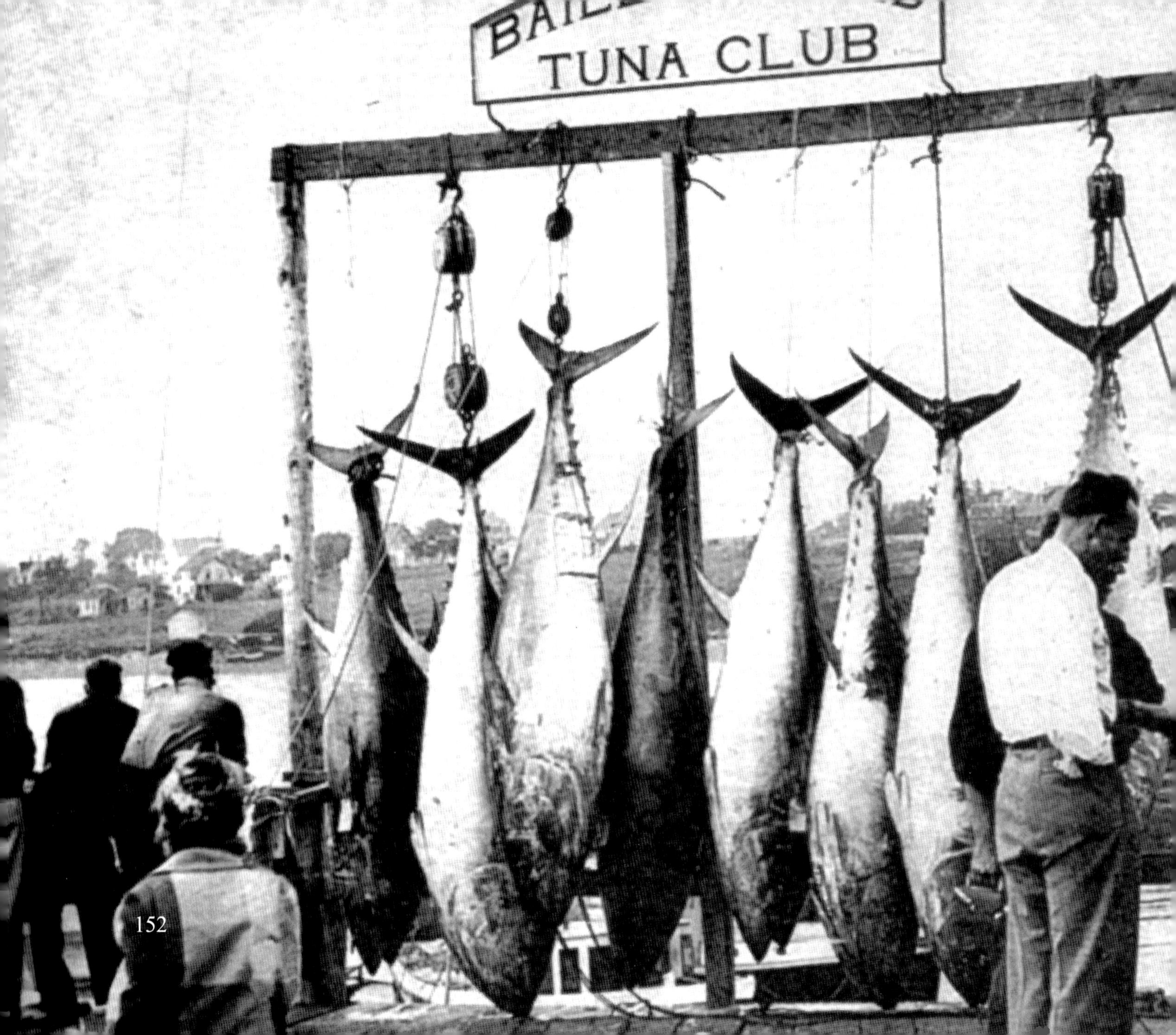
TUNA CLUB

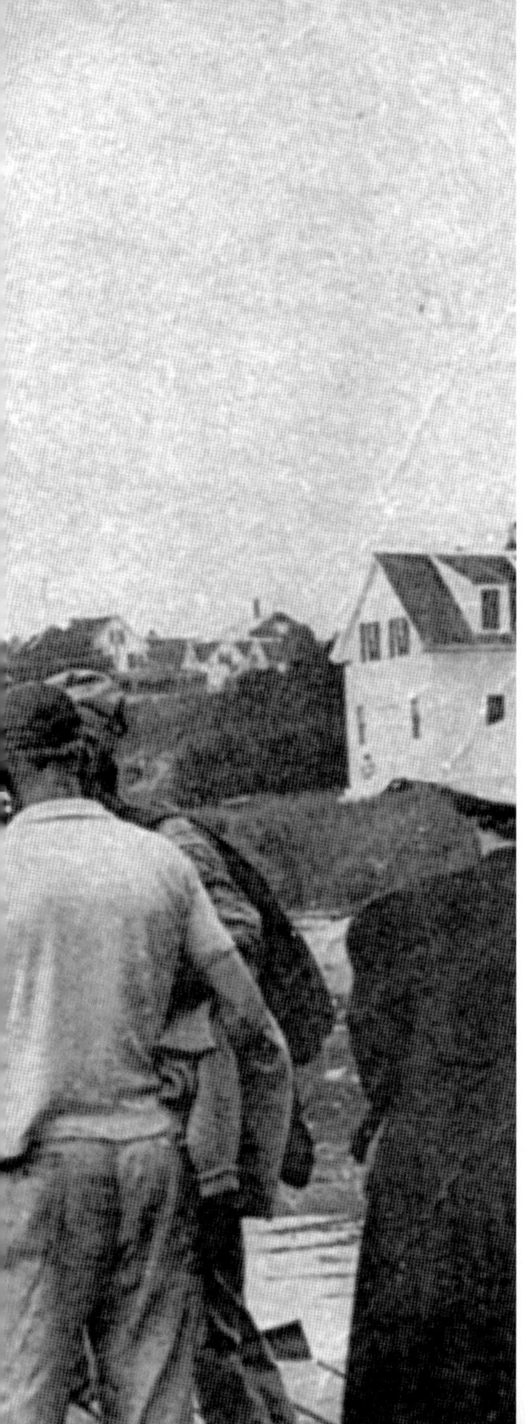

Tuna Fishing

Janet Freeman Baribeau

Tuna fish had very little value during the late 1800's, fish oil being the only marketable part of the fish. The main purpose of going after the big fish, known as horse mackerel, or as the locals called them, "hoss" mackerel, was to decrease their population. The "too-plentiful tuna" would eat schools of mackerel, an important fish to the fishermen's livelihood.

The minimal gear needed, the excitement of the "chase" and the thrill of capturing the big fish made tuna fishing popular with the local men.

A fisherman mending his lobster traps on the shore might spot a tuna coming into the cove. He'd grab his iron, 150 feet of warp (rope) and pole, run for his 10 foot square-ended punt, and shove off from shore. When he'd get close enough to the fish to throw his iron, he'd make the throw and hopefully hook his prize. Then he'd brace his feet for the wild ride around the cove until the fish had become tired enough to be brought into shore where it would be beached.

After the head and tail had been removed, the fish would be cut up into "junks." The people of the island would come to the shore and help themselves to as much of the fish as they wanted. They would usually fry up the fresh tuna steaks or salt down the rest for the cold winter months. The liver and unused portions of the fish would be put into barrels and left to dry in the sun. Later the oil would be drained from the barrels and sold for use in medicines, paint and lubricants.

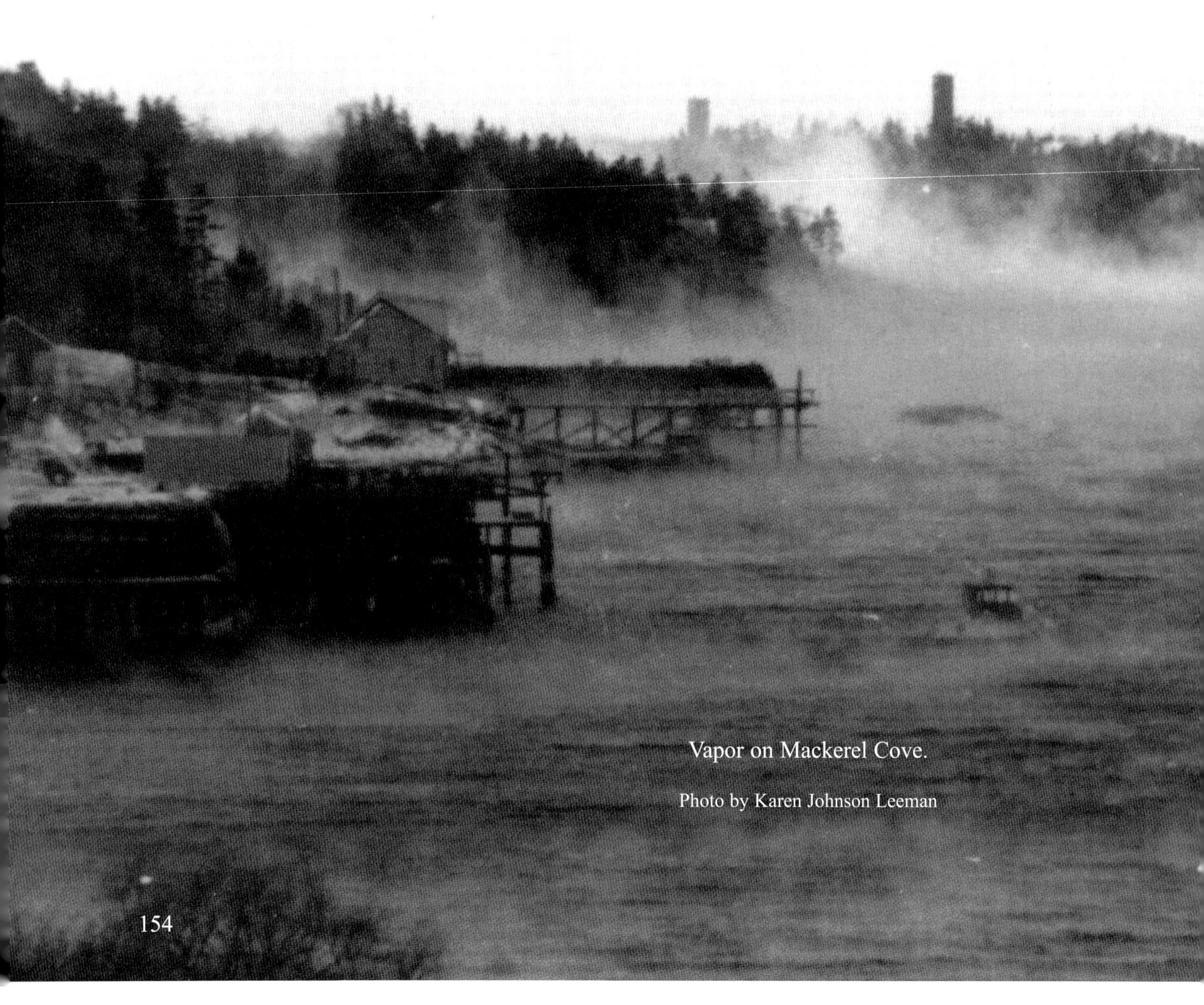

Vapor on Mackerel Cove.

Photo by Karen Johnson Leeman

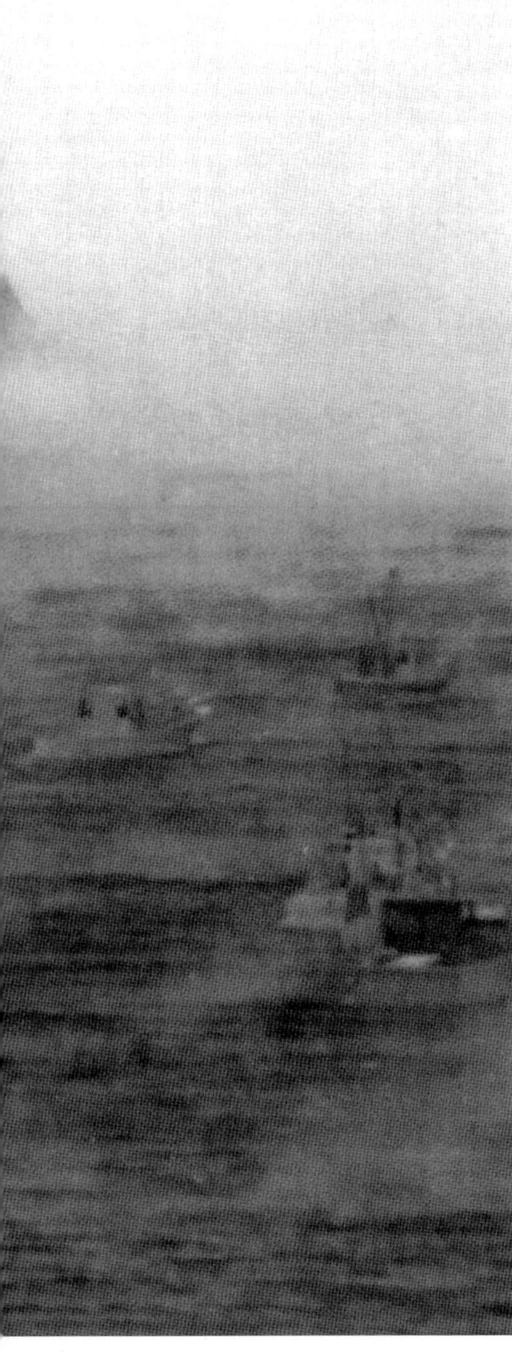

In the late 1930's the young island preacher Jim Herrick, Jesse and Elroy Johnson, brothers, and John Gould, *The Brunswick Record* editor, got together and went to the state capital at Augusta to talk with the appropriate authorities there. The Bailey Island Tuna Club finally got its start.

The first official Tuna Tournament was held in 1939 and attracted 5,000 spectators. Field events, yacht races, swimming and clambakes all added to the excitement and fun of the tournament. There were many concession stands at the head of Mackerel Cove.

One of the favorite sports events of the tournament was the baseball game between the "Old Timers" and the "Youngsters" of Bailey Island. *The Brunswick Record* reported the game.

Rip Black ascended the mound as the Old Timers' pitcher. The Youngsters were about to "face a man who could toss a cod-fish across Mackerel Cove." Rip was also a man who had won the bronze medal for the hammer throw in the 1928 Olympics.

Larry Johnson and Stan Johnson, both close relatives of Rip Black, were two other renowned hammer throwers from Bailey Island.

The State of Maine sponsored the epoch-making Tournament of 1941. Fifty fish, totaling 26,065 pounds, were caught. The largest fish of the tournament was caught by a woman and set a world record. It weighed 818 pounds.

The Tuna Tournament continues to this day and is held in July. Registered boats and fishermen embark from Cook's Wharf at Garrison Cove on Bailey Island and return at the end of the day with their catch. Most of the tuna are sold to the Japanese.

An interesting footnote: Jim Herrick, now in his late 90's, still serves Bailey Island, officiating at many weddings and funerals.

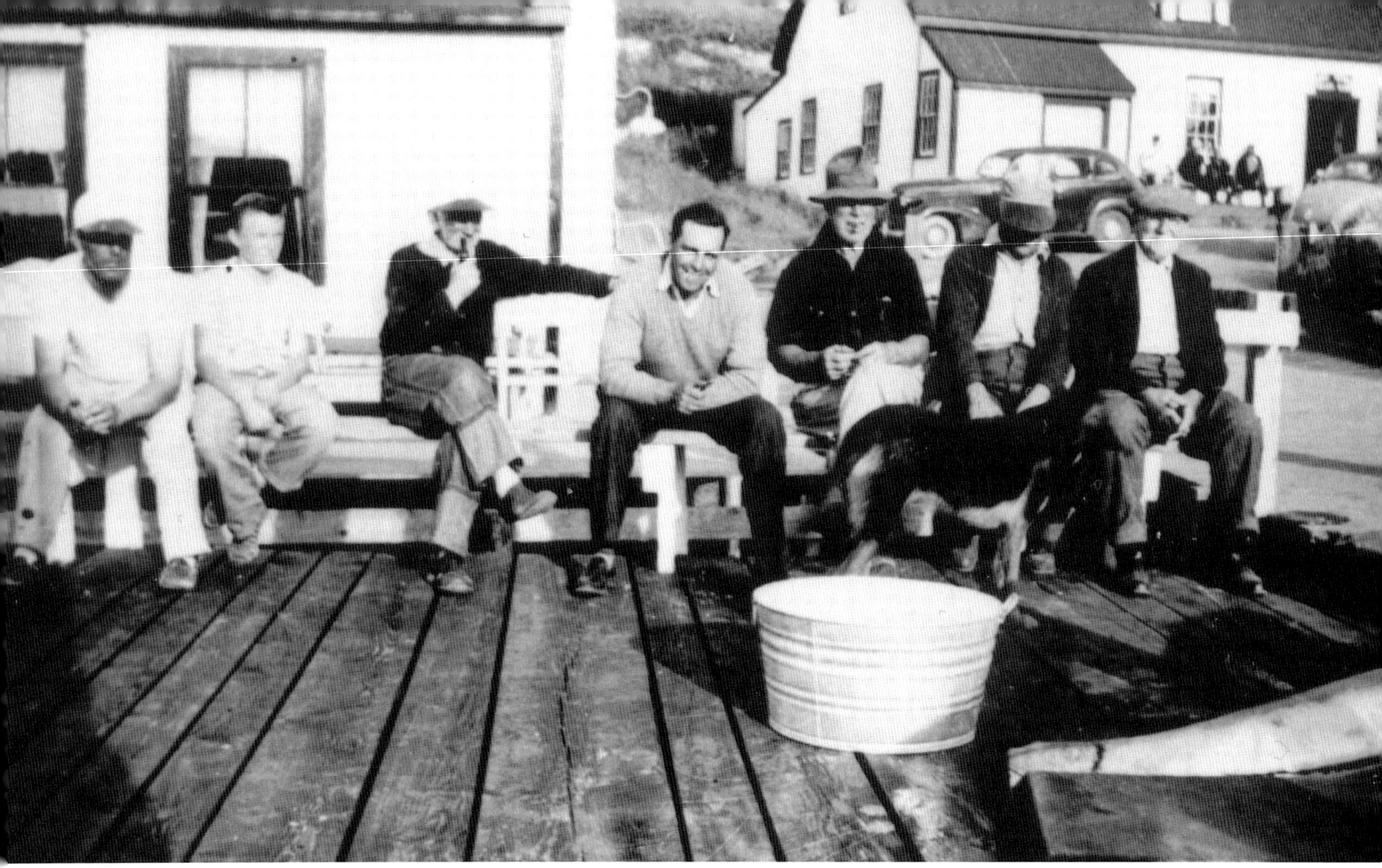

Left to Right: Herman Coombs, Aldie Leeman, Bishy Orr, Link Gardner, Bill Black, Muffin Sinnett, Ernest Gardner.

My mother always laughed when she showed us this picture, taken around 1950. She had been trying to take a photograph of the local men watching the cutting-up of the daily catch of tuna. As she stepped back she rubbed up against the tuna and got all bloody, causing quite the laughter from the fishermen!

Tip Top, the house still standing on one of the highest points of Bailey Island, was built around 1890.

Photo by Karin Jensen Sammons

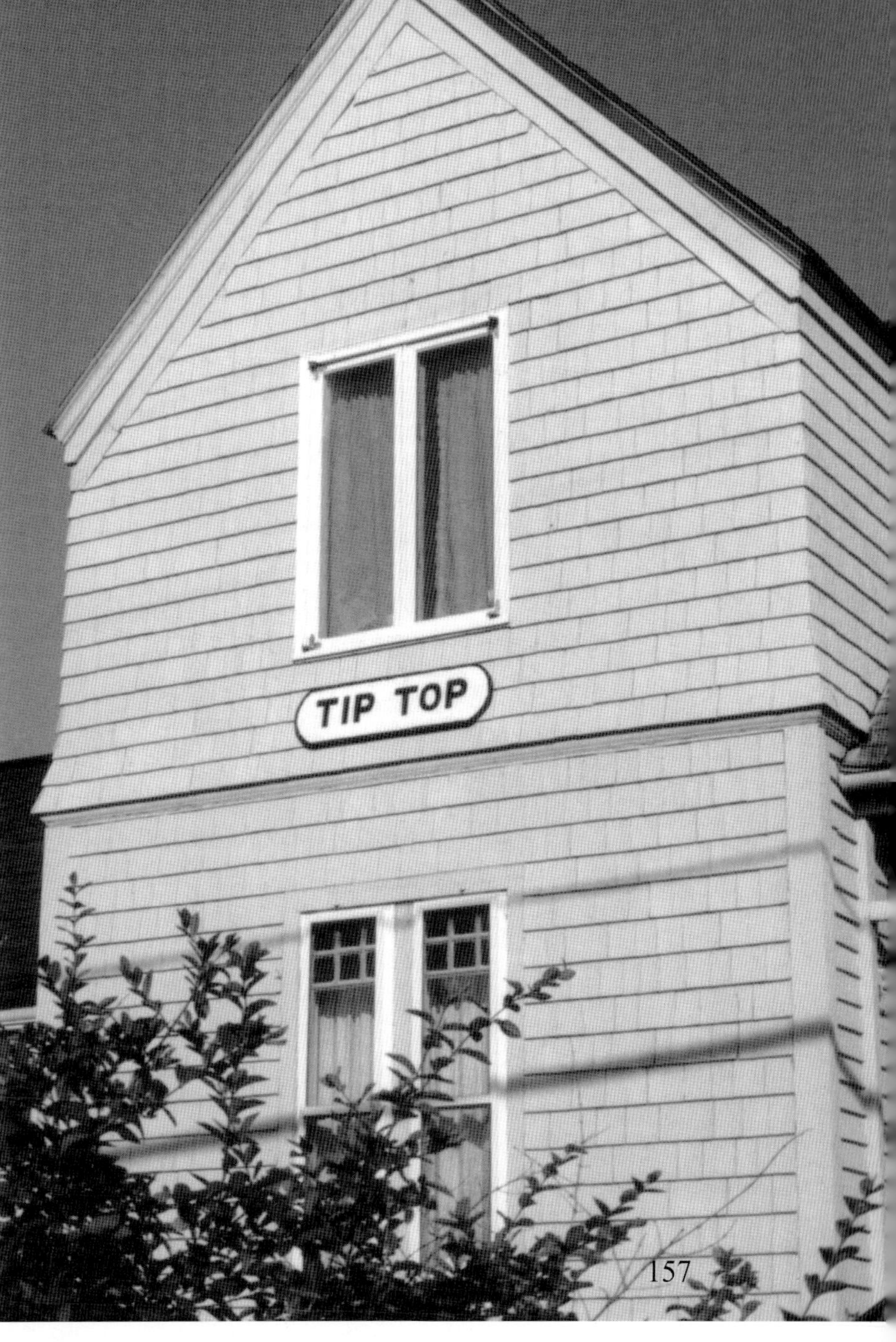

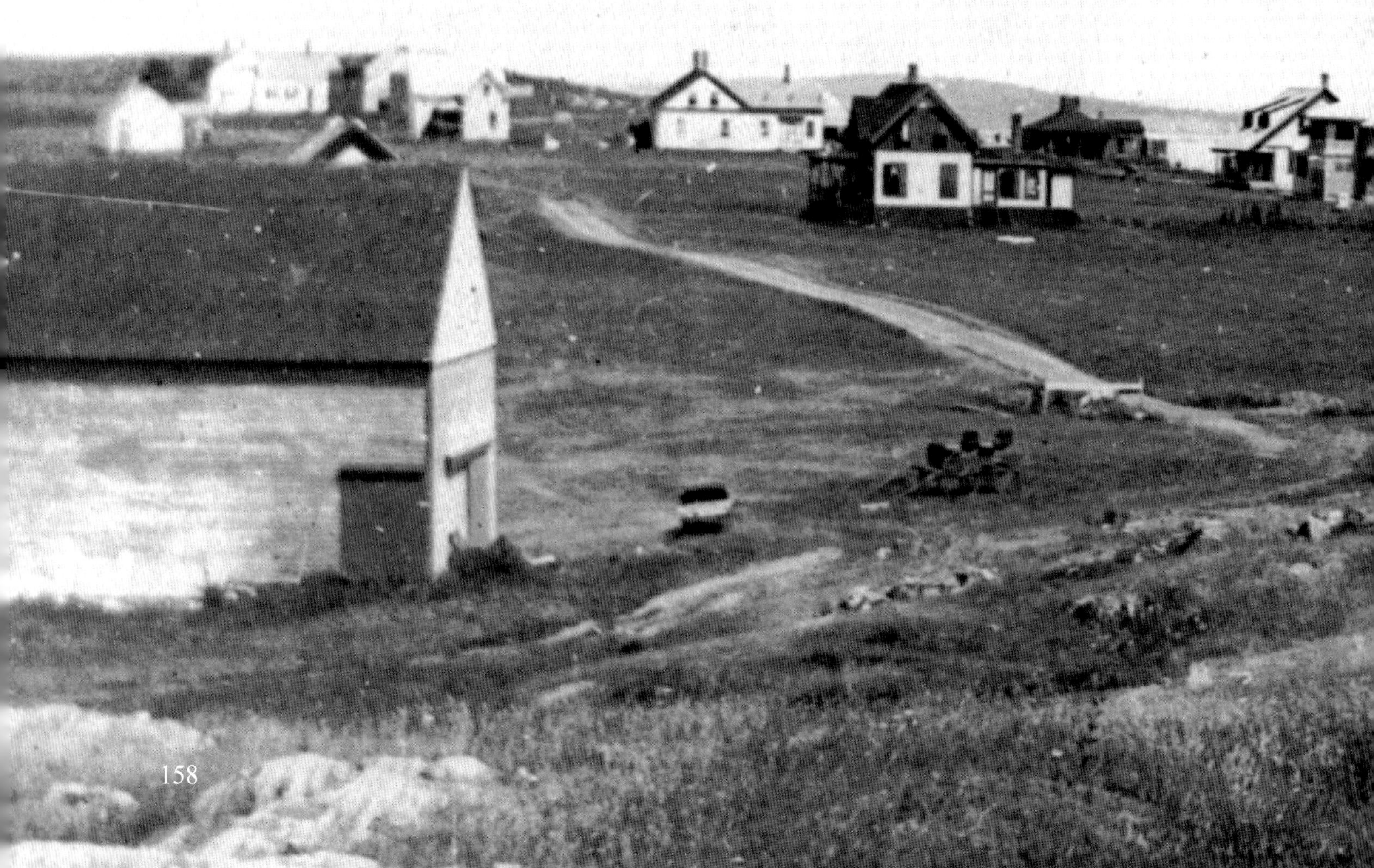

From Tip Top, looking north along Sea Bank. Perry Sinnett makes deliveries in his wagon—1887.

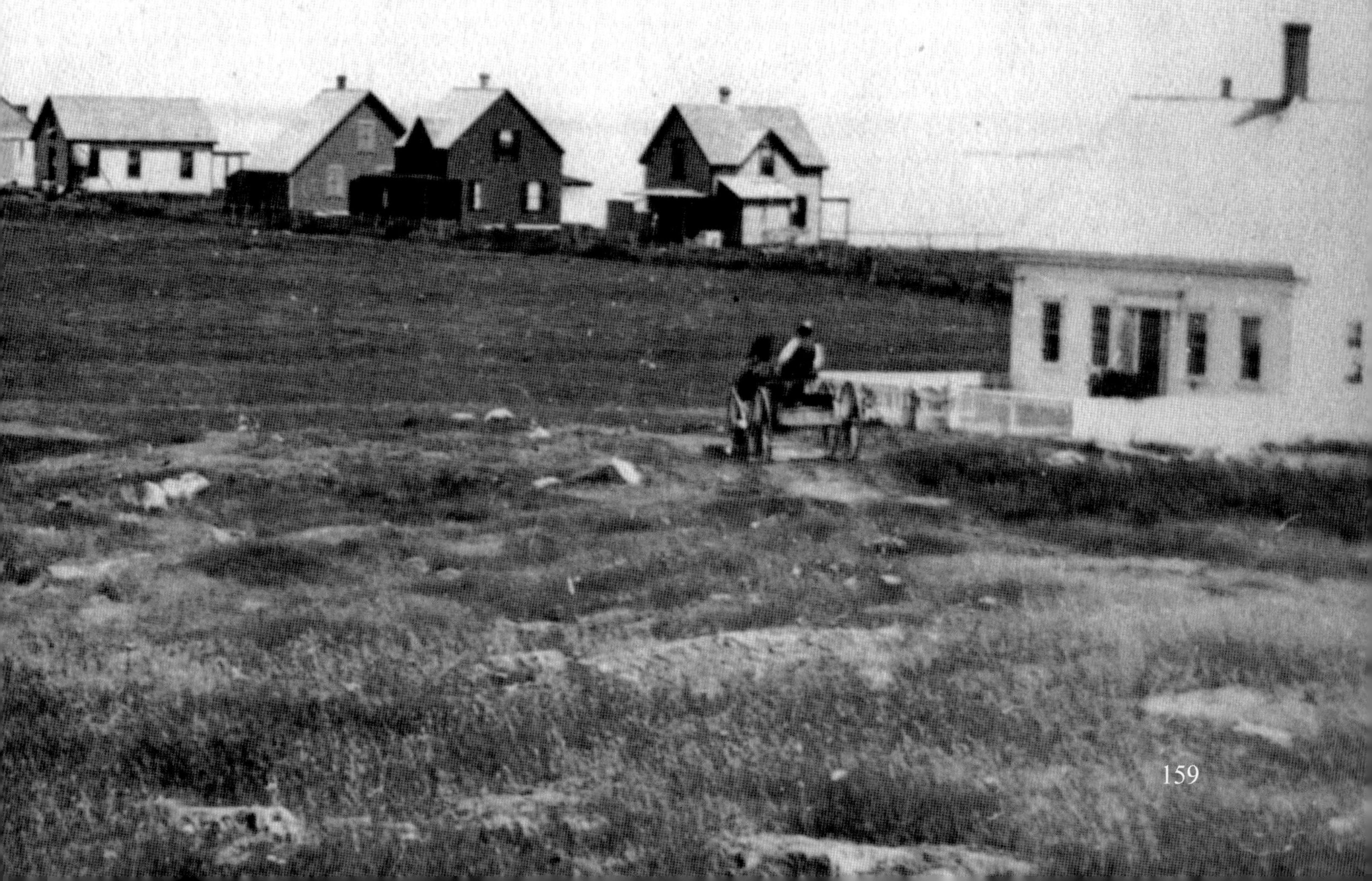

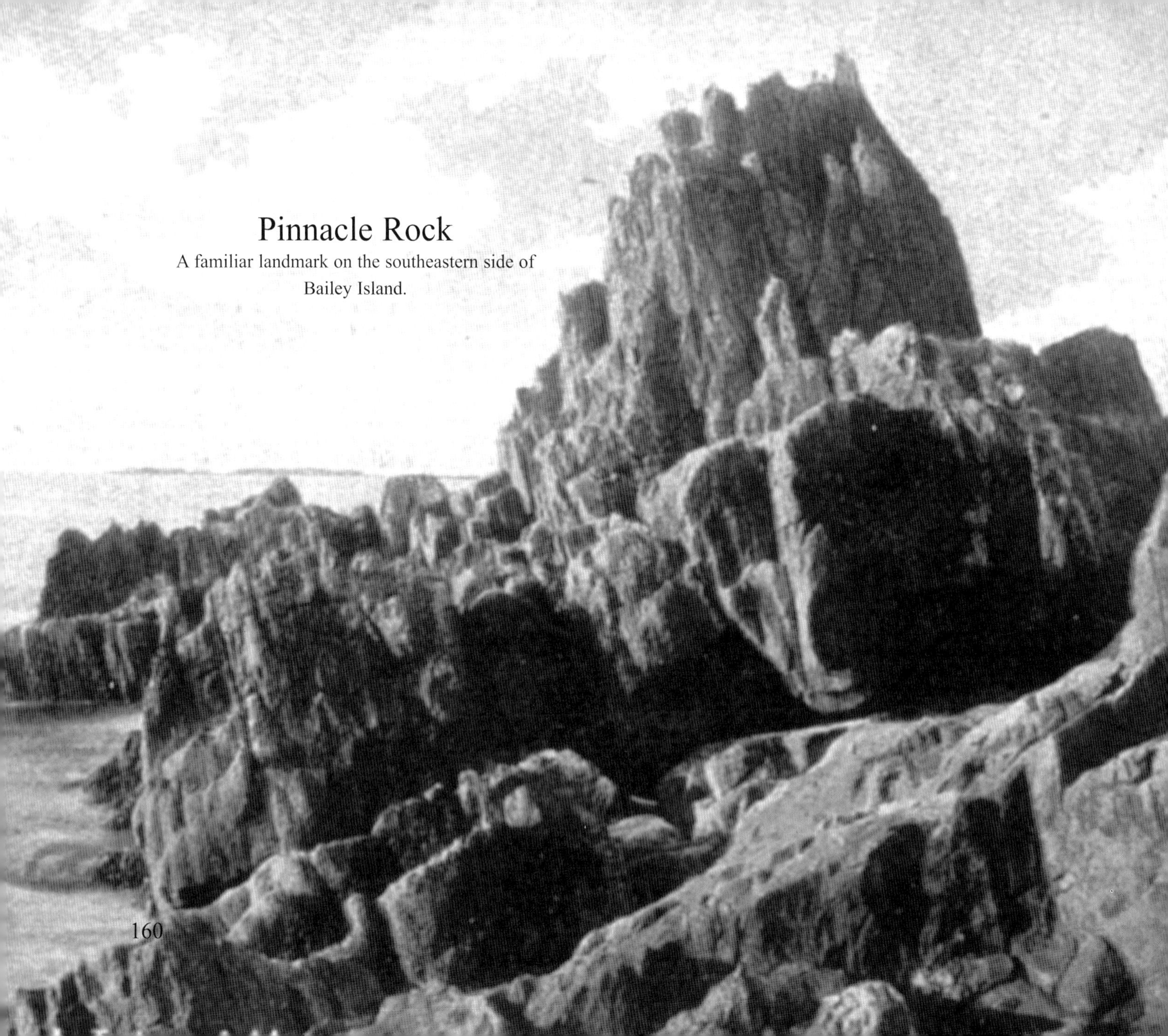

Pinnacle Rock

A familiar landmark on the southeastern side of Bailey Island.

Giant Stairs (The Devil's Stairway)

Giant Stairs, located on the southeastern shore of the island are steps cut evenly by nature out of the solid cliff. At low tide all of the steps are exposed. The land around this picturesque site was a gift to the public by Captain Henry Sinnett.

Sinnett, a lifelong resident of Bailey Island, was a very active and colorful man of the island. He was well known among the summer residents; many photos and postcards were taken of him. His involvement in affairs of the island included securing the original grant for the Bailey-Orr's Island Bridge from the State Legislature.

Captain Sinnett owned a large piece of land on the southeastern side of the island. He sold a number of cottage lots there. With the increased tourist trade, hotels and boarding houses had to be built to accommodate those without cottages.

"When Captain Henry Sinnett sold cottage lots in this area, he did not convey land to the water, but reserved a strip which he later conveyed to the town for the use of the public. This means that anyone can enjoy the surf and scenery without trespassing on other people's property."

—*Brunswick Times Record*, 1978

The Giant Stairs is a favorite spot for people wanting to witness the ocean's power and to see the surf as it breaks on the ledges below.

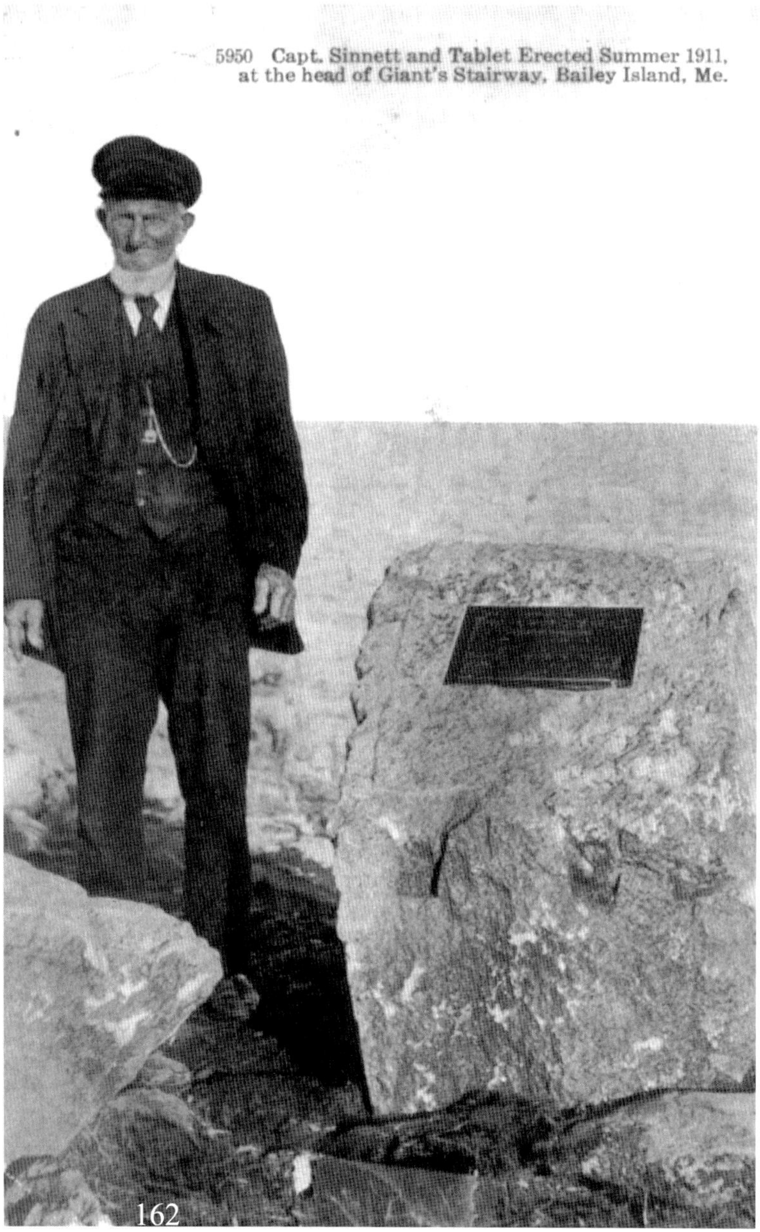

5950 Capt. Sinnett and Tablet Erected Summer 1911, at the head of Giant's Stairway, Bailey Island, Me.

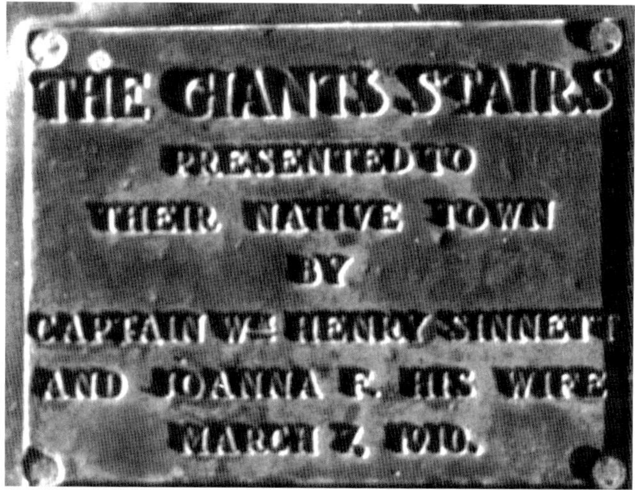

Captain Sinnett's gift is commemorated by a bronze plaque set in a rock at the top of the Giant Stairs.

At left: Captain Henry Sinnett—1911.

The Nubble—some say the most photographed fish shack on the coast of Maine.

Photo by Nancy Jensen

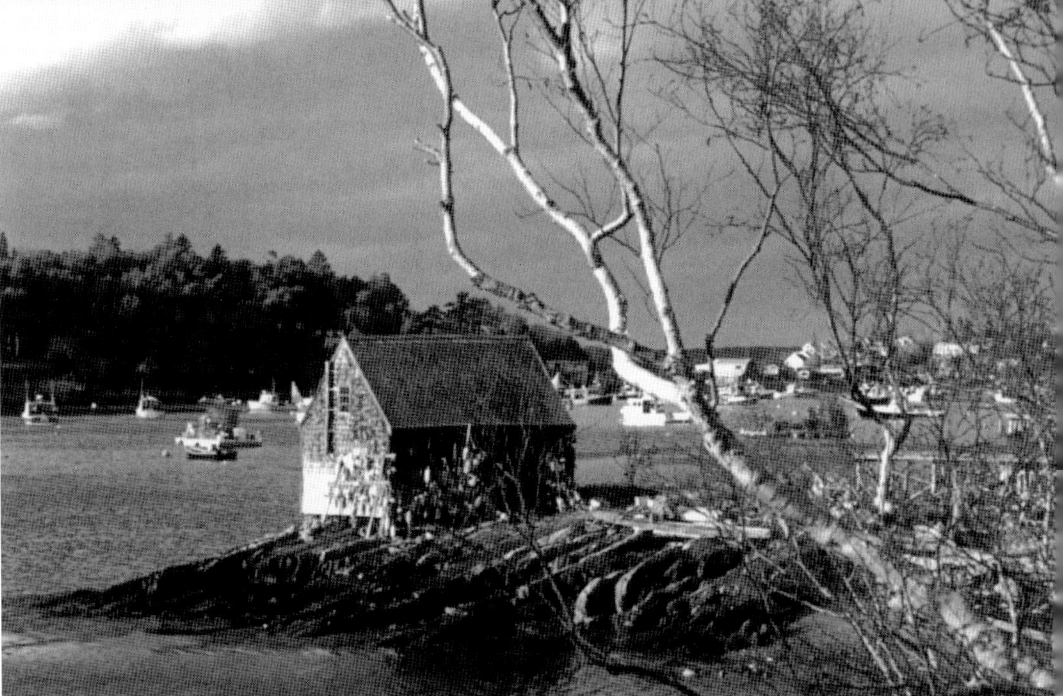

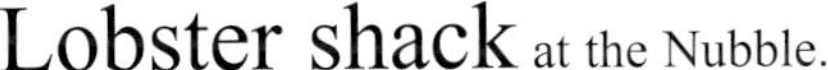

Lobster shack at the Nubble.

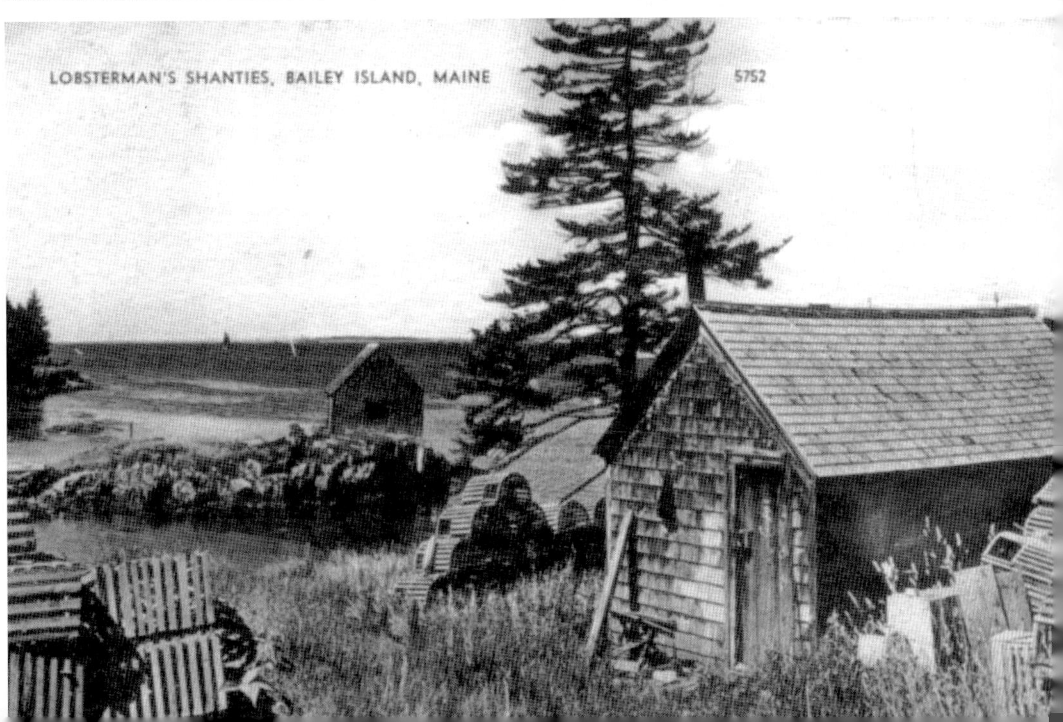

As youngsters on Bailey Island we rarely left the island, so we had to entertain ourselves. One of our regular activities in the summer was to walk to **Land's End**, the southern tip of Bailey Island. There we could get a good look at all the "highlanders" who drove down to view the ocean and walk along the shore. It was our window to the world. Then we'd head for the back shore to look for garnets—deep red semiprecious stones—attached to the ledges. Below is a little gift shop at Land's End. Note the sea foam covering the beach left from a storm.

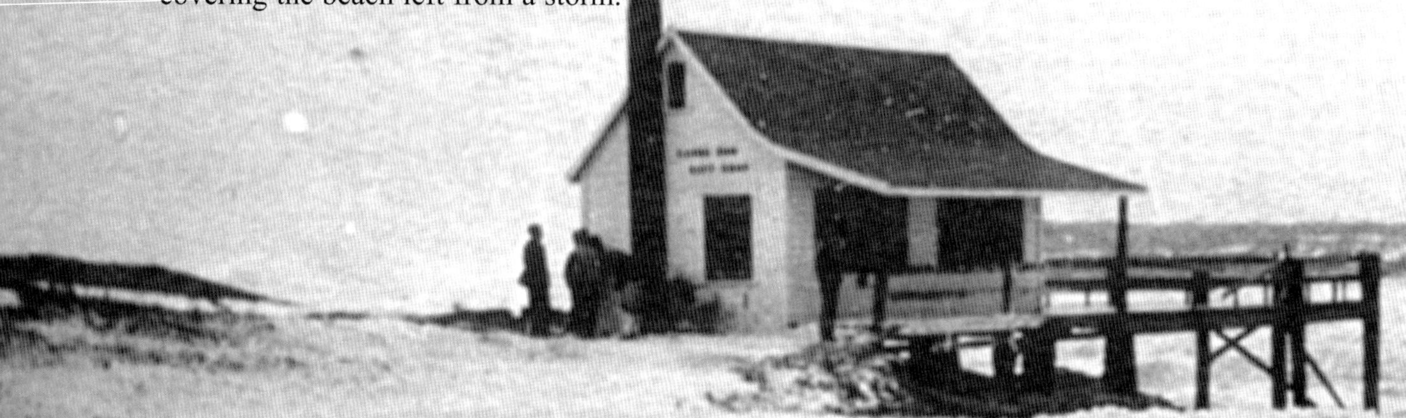

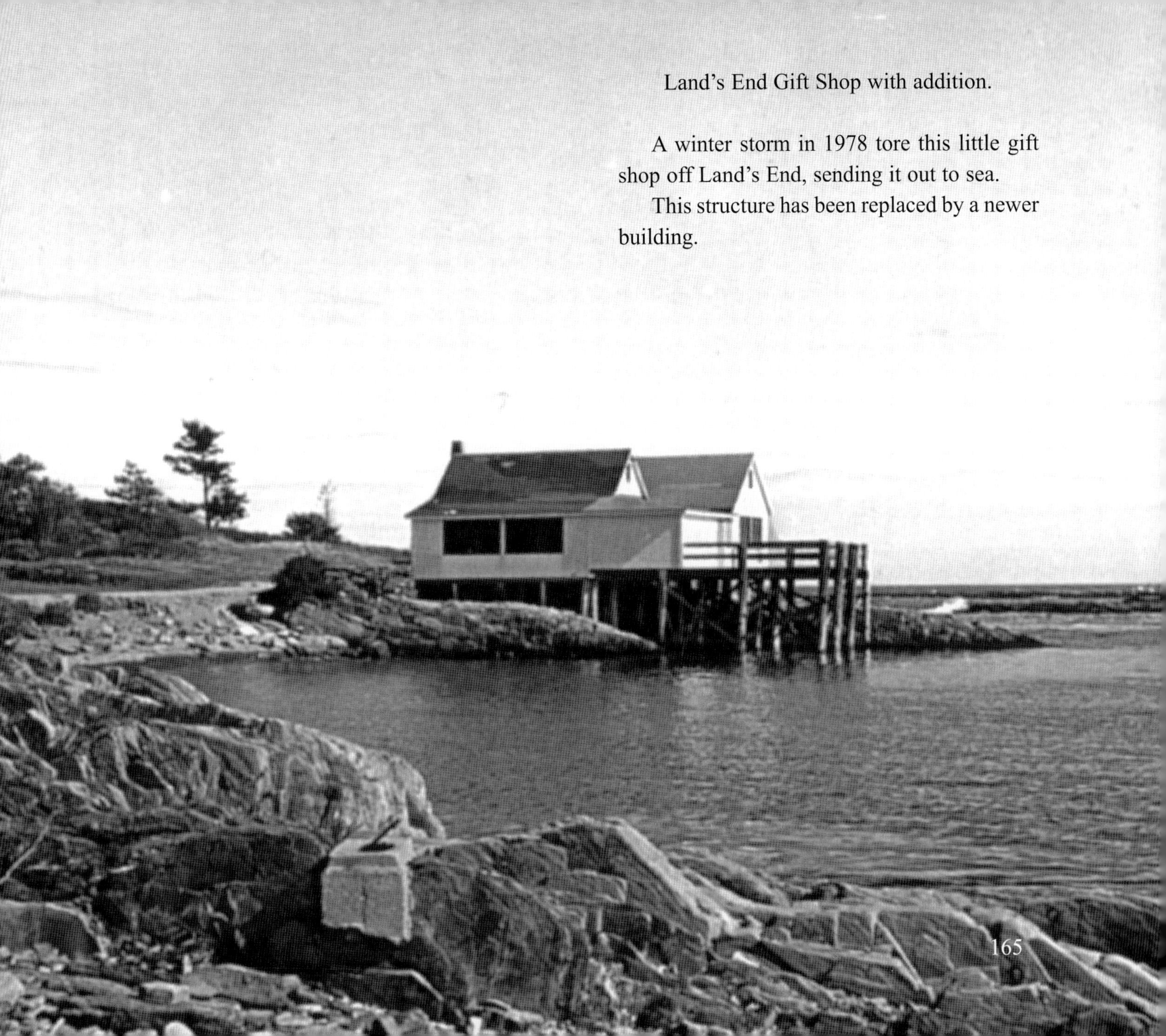

Land's End Gift Shop with addition.

A winter storm in 1978 tore this little gift shop off Land's End, sending it out to sea.

This structure has been replaced by a newer building.

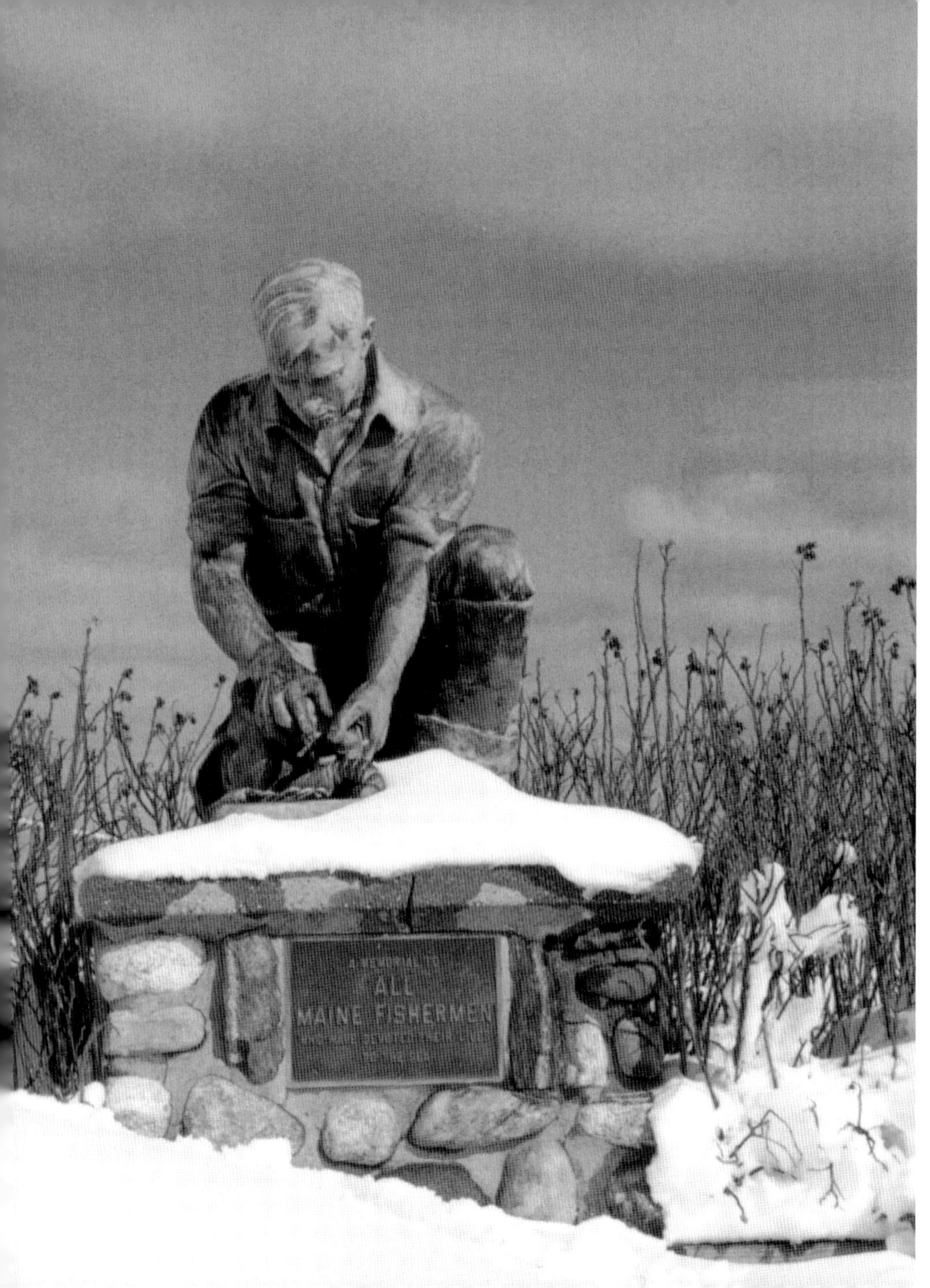

H. Elroy "Snood" Johnson, a resident fisherman of Bailey Island, was a model for a statue sculpted for the 1939 World's Fair. One replica is in Washington, D. C. on Maine Avenue; and another at the Civic Plaza in Portland, Maine. A bronze version was made for Land's End on Bailey Island.

The Plaque reads:

A Memorial to
ALL MAINE FISHERMEN
who have devoted their lives
to the sea.

Photo by Nancy Jensen

Bailey Island Towers

In 1942 the U. S. Navy and Army came to Bailey Island and built two towers for surveillance; one to watch for offshore boats, submarines, and planes, the other to watch for blasts from guns on islands off the coast. The service men lived in barracks near the towers. Local houses were used as living quarters for the military officers. A cable was laid under water, running from Bailey Island to Halfway Rock, used to detect any boat or submarine going over it.

Both abandoned military towers still stand on Bailey Island near Land's End. Many times as children we sneaked inside to climb the narrow stairs to the top to catch a wonderful view of the bay and surrounding islands.

We were not supposed to trespass because this was government property. The towers were boarded up, so to get in we had to roll logs over to the windows, climb up, and squeeze through the narrow opening. After the war Esther Adams bought the property, including the towers, and built a home, which her family still owns and returns to in the summer.

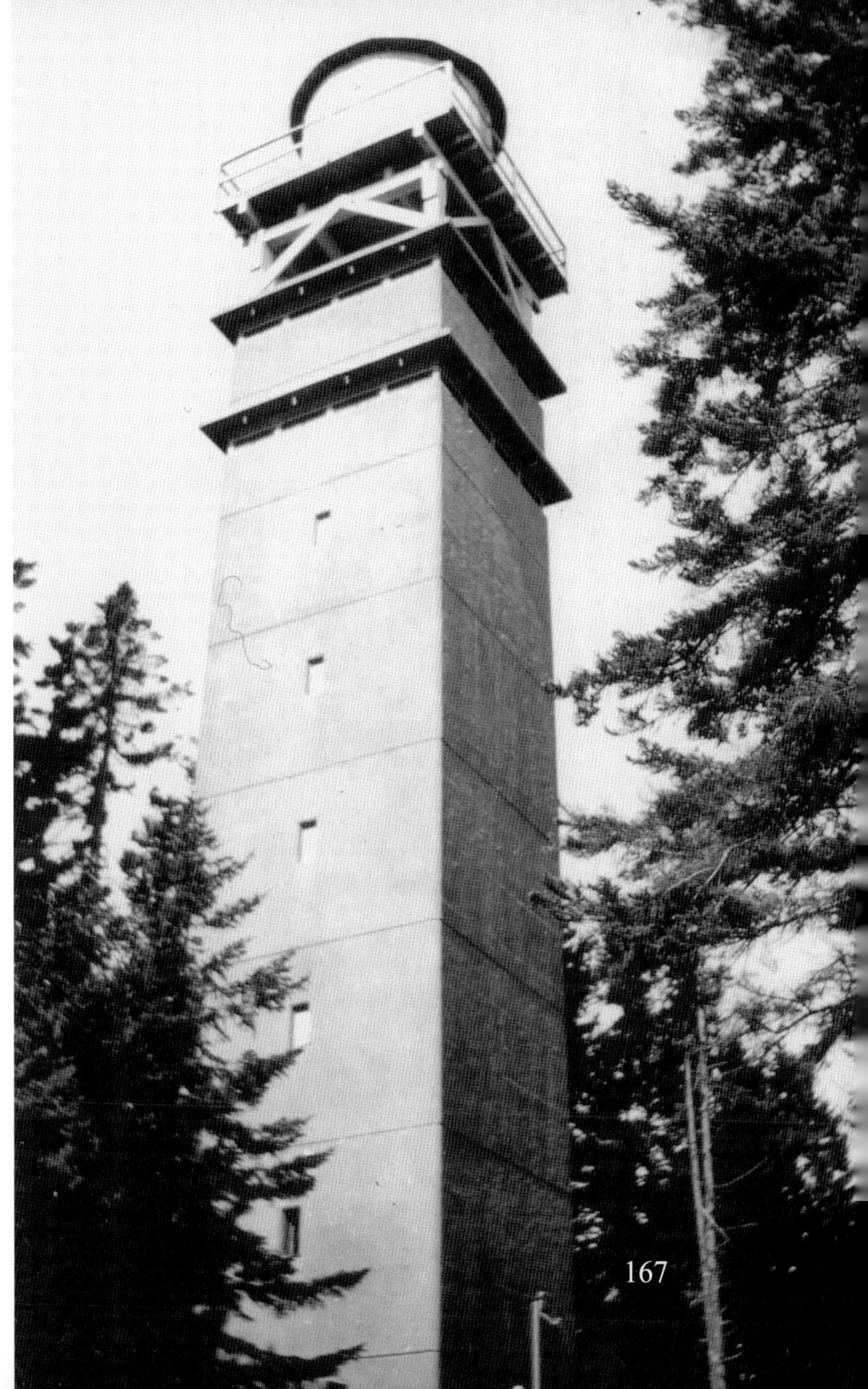

Offshore

The main island road, Route 24, abruptly comes to a halt at Land's End, at the southern end of Bailey Island. From this point, looking south, you can see Jaquish Island, Turnip Island, Mark Island and Halfway Rock. Looking east you can see Ragged Island and Pond Island.

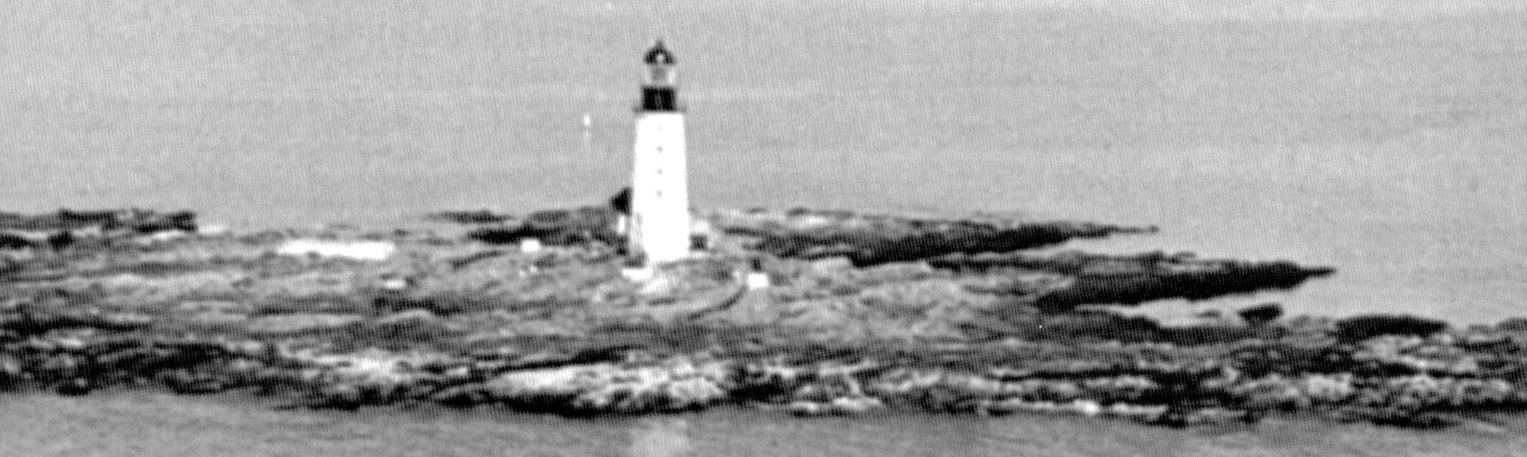

Halfway Rock—looking south from Land's End, four and a half miles out from Bailey Island, located halfway between Cape Small and Cape Elizabeth. The light was first turned on in 1871.

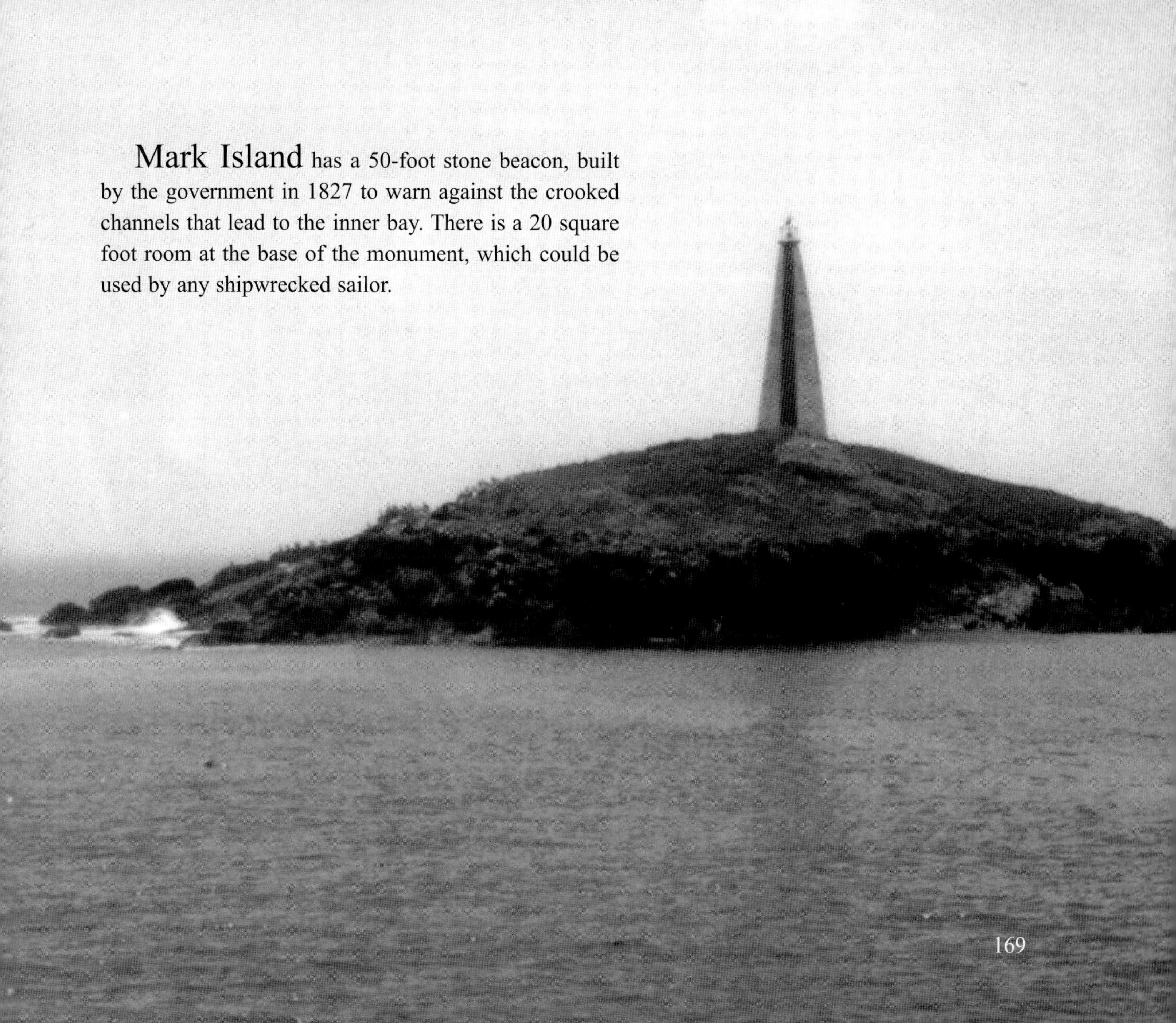

Mark Island has a 50-foot stone beacon, built by the government in 1827 to warn against the crooked channels that lead to the inner bay. There is a 20 square foot room at the base of the monument, which could be used by any shipwrecked sailor.

Jaquish Island is across the narrow strait of water at Land's End. It is named for Captain Richard Jaquish, who, during the French and Indian War, led the island men from Casco Bay in the expedition against the French at Louisbourg, Nova Scotia.

Memories of Jaquish Island

Janet Freeman Baribeau

My mother, Celina Freeman, remembers Jaquish Island and conjures up images of puntloads of fellow classmates and their teacher, Margaret Skillings, rowing out to Jaquish Island for their year-end Bailey Island School Picnic.

"We would come ashore on the beach at Jaquish and not a cooler or picnic basket was in sight. Margaret hand-carried a canvas bag that held her cast-iron frying pan, a few cooking utensils, flour and grease. A green 5-gallon army surplus metal can, with a good carrying handle, held their drinking water for the day. Lots of small bag lunches, a couple of galvanized buckets and a few clam hoes emptied the punts of their cargo.

"First thing we'd all do is go along the shore and gather up driftwood until we had a good-sized wood-pile. Margaret and the boys would build a small rock fireplace and get a good hot fire going. Us kids would start taking turns with the clam hoes.

"Each one of us would dig a dozen or so clams, then pass the clam hoe on to the next in line. You would take the clams you'd dug, clean and shell them, and bring them over to where Margaret had set up quarters on a ledge next to the fire.

"First she'd dip the clams in a little egg wash and then drop them into the flour mixture in her cheesecloth bag. She'd gently shake the bag, coating the clams with a fine layer of egg 'n flour. Then she'd drop the clams, one-by-one, into the hot grease of the old black cast-iron frying pan. Each addition would pop, sputter, and spatter as the freshly dug clams hit the hot fat. The child who had dug the clams she was frying at the time, patiently stood by waiting for his or her clams to be cooked and ready to eat. This process would go on until each of the kids had a chance to eat the clams that they had dug, cleaned and shelled.

"I can still see Margaret to this day, sitting there on the ledge, with her dress spread out around her, frying clams for all us kids."

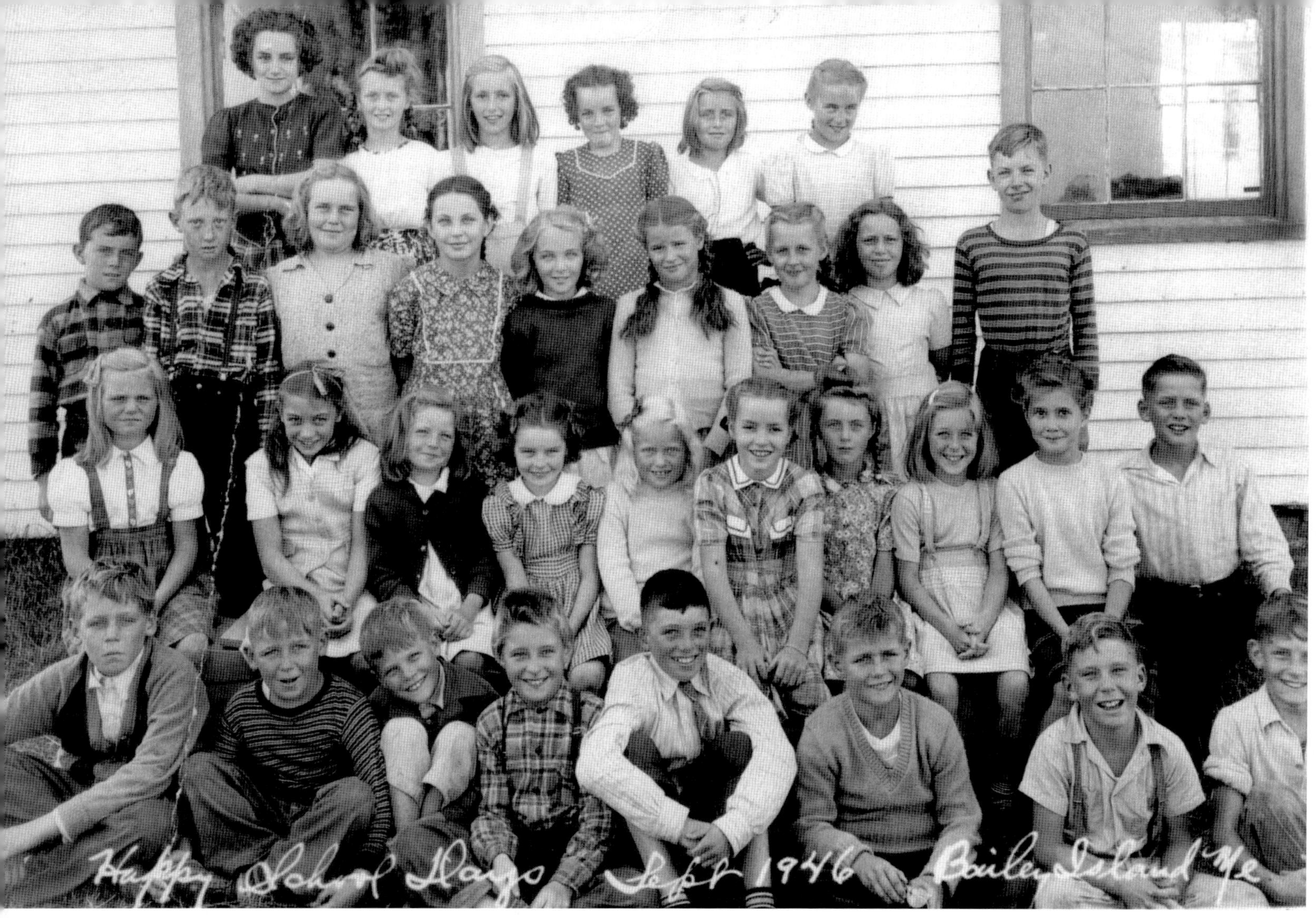

Bailey Island Students-1946: Front row, left to right: Billy Dunlap, Edwin Dunlap, Oliver O'Neill, Wayne Johnson, Don Rogers, Jerry Leeman, Richard Crowe, "Bump" Orr. Second Row, left to right: me, Sandra Williams, Sandra Stevens, Jackie Williams, Janet Freeman, Judy Harris, Shirley Shea, Donna Leeman, Yvonne Sylvester, Bucky Swan. Third row, left to right: Russell Wilson, Alfred Perry, Evelyn Moody, Doreen Cotter, Mary Crowley, Alice Herrick, Lucille Snow, Ruth M. Johnson, Robert Stevens. Back row, left to right: Carol Thurston, Patricia Shea, Ruth V. Johnson, Glennis Reid, Madelyn Stilphen, Lorraine Snow.

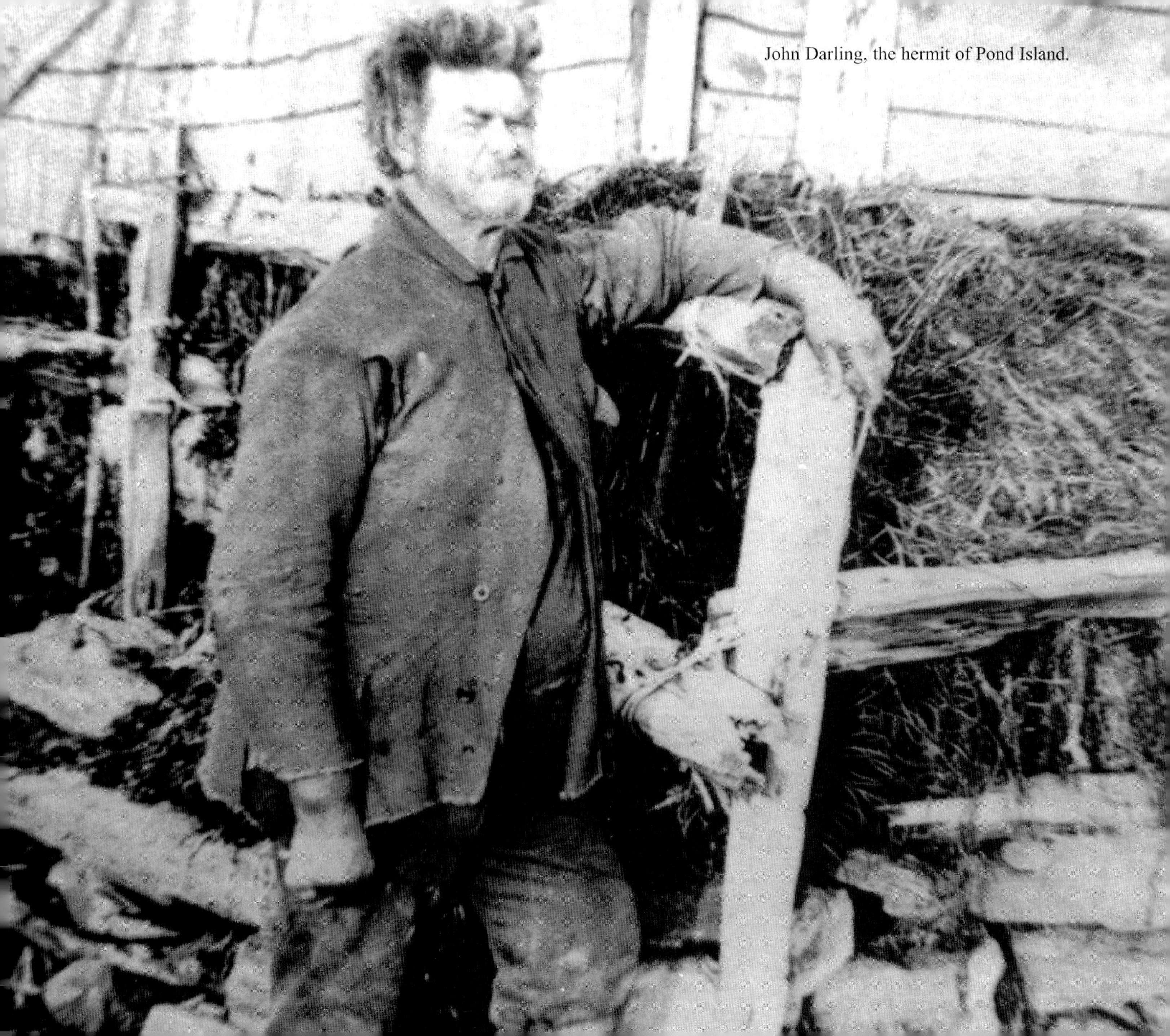

John Darling, the hermit of Pond Island.

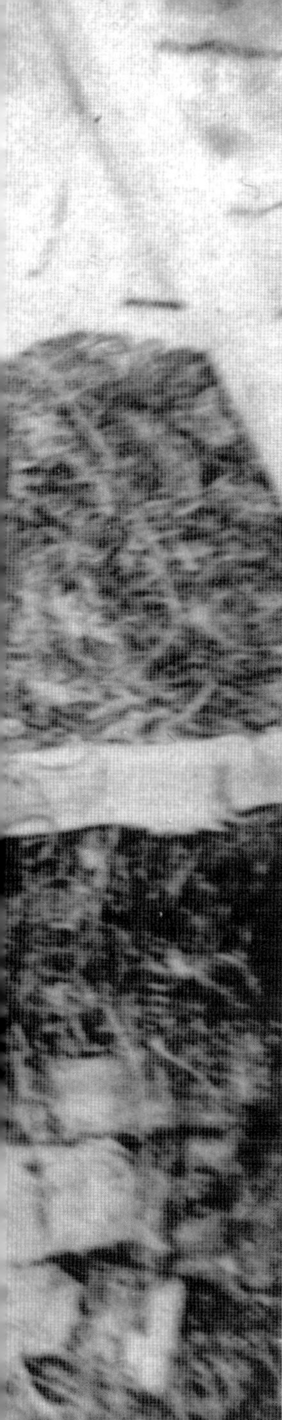

Pond Island lies just east of Bailey Island. It was once believed that pirates had buried silver, gold and jewels on Pond Island. Stories have also been told about strange noises and lights occurring on the island that some say can only be attributed to supernatural causes. The famous poet and professor at Bowdoin College, Robert Peter Tristam Coffin, once owned Pond Island.

There are several accounts about John Darling who lived as a hermit on Pond Island for many years in the early 1900's. One such account states that he was considered an undesirable citizen by the Town of Harpswell and therefore condemned to Pond Island. There were no trees on Pond Island, and the only fresh water came when it rained. John Darling had to build his shack from driftwood, traps, or any scraps of wood that might show up on the shore. He lived on lobsters, crabs, and clams he caught as well as seagulls he trapped. The same citizens who condemned him also supplied him with some necessities such as clothing and basic cooking supplies. In the summer tourists naturally became very curious about this man who survived against all odds, living alone, marooned on an island. They took excursions to Pond Island and gave him gifts of tobacco and other luxuries. When winter came he did not see another human for months, but managed to survive in the cold, northeast weather. Some say he eventually froze to death on Pond Island.

The town records show quite a different story. John Darling lived on Pond Island with his family. He was employed at Prince's Wharf on Orr's Island in the summertime. He helped unload cargo from fishing vessels and assisted with salting down fish. He rowed his children to school in his dory to Orr's Island. His wife became very ill, so the family had to be separated. Darling died in a Portland hospital in 1918 at age 68. Those who knew him said he was extremely strong and self-sufficient.

Ragged Island

Edna St. Vincent Millay

There, there where those black spruces crowd
To the edge of the precipitous cliff,
Above your boat, under the eastern wall of the island;
And no wave breaks; as if
All had been done, and long ago, that needed
Doing; and the cold tide, unimpeded
By shoal of shelving ledge, moves up and down,
Instead of in and out;
And there is no driftwood there, because there is no beach;
Clean cliff going down as deep as clear water can reach;

No driftwood, such as abounds on the roaring stove;
Barrels, banged ashore about the boiling outer harbor;
Lobster buoys on the eel-grass of the sheltered cove;

There, thought unbraids itself, and the mind becomes single.

There, you row with tranquil oars, and the ocean
Shows no scar from the cutting of your placid keel;
Care becomes senseless there; pride and promotion
Remote; you only look; you scarcely feel.

Even adventure, with its vital uses,
Is aimless ardor now; and thrift is waste.

Oh, to be there, under the silent spruces,
Where the tide, quiet evening darkens without haste
Over a sea with death acquainted, yet forever chaste.

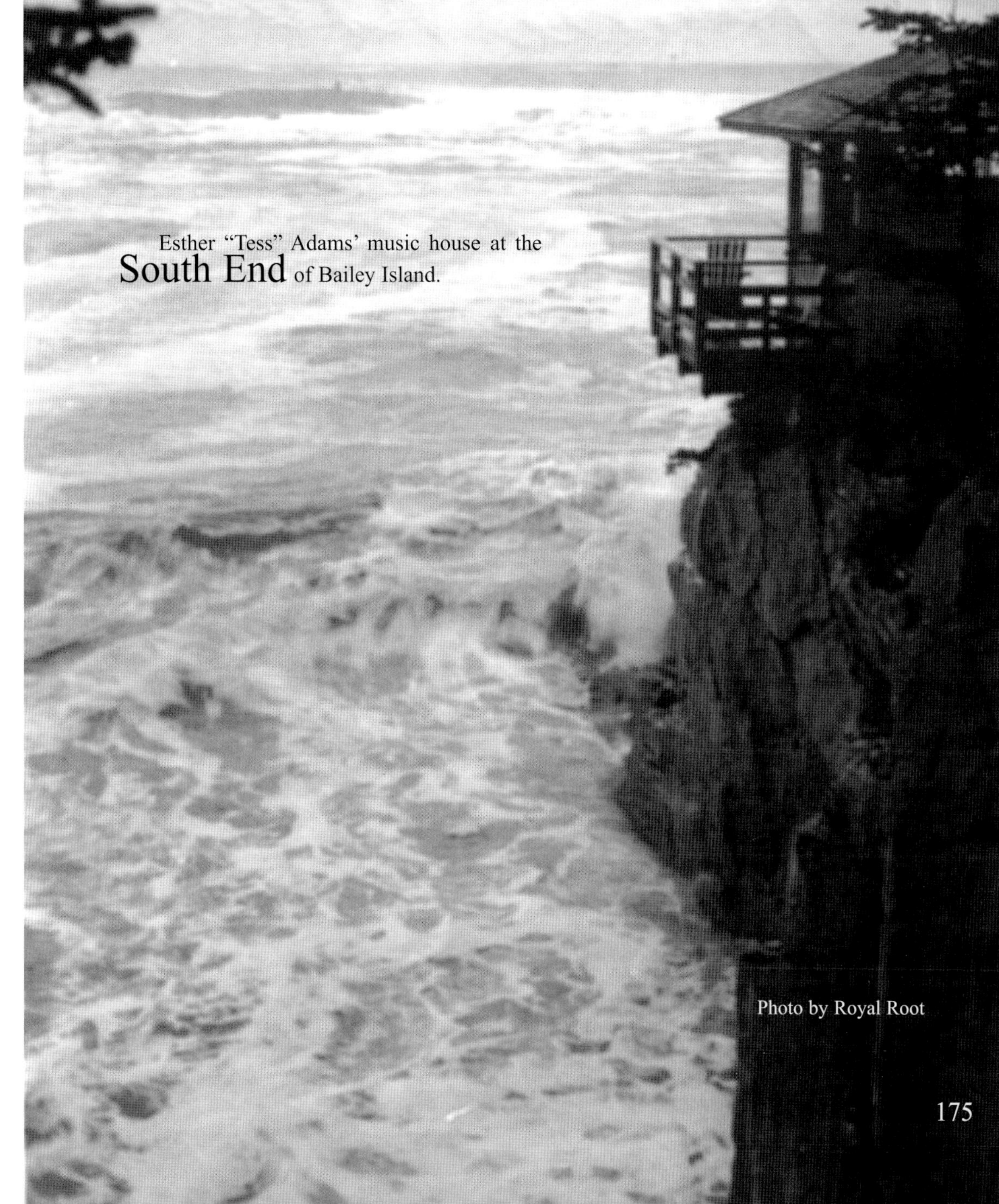

Esther "Tess" Adams' music house at the South End of Bailey Island.

Photo by Royal Root

Ragged Island, a wooded island over two and a half miles east of Bailey Island, was called Rugged Island on a 1780 chart of Casco Bay. The famous Harpswell citizen, Reverend Elijah Kellogg, often went out to Ragged Island, and there he was inspired to write the Elm Island series of boy's books.

For seventeen years Ragged Island was the summer home of the famed poet, Edna St. Vincent Millay. Millay won the Pulitzer Prize in 1923 for her poetry. She often came to Bailey Island to visit her good friend from New York, Esther "Tess" Adams, who summered on Bailey Island. Esther was the wife of the late Franklin Pierce Adams, (FPA), humorist and columnist for the *New York Times*. He was a regular member of the "Information Please" radio program from 1938 to 1948.

In *The Indigo Bunting: Memoirs of Edna St. Vincent Millay*, Vincent Sheean tells of the visit he made with Edna and her husband, Eugen Boissevain, to Bailey Island. They stayed at Esther's house a night or two until the fog cleared, then took a motored dory to Ragged Island, two and a half miles to the east, loaded down with all their supplies for the weekend.

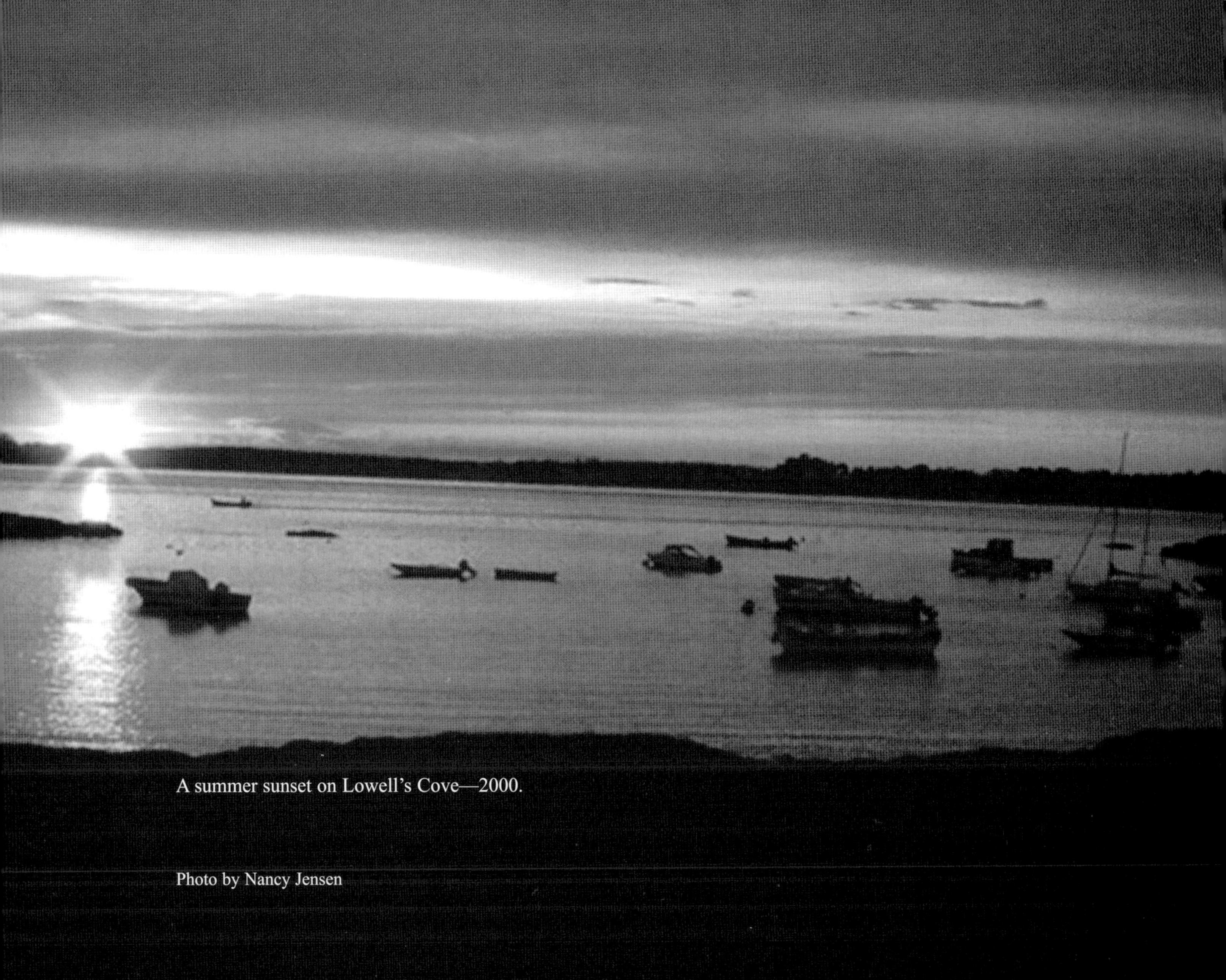

A summer sunset on Lowell's Cove—2000.

Photo by Nancy Jensen

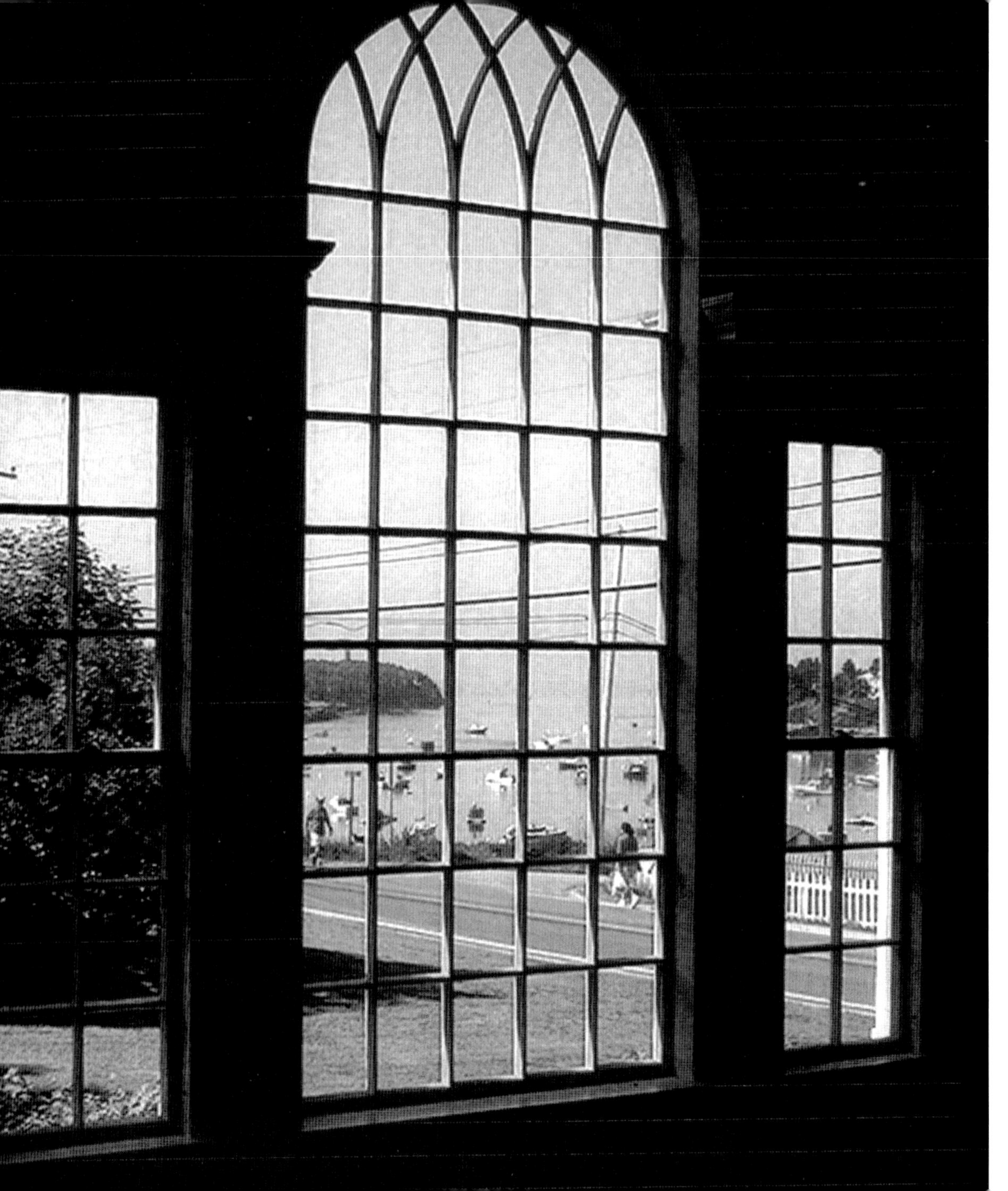

Library Hall window overlo
ing Mackerel Cove.

Photo by George Kotuby, resi
of Bailey Island

In June 2001, I asked Jesse Johnson, a 97 year-old lifelong resident, "What are your memories of Bailey Island?"

With a smile he replied, "It was a damn nice place to live."

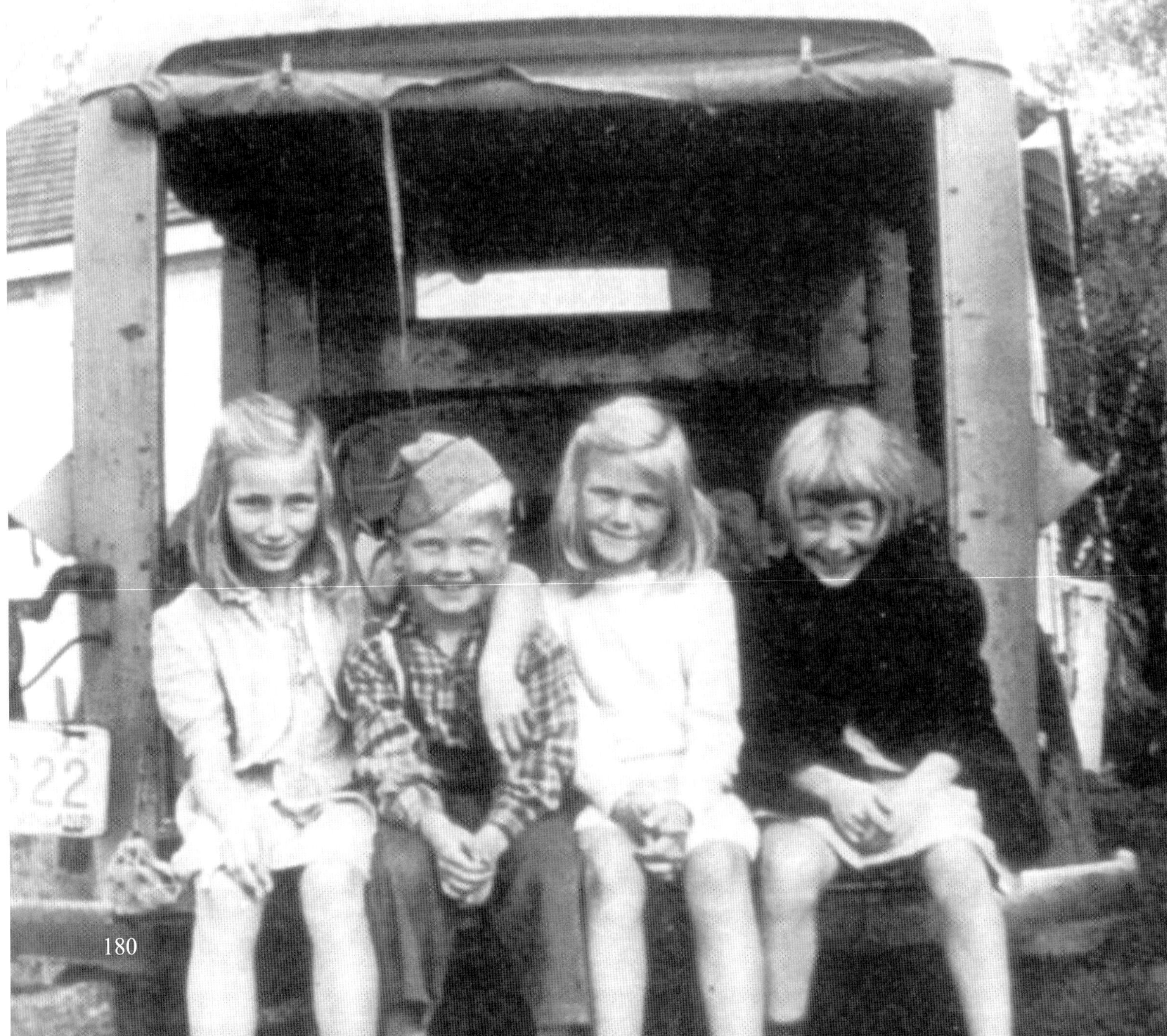

Sources

Most of the photos and old unidentified postcards are from the collection of my father, the late Linwood Johnson, who knew and loved his island heritage and whose ancestors lived in Harpswell since the mid 1700's. There are also many fine photos taken by the late Royal Root, a summer resident.

Anson Gilman was a summer resident of Bailey Island in the late 1800's. He may have taken some of the wide, landscape photographs seen in this book. Another great photographer of that era was Charles E. Davis, whose booklet we have reprinted.

Annual Reports of the Town Officers of the Town of Harpswell, 1874-1956.

Burnham, Clara Louise. *Doctor Latimer: A Story of Casco Bay*. Grosset & Dunlap, Publishers, New York. 1893.

Casco Bay Breeze Publication. Harpswell, Maine.

Casco Bay Directory. Portland, ME: Breeze Publishing Co., (Crowley & Lunt, Publishers), 1901-02; 1920-22.

Clifford, Harold B., *Charlie York: Maine Coast Fisherman*. International Maine Publishing Co. Camden, ME. 1974. Printed by permission of The McGraw-Hill Companies.

Frappier, William J. *Steamboat Yesterdays on Casco Bay.* Boston Mills Press, Toronto, Canada. 1993.

Hill, Beth. *The Evolution of Bailey's Island*. 1992.

Johnson, Marjorie. *Songs From an Island*. The Golden Quill Press, Francestown, N. H. 1975. Reprinted by permission of heirs.

Jones, Herbert. *The Isles Of Casco Bay-In Fact and Fancy.* Jones Book Shop, Portland, ME. 1946.

Lewiston Sun Journal, Lewiston, Maine.

Lucas, John. "The Maine American and the American Lobster." *National Geographic Society, Vol. LXXIV, No. 4, April, 1946.*

Mitchell and Campbell. *The Harpswell Register 1904*. Brunswick, ME: H.E. Mitchell Publishing Co., 1904.

Northeast Archives of Folklore and Oral History, Maine Folklife Center, University of Maine, Orono, Maine. Permission to quote from David Taylor's taped interview with Linwood Johnson. T1961.

Pejepscot Cryer, 1989 issues.

Pejepscot Historical Society, Brunswick, Maine.

Rich, Louise Dickinson. *The Coast of Maine*. New York: Thomas Y. Crowell Co., 1956.

Sheean, Vincent. *The Indigo Bunting*. New York: Harper & Brothers, 1951.

Sinnett, Rev. Charles. *Genealogies of Sinnetts, Orrs, Johnsons and Stovers*.

Taylor, David A. Interview with Linwood Johnson, 1975, Bailey Island, Maine. *Northeast Archives of Folklore and Oral History*, accession number T1961. Maine Folklife Center, University of Maine, Orono, ME.

Todd, Margaret and Charles. *Beautiful Harpswell*.